CW00793774

A GUIDE TO

THE BLUE PLAQUES

KNOWLE COTTAGE

Life & Times in Sidmouth

New Updated & Enlarged Edition

Published by the Sid Vale Association

MMXIX

First published 1992 © Julia Creeke
Revised 2013 © Julia Creeke and Sid Vale Association
Revised 2019 © Sid Vale Association
Illustrations © Sid Vale Association unless otherwise acknowledged.

All rights reserved. No part of this publication may be reproduced,
stored in a retrieval system or transmitted in any form or by any
means without the prior permission of the publisher.

ISBN 978-0-9934814-8-2

*We have made every effort to obtain the necessary permission to
reproduce copyright material in this work, though in some cases it has
been impossible to trace the current copyright holders. Any omissions
are entirely unintentional and if any are brought to our attention, we
will be most happy to include the appropriate acknowledgements in
any future reprinting.*

Sidmouth's Blue Plaques

The Sid Vale Association is the oldest Civic Society in Britain, founded in 1846. Amongst its objectives are to promote, for the benefit of the public, maintenance of the town's beautiful surroundings, care of the built environment, and to advance awareness of Sidmouth's history. The Association considers that its Blue Plaque scheme plays an important role in this and in 2017 formed a committee to bring Sidmouth's existing Blue Plaque scheme up to date, further extending it, and publish the third edition of the guide to the Blue Plaques. Members of this committee were:

Richard Thurlow, Chair, and Chairman of the Sid Vale Association
Kelvin Dent, Sidmouth Town Council
John Dowell, Chair of SVA Publications Group
Julia Creeke
Nigel Hyman
John McCarthy
Andrew Rugg-Gunn

The Sid Vale Association, through the Keith Owen Fund, has financed the production of the Blue Plaques, the book and the accompanying mini-guide. Most of the Blue Plaques are located on private property, but all are situated where they can be seen easily by the public without trespassing.

Sidmouth beach looking east, dating from around 1868. Courtesy of Mrs Sue Bartlett

PREFACE

This is the story of Sidmouth's 64 Blue Plaques. This large number indicates the interesting history and heritage of this 'Regency seaside town' which nestles between the red cliffs of the south Devon coast. Within the descriptions of each location lies a treasure-trove of information on colourful residents, visiting royalty, rogues, innovations, pastimes, fashionable architecture and exotic gardens. The Introduction, which follows this Preface, provides the context for Sidmouth's Blue Plaque scheme through a short history of our town and its inhabitants. This will help the reader to understand how each of the locations, and the people associated with these locations, fit into the rich fabric of Sidmouth's past. The texts associated with the 64 blue plaques are presented in alphabetical order with the author's name at the end of each. Maps are provided to help you locate each Blue Plaque.

A pocket-size booklet is available separately, helping you to find each of the 64 plaques, and provides a convenient summary of the scheme.

Sidmouth's Blue Plaque Scheme was launched in 1992, 27 years ago. The first edition of the Guide, *Life and Times in Sidmouth*, was written by Julia Creeke and published in the same year by the Sid Vale Association, with financial support from the East Devon District Council. In its 56 pages it described 32 locations. It proved to be very popular with Sidmouth residents and visitors, so that a revised edition was published ten years later, in 2012, again written by Julia Creeke. The number of locations rose to 35. Julia received many comments of appreciation from those who had stopped to read the informative blue plaques as they walked around the town. Again, this guide was much in demand, with all copies sold by 2016. This prompted the Sid Vale Association to form a committee, with the dual aim of writing a new Guide, with further expansion in the number of plaques, and replacing all of the Blue Plaques, many of which had deteriorated in Sidmouth's salty air.

Revising the Guide to the Blue Plaques was a major task and other authors joined Julia Creeke in compiling the text and collecting the photographs which accompany each description. Many of the photographs in this book come from Sidmouth Museum's collection. Apart from the four authors listed below who had the principal task of compiling this book, chapters were also contributed by Vicki Campbell, Mary Coghill, Brian Golding, Martin Mallinson, Maureen Thurlow and Alastair Watson. The work of getting this book from drafts into its published form has been undertaken by John Dowell, who also contributed a number of photographs. The principal team of four, below, are most grateful for his expert contribution.

Criteria for eligibility remain the same as those used by the Society of Arts when they established the first Blue Plaque Scheme in London (the first in the world) in 1866: a location should have been lived in or visited by a famous person, have been the venue for an important event, or the site of a significant building. Examples of each can be found within our 64: the infant Princess Victoria stayed at Woolbrook Cottage, now the Royal Glen Hotel; the Assembly Rooms of the London Hotel hosted fashionable Regency balls for many years; Knowle Grounds was the site of the spectacular Knowle Cottage.

Finally, this book contains much new material. Accuracy of this information has been the aim but doubtless, with time, errors and omissions will come to light. If this is so, please let the SVA know.

It is hoped that you will enjoy reading this new *Life and Times in Sidmouth*, in wandering around Sidmouth reading the Blue Plaques and looking at the buildings they adorn.

Julia Creeke
Nigel Hyman
John McCarthy
Andrew Rugg-Gunn
January 2019

CONTENTS

INTRODUCTION

A broad chronological summary of the town's history may allow the reader to better understand the context of the Blue Plaques. Blue Plaque chapter numbers are inserted where relevant.

EARLY HISTORY

In the 11th century, Sidmouth was part of the Manor of Otterton. After the Norman Conquest, the Manor, previously held by Countess Gytha, the mother of King Harold, was seized and given to the Abbey of Mont St Michel in Normandy. In the 12th century Sidmouth was overseen by a Priory, again based in Otterton. Priory memoranda of 1260 are preserved in a Cartulary, a register of charters and title deeds, and the monks may have visited St Peter's Chapel where a section of wall remains. (**53**)

Shipbuilding locally dates to at least the 14th century and in 1336 Edward III issued a writ to ports on the south coast for both ships and men. Sidmouth provided three ships and 62 men. (**56**)

In 1415 the Manor of Otterton, including Sidmouth, was given by Henry V to the Abbey of Syon who failed to maintain the Priory. From that time the growth of Sidmouth meant that it overtook Otterton in importance.

Tudor Cottage, in Chapel Street, is thought to date from the 1400s and to have been the administrative centre for the Manor and possibly the most important building in the growing town. A screen dividing the ground floor hall has beautiful paintings on both sides and dates from the reigns of Edward VI or Elizabeth I. (**60**)

The Old Ship, now a coffee house, on Old Fore Street dates from the 15th century and was a tavern from the 17th century. The interior is well preserved. (**48**)

Another mediaeval building of great architectural significance is Woolcombe House, also dating from the 1400s. The roof is an excellent example of the 'jointed cruck', a ubiquitous type of truss seen in Devonian rural houses. (**64**)

Saxton's 1575 map of Devonshire shows three places on the south coast in bold print, Plymouth, Dartmouth and Sidmouth, reflecting the town's significance. In the 1600 and 1700s local fishermen and ship owners contributed to the lucrative but demanding 'Newfoundland Trade'. It consisted of crews collecting salt from Spain and Portugal, and then crossing the Atlantic to the Newfoundland fishing grounds. The preserved fish was brought back to the Iberian Peninsula and some of it exchanged for wine and oil before finally returning to Devon. (**56**)

In 1630 the topographer and author of survey of the County of Devon, Tristram Risdon, wrote that Sidmouth was 'one of the especialest fischar towns of this shire.' Even then it may well have lost its harbour as the River Sid was said to be 'choked with chisel (gravel) and sands due to vicissitudes of the tides.'

REGENCY PERIOD

The decline of the fishing industry through the 1700s was offset, towards the end of the century, by the rapid growth of a new industry. Sidmouth became a 'watering place' or 'resort' and followed the example of Exmouth and Teignmouth. It was strongly believed that sea water and sea air, combined with an agreeable climate, must have health-giving properties. There were several hot, sea-water bath establishments in the town for those not brave enough to face the waves.

Inland spas, such as Bath or Harrogate, were becoming increasingly expensive and the development of south Devonshire resorts was an attractive proposition for speculators. The French Revolution and subsequent Napoleonic Wars (1789 – 1815) were a definite catalyst as

Sidmouth from Salcombe Hill, from an old print after the painting by George Rowe, 1796 (Sidmouth Museum)

Seacourt, Seafield Road

there were evident dangers crossing the Channel. The wealthy discovered that the winter climate in Sidmouth was usually mild and that it was agreeable to either overwinter or take up permanent residence. The town became popular with retired East India Company officials and either retired or half-pay army and naval officers. It has been suggested that 'ex-colonials,' especially those that had served in India, may have influenced the architectural style favouring first floor balconies, leaded canopy roofs, wide verandahs and white stucco exteriors. In the 1820s, two distinguished naval men with colourful careers, Admiral Henry Digby and a former colleague, Rear Admiral James Macnamara, spent time in Sidmouth; Digby at Woodland Cottage (**63**) and Macnamara at the adjacent Spring Garden. (**58**)

Most properties were leased as the hotel industry was in its infancy but the York Hotel was purpose built in 1807. (**52**)

Several individuals were crucial in the development and success of the early resort.

Emmanuel Baruh Lousada was beyond doubt the most influential. He came as early as 1788, and initially leased and then bought 20 acres (8 ha) on Peak Hill. His background was from a wealthy Jewish Sephardic family. He may have reasoned that it would be easier to buy land and build houses in this remote part of England rather than in the London area. His base was Peak House and his importance to the town was that of both philanthropy and also encouragement to family and friends to move to the flourishing small town. (**50**)

Thomas Jenkins, although born in Honiton, made his fame and fortune in Rome. He developed a service specifically for travellers on the Grand Tour which included banking, selling works of art and dealing with all aspects of their travel arrangements. In his middle sixties his thoughts turned towards returning to Devon and he purchased the Manor of Sidmouth. He commissioned the building of Fortfield Crescent and he decided to return to England following the early death of the architect plus the advance of Napoleon's troops towards Rome. He died soon after landing in Great Yarmouth and part of the crescent's western section was never completed. Nevertheless, the town had a crescent of sorts and the leased houses were occupied, at times, by the rich and famous. (**25-28**)

John Wallis came from London in 1803 and established a library at the eastern end of the front. In 1813 he moved his business west to the site of the present Bedford Hotel. The importance of his enterprise cannot be overestimated. The subscription Marine Library offered much more than books and included newspapers, prints, magazines, telescopes for hire and a billiard room. But, above all, it was a daytime meeting place for the gentry and was perfectly situated on the Mall overlooking the sea. Wallis commissioned the Exeter artist, Hubert Cornish, to paint a panoramic view of the front with, naturally, his establishment in the very centre. The subsequent Long Prints were sold in the town but also elsewhere giving publicity to both Sidmouth and Wallis, who, tellingly, dedicated the print to Lousada. (**5**)

Libraries faced trading difficulties and public taste was fickle. The Marine Library closed in 1835 due to lack of business.

Sir John Kennaway made his military reputation in India and in association with his brother's commercial success in the British East India Company they returned to England and built Escot. When it was destroyed by fire in 1808, Sir John bought and developed Fort House (**34**) which became an important social centre for the aristocracy and gentry. He also owned the land on which Hope Cottage (**31**) was built in 1815 and the attractive Coburg Terrace (**17, 18**) in the 1820s. He also granted the land on which All Saints Church was built in 1837 although he died the year before.

The Reverend Edmund Butcher was a Unitarian Minister but his significance, both then and now, was his splendid guide, *The Beauties of Sidmouth Displayed*, first published in 1810. The later editions carried illustrations, and we learn about the fine houses, the inns, the shop-keepers and the fishing industry. The London Inn is described and was the town's Assembly Rooms. The evening card games and weekly balls perfectly complemented the day-time Wallis facilities. (**40**)

This period could be described as Sidmouth's Golden Age, roughly spanning 1790 to 1830. The architecture was varied and striking: the Gothic Revival Woolbrook Cottage (Royal Glen **51**), the imposing Fortfield Terrace (**25**) and the plain but elegant Georgian, Fort House (Kennaway House **34**). The town was famous for its cottage orné, a highly decorated 'rustic' style, such as Marino Lodge (**49**) and the 1820s villas in Elysian Fields (**55**) but the Knowle (**36**) was its most perfect example.

There were setbacks. In 1824, the Great Gale struck Dorset and eastern Devonshire and wrecked many Sidmouth buildings especially on the front. (**4**, **5**) Five years earlier, Edward Duke of Kent came to Woolbrook Cottage with his wife and small child, the future Queen Victoria, for what was planned to be a significant period whilst he attempted to reduce his debts. What better promotion for the town than the approval of a possible future king? Wallis presented him with his Long Print. His death after less than a month was, to say the least, unfortunate. (**51**)

1831 brought another royal visit but with a happier outcome. The sister-in-law of the Russian Czar, Helena Pavlovna, and high ranking Russian aristocracy stayed at Fortfield Terrace. Her personal band found accommodation nearby. She held receptions and was very gracious. The townspeople were delighted and, later, commemorated her visit with a double-headed Russian Eagle on the pediment of numbers 7 and 8.

A year after the visit, a then unknown and unwell Elizabeth Barrett came with her father and eleven siblings and stayed at the same address. Elizabeth's finest poetry came later but in a letter describing her new home close to the sea there is no doubting her promise: '...I was lulled to sleep last night by the rolling reverberating solemn sound of its waves'. (**26**)

Sidmouth has been fortunate in its early print history. Hubert Cornish's panoramic 1814 watercolour, in the Museum, became the 'Long Print' a year later. (**5**) George Rowe was 40 years younger than Cornish. His 1826 '48 views of Cottages and Scenery at Sidmouth' are a valuable record – see Richmond House print (**55**). Henry Haseler, a drawing teacher and contemporary of Rowe, lived at Clifton Cottage. (**15**) Many of his fine drawings and watercolours are in the Museum.

The population grew three-fold from 1,252 in 1801 to 3,441 in 1851 but a description of the rich and famous overlooks the fact that the majority of the townspeople remained impoverished. Fishing was already in slow decline and common land, for example on Salcombe Hill, was diminished by successive Enclosure Acts.

Teaching children to read and write depended upon parochial schools associated with the churches. The first is thought to have been on High Street and on the same site as the Poorhouse, now the Potburys location. The 'new' Poorhouse was built in the early 19th century on Mill Street and in 1811 the Parochial Boys School was built nearby. Despite its name, girls shared with the boys until 1858. The original building can still be seen, Counters Court, with separate faded inscriptions, 'Boys' and 'Girls', above each stone porch. Next door is The Masters House, still so named. The Marsh Chapel (Independent Calvinist Church) on what is now York Street had an Infants School, established in 1821 and was to become the Girls and Infants School.

Other schools included All Saints and the British School, both founded in 1848. The latter was on the site of the Congregational Church in Chapel Street and after the Education Act 1870, it closed as free, compulsory, non-religious education was now available to all. Schools for the wealthy flourished in the 19th century and fee-paying 'academies' were established in private houses. For example, the Sidmouth entry in the Pigot's 1838 Directory lists six academies.

VICTORIAN AGE

If the Regency period reflected rapid growth, then the long Victorian era could best be described as a period of stasis or even relative decline in the town's fortunes.

There is uncertainty whether the mouth of the Sid had a harbour in mediaeval times. An ambitious scheme to build a

Parochial Boys School (now Counter's Court)

harbour at the western end of the beach, which included an industrial railway, started with great ceremony in 1837 but was scrapped a year later after farcical mismanagement. (**1**)

Sidmouth's best attraction was the spectacular Knowle Cottage where the wealthy and eccentric Thomas Fish opened the property on Mondays in the summer months. The house contained an extraordinary collection of paintings, china and ornaments. Among the fine trees and shrubs in the grounds could be seen kangaroos, emus, parrots and a camel. Mr Fish's death in 1861 brought a sudden end to this remarkable 40 year venture. (**36**, **37**)

In 1846 the Sidmouth Improvement Society was formed and John Carslake, in earlier life a midshipman on HMS *Victory* at Trafalgar, was the first chairman. (**20**) Early items for discussion included smoothing the walk on the beach (the forerunner of the Esplanade). Chairs on the beach were provided but there was dismay that they were 'being occupied by Sailors and low people to the annoyance of those for whom they were especially intended'. (In 1909 the Society changed its name to the Sid Vale Association) In 1847 the town enjoyed its first Sailing Regatta. (**56**)

Probably the single most outstanding new building in the early Victorian period, although not seen by most Sidmothians, was the Ball Room in Richmond Lodge (Sidholme), the home of the 6th Earl of Buckinghamshire. Built in 1854, it was then separate from the main block, neoclassical in style and containing ideas gleaned from the 1851 Great Exhibition including magnificent chandeliers lit by 236 gas burners. (**55**)

The town was fortunate, in the second half of the century, to have a very able chronicler, Peter Orlando Hutchinson. (**18**)

Railway Station (Sidmouth Museum)

Although now best known for his diaries, he was very much the Victorian polymath; a water colourist, local historian, geologist and musician. He was an important participant in an extraordinary episode in 1860 when the peaceful town was riven with polarised religious views resulting in fury and insults. The cause was the proposed 'improvement' of the Parish Church in which extensive rebuilding was planned including the installation of a window to be donated by the Queen. The dispute lasted a further six years by which time the conflicting parties had forgotten the reasons for their outrage and an amicable outcome resulted. (**59**)

Our main artistic record of this era comes from the brush of Hutchinson whose output was prolific and is archived in the Devon History Centre and online. The artist and sailor, Robert Leslie, lived in Sidmouth and his 'Waterbiography' includes local marine illustrations. (**28**) The landscape artist, euphoniously named Hopkins Horsley Hobday Horsley visited Sidmouth in the 1860s staying at Marine Place (Hotel Riviera). The original Alma Bridge is shown in the fine 'Mouth of the Sid' oil painting in the Museum. (**1**)

The 1860s saw further sailing regattas and the launch of the first lifeboat. (**38**, **56**) However, a series of misfortunes was associated with another type of transport, the railway.

In 1844 the Great Western Railway (GWR) Paddington-Exeter line opened and soon afterwards the South Devon Railway Company extended the line to Plymouth via the coastal resorts situated west of the Exe – Dawlish, Teignmouth, Torquay and Paignton were connected by 1849. Sidmouth, east of the Exe, continued to be served by coach and horses. In 1856 the town's attempt to raise funds for a shared branch line to Exeter failed, its population was static and house prices were falling. In 1874 the Sidmouth Railway Company eventually had the capital, £70,000, to build the line which was operated by the London & South West Railway (L&SWR). It ran from Feniton, renamed Sidmouth Junction, to Bulverton on the edge of Sidmouth, some eight miles (13 km). Earlier branch lines had been established in Exmouth in 1861 and in Seaton in 1868.

The anticipated increase in visitor numbers never happened. The GWR had excellent connections with the West Midlands, South Wales as well as London and the burgeoning middle classes had ready access to the resorts west of the Exe. By 1892 it was possible to get a through train from the north of England to Torquay. Between 1841 and 1891 the Torquay population grew from 5,982 to 25,534 compared with Sidmouth's trivial increase from 3,309 to 3,758.

The late Victorian era saw the rise of the day tripper and working class families from Exeter who had the opportunity to spend a day at the seaside. Rail fares, especially excursion day trips, were affordable and Exmouth, with its fine sandy beach and station on the front, was far preferable to Sidmouth with its shingle beach and mile long walk to the front. The L&SWR had fewer excursions but those that came from London generally chose Seaton as it was the first stop in south Devonshire.

The consequence of bad luck and bad management meant that Sidmouth never had the building boom of Exmouth and Torquay. An unintended consequence was that much of the town's old fashioned charm, including the Regency architecture, was not destroyed by developers.

A thriving retail industry is the lifeblood of any town and Sidmouth had both thriving and quality shops which attracted the carriage trade: in 1813, Stone and Gore in Fore Street later became Trumps, Grocers, Bakers, Wine Merchants. In High Street, a cabinet makers' business, Farrants, became Potburys and, apart from furniture, it offered removal and auctioneering services. Drapers' premises in Market Place were bought up by the enterprising John Field and the town had its first 'department store' in 1893. Ladies clothes were sold but, additionally items such as baby linen and mourning clothes, the so-called 'womb to the tomb' approach. Field had a separate 'Tailor, Outfitter and Hatter' business in Fore Street.

The lace industry (**3, 10**) was of enormous importance commercially despite the exploitation of child labour in the lace schools. It was not the only industry for female workers. The splendidly named Mr Sleep of Knightsbridge opened a factory in 1884 in Holmdale, not for bed production, but rather for producing hand-made gloves.

At one time in the 19th century the town had three breweries. The first, Marsh Brewery, was sited off Mill Lane and in operation from 1815, but was the first to close. The Town Brewery dates from the 1840s and continued until the end of the century. The building can still be seen as Lennard's Court off Old Fore Street. The most successful, and the largest, was started by the Searle brothers in the 1830s but eventually acquired by the Vallance family, and was located on the junction of Temple Street and Brewery Lane – the site was demolished in 1980.

Public utilities garner no Blue Plaques but were, and are, vital to the health and comfort of the townspeople.

The first Water Works were built in 1844 in Cheese Lane in response to the insanitary town wells which locals were reluctant to abandon. Cholera, due to drinking infected water, was a

Town Brewery from 4 Coburg Terrace, 1848
Painting by PO Hutchinson

deadly disease. During a London outbreak in 1848, Hutchinson anxiously noted in his diary that the disease was said to travel at a rate of 280 miles a month, that is about 10 miles a day, and he expected it in Devonshire shortly; Sidmouth escaped but Torquay was less fortunate. Eventually a far better water supply was provided by the Manor Water Company in 1888 which consisted of a reservoir and filtering beds on Peak Hill.

The first Gas Works in 1837 were off Temple Street and privately owned. It moved to Bulverton (the present Alexandria Estate site) and finally to The Ham in 1875. This was convenient as coal ships could unload directly to the Works which now belonged to the Manor. The public disliked bright light which was thought damaging to the eyes, and congregants complained of the glare in the Parish Church. The street lamps, now lit by gas rather than oil, were not lit on the three days before and after each full Moon.

The saga of the town's electrical supply was an unhappy one. The Manor wished to add electricity to its gas and water companies. This was blocked by Sidmouth Urban Council who signed a contract for electric street lighting in 1903, but the lights were not switched on until 1923 and, even then, it was initially confined to a string of lamps in the Market Place. The 20 year delay provoked acrimonious letters in the newspapers signed with noms de plume such as 'A Mere Tradesman' and 'Vigilans'.

The long delay was due to uncertainty about this new source of light, the rapidly changing manufacturing costs and the Great War. Several hotels and many businesses, tired of waiting, installed their own generators. The electricity was generated by two noisy coal-powered engines at the Ham, adjacent to the Gas Works.

As the century drew to a close, medical facilities for the poor improved with the establishment of four beds in May Cottage. It was so successful that a purpose built Victoria Cottage Hospital, with ten beds, opened in 1892. (**43**)

Soon afterwards, in 1895, The Baths, owned by the Manor, opened on the front and offered hot and cold water treatments. (**35**) The Lord of the Manor, Colonel Balfour, owned other companies including water, gas, some hotels and the railway.

THE 20th CENTURY

Annie Leigh Browne and her sister Mary Lockyer were both very influential in town life. Annie created facilities at Woolcombe House to enable people of all ages to learn new skills as well as providing expert advice to nursing mothers. Her life's work focused on the empowerment of women through education and welfare. (**64**) Mary, although very involved in her husband's Hill Observatory, was, like Annie, a life-long suffragist. She was secretary of the Sidmouth & District Women's Suffrage Society which was an active group with its own banner.

The Crimean War in the 1850s and the Second Boer War at the turn of the 20th century had little impact on the townspeople. However, the Great War directly or indirectly touched almost the entire population. Black-out regulations were enforced and public houses closed early. Many fishermen belonged to the Royal Naval Reserve and were automatically called up in 1914 causing major disruption to the fishing industry. Stephen Reynolds, the fisherman/author,

was in charge of the inshore fisheries for the entire South West from his base in Hope Cottage. (**31**) A Volunteer Training Corps for the older men was set up and well subscribed. Conscription in 1916 saw most of the young men called up to the army or navy. Small shrines, consisting of flowers and the names of the dead and missing, appeared at the ends of some streets. There are 117 listed dead on the war memorial tablets in the Parish Church although a more accurate figure is nearer 150.

The War had seen the rise and popularity of moving pictures. The Cinema Picture Palace, with 350 upholstered, tip-up seats in Fore Street, belonged to the photographer Arthur Ellis, a now forgotten name, but a very important figure in the first quarter of the new century.

Many buildings between the 1890s and 1930s were designed or influenced by the Manor architect, RW Sampson. Arts and Crafts style predominated in the developing Bickwell Valley. (**42**) He was very versatile and was responsible for the highly regarded Arcot Park council development, as well as the fine rebuild of Rock Cottage (**13**) and, almost directly opposite, the 1904 Victoria Hotel. (**61**)

Former military men retired to Sidmouth in the first quarter of the 20th century following a similar pattern to those of a century earlier. Colonel The Honourable John Pleydell-Bouverie moved to Blackmore Hall in 1914 (**7**) having served in South Africa and India. Colonel Charles Grant served in the British Indian Army and was awarded the VC after the Battle of Thoba in 1891. He retired after WW1 to Western Field. (**62**) General Sir John Hart Dunne (**57**), a veteran of the Crimean War, retired to 6 Fortfield Terrace. Berkley Levett was a Major in the Scots Guards, an aide-de-camp in India and, in later life, the equerry to Arthur, Duke of Connaught, himself a former Field Marshall and the third and favourite son of Queen Victoria. In 1920 Levett lived at Cottington on Cotmaton Road and probably influenced the Duke's decision to overwinter in Sidmouth in the 1930s. The Duke's health, fortunately, was better than that of his grandfather in the town over a century earlier. He was a popular figure and opened the new gardens in his name in 1934. (**19, 54**)

Eminent scientists, all Fellows of the Royal Society, have associations with the town.

Sir Aubrey Strahan had his childhood at Blackmore Hall. (**7**) He became President of the Geological Society and Director of the Geological Survey. Churchill's 'Prof', Frederick Lindemann (Viscount Cherwell) was brought up in Sidholme. (**55**) The eminent astronomer, Sir Norman Lockyer, built the then called

Victoria Cottage Hospital 1904 (Sidmouth Museum)

Hill Observatory in 1913. (**45**) Sydney Brown, a prolific inventor, also retired to Sidmouth to live in the former house of his friend, Lockyer, which he named Brownlands. Sir John Ambrose Fleming, the inventor of the first thermionic valve, died in 1945 having retired here in 1926. (**30**)

In the early 20th century Beatrix Potter painted several charming local landscapes. (**33**) The architect RW Sampson was a talented amateur artist of the local scene in the same era. The artist and poet David Jones painted several very fine works from the roof of the Fort Hotel in the 1930s. (**23**)

Authors, likewise, have stayed for prolonged periods. These have included JRR Tolkien (**2**) and Ron Delderfield. (**21**) John Betjeman made many visits from the 1930s to old age. (**61**)

Tourism in the interwar years was reasonable without the glamour of Torquay or popular attractions of Exmouth. The paddle steamer, the Duchess of Devonshire, plied its trade between Torquay and Lyme Regis before disastrously going aground off the Sidmouth shingle in 1934 and subsequently breaking up.

Entertainment included the Town Band which dated back to 1862. The Sidmouth Amateur Dramatic Society was founded in 1922 with productions at the Manor Hall, now the Manor Pavilion Theatre. The Cinema Picture Palace was replaced by the Grand Cinema in High Street and the Radway Cinema, both in 1929.

The Grand burned down in 1956 but the Radway remained.

World War 2 brought blackouts at night again. Barbed wire was placed on the Esplanade with scaffolding defences on the shingle and under Alma Bridge. Bren gun positions were located on the Fortfield and a Pill Box was erected in Connaught Gardens. Between 1943 and 1945, the town became the RAF's Medical Training Depot. Hotels were requisitioned and converted for accommodation and teaching. (**29**)

In 1950 the first Museum opened on the first floor of Woolcombe House. (**64**) In 1970 it moved to Hope Cottage, at the top of Church Street. (**31**)

Colonel Balfour died in 1952. He was the last Lord of the Manor and the only one to live in the town. He had a reputation for feudal patronage, and towards the end of his long life it was clear that his role was increasingly anachronistic. In old age he said that he regretted that the town had been suspicious of the Manor and its schemes for improvement. His various acts of philanthropy should be remembered including the gift of the grounds for the Victoria Cottage Hospital. (**43**)

Grand Cinema (Sidmouth Museum)

In 1955 a small event, organised by the English Folk Dance and Song Society, took place. It was to become The Sidmouth International Festival of Folk Arts and for many people, in both this country and abroad, the name Sidmouth is associated with the Folk Festival.

From 1960, and for 20 years, the Alexandria Works (now the Industrial Estate) assembled so-called 'caravettes'; Volkswagen vans converted into a living space, similar to a caravan. At its peak there were 150 workers, many of whom were skilled craftsmen, inside the factory and a further 100 out workers. In the early 1960s over 1000 caravettes were produced annually. (Early models are highly prized)

The history of Sidmouth did not end in the 1960s and, in recent decades, unlike many other seaside towns, it has prospered. For over two centuries it has attracted, and continues to attract, incomers with a wide range of interests and backgrounds. The Victorians were anxious that the failure of a building boon would spell its eventual death knell but the very opposite happened. It has retained its charm without losing its vitality.

The Sid Vale Association is pledged to record the local history of the Sid Valley and the Blue Plaques help fulfil that undertaking.

Nigel Hyman

Acknowledgements
The authors wish to thank the following for their kind assistance:
Mary Atkinson, for commenting on an early draft. Peter Yule
Booth, for information on the Carslakes. Peter Child, former
Devon County Council Historic Buildings Adviser, for information
on Woolcombe House. Jane Inder, for details of the Cornish
family. David Strange for information on the Norman Lockyer
Observatory. Ann Tanner, for help identifying photographs in
Sidmouth Museum archives.

Sidmouth's Blue Plaques

Site of the original

 ALMA BRIDGE

A footbridge was first built across the mouth of the River Sid in 1854, to be replaced in 1902 by one designed by RW Sampson, and replaced by a new bridge further upstream in the 21st century.

By the 1840s there was increasing agitation to provide a new convenient crossing of the Sid nearer its mouth to shorten the distance for foot travellers to and from Salcombe Regis. In the early 18th century, probably the only foot crossing below Sidford was close to the present Mill Ford water-splash, but a document of 1619 cites evidence of 80 years before, i.e. 1540, that the area where the King's Mill leat flowed into the Sid was at Stoney Bridge, so there must have been a bridge in existence since at least early Tudor times (the ancient King's Mill was on the site of present day Tesco Express). The bridge probably consisted of a large tree, most likely felled on the spot and allowed to fall across the river, the top side adzed reasonably flat and a rough hand rail fitted, it remained the only foot-crossing close to the town until the building of the stone bridge just upstream in 1820.

In 1855, the Sid Vale Association (SVA) undertook the construction of a new bridge, just above the mouth of the Sid alongside the Ham in an area then known as 'The Marsh'. The SVA had been founded in 1846 as The Sidmouth Improvement Committee, by a group of influential residents primarily to keep open and maintain, by walking over them regularly, the vast network of over 70 miles of footpaths which criss¬crossed the valley. At this time, farms were being amalgamated and lands enclosed, and owners frequently attempted to block or divert the old rights of way.

The bridge would probably have been built shortly after the Committee's formation but for the refusal of Mrs Cornish, widow of the Lord of the Manor of Salcombe Regis, to grant any additional access or right of way over Manor lands. In 1852, Mr Trump and Mr Pile visited her to discuss using the abandoned railway tunnel through the cliffs. This was built in order to gain access to a supply of stone at Maynard's Cliff (to the east of Salcombe Hill), but left unused when the harbour project failed. She objected strongly, eventually agreeing to an iron bridge and so a Bridge Fund was set up. The cost of the new bridge was estimated at £70. There were however problems: the money was not forthcoming and in July 1854 a deputation was sent 'to wait on Mrs Cornish and explain the matter to her and see what could be done in throwing an inexpensive wooden bridge across the Sid'.

Eventually, after almost nine years, construction of a much more modest timber bridge began. The ship *Laurel* had not long before grounded on the beach and broken up, and some of her timbers were salvaged and put to use in building the new footbridge, a simple structure supported on five pairs of inverted V-shaped legs with a handrail on curiously shaped uprights, which belied their nautical origin. Its foundations used part of the old foundation for the bridge which carried the harbour railway track across the river. Steps were cut in

Alma Bridge in 1870, built in 1855 with timbers from a wrecked ship (Sidmouth Museum)

the Hanger to join up with the cliff path. The remains of the steps still exist today although cliff erosion has caused their closure.

The bridge was 24 inches (61cm) wide and 125 feet (38m) long, cost £26.10s (£26.50) and was called the Alma Bridge, after the Battle of Alma, fought and won in 1855 in the course of the Crimean War. A fine painting in Sidmouth Museum shows the bridge in detail.

The railway track mentioned above was intended to facilitate the bringing of stone from Hook Ebb for the proposed harbour at the western end of Sidmouth. Funds had been subscribed totalling £18,000 in 1836 and a tunnel dug through about a third of Salcombe Hill. The line emerged onto the beach and continued east of Salcombe Mouth terminating close to Hook Ebb (below Maynard's Cliff).

A steam engine was ordered and delivered by sea, but unloading proved impossible at Sidmouth so it was discharged at Exmouth and towed over Peak Hill to Sidmouth by a team of horses with the engine decorated with ribbons. A track had been laid along the promenade and the engine was put onto the rails. Alas, it proved too large to go through the tunnel. By now all the money had been spent. It is said that the engine gave visitors rides up and down the promenade for a summer and was then sold. Thus ended the harbour project.

The Esplanade did not then stretch as far as the mouth of the Sid and the area beyond the end of the promenade was a working area with a shipyard and timber yard both owned by a Captain Andrews who ran a shipping business, bringing in coals and shipping out timber, mostly elm. This latter trade brought him into conflict with Sidmouth's residents who accused him of taking so much elm that the hillsides and field banks were rapidly becoming denuded of trees. Captain Andrews paid an above average price of 9 pence (5p) a foot for timber that, until then, was considered of little value as it had few uses. He would take all he could get, shipping it off to Lowestoft for the shipyards there, where it was in demand for ships' keels. Captain Andrews and his brother had various business interests, but got into financial difficulties and their Sidmouth properties were sold. By 1861 the two brothers were in prison for debt.

The first bridge was not a very robust construction and was quite badly damaged by storms in 1877 which necessitated repairs and strengthening that cost £34. Lethaby's Journal of 1888 reported that 'until Mr Dunning interfered and made the approach from the Sidmouth side so awkward and unsightly as it now is, it was more picturesque'. It seems a large rubbish tip

Replacement bridge completed in 1902 to a design by RW Sampson (Sidmouth Museum)

had disfigured the land at the very end of the promenade and there were also complaints about the state of the stepped path up the cliff. Mr Dunning had purchased part of the Ham in 1875 and erected a gas works. He had also constructed a rather ramshackle jetty for unloading his coals, but this was not satisfactory and was knocked to pieces in a storm in 1877 at which time his crane was also washed away.

The gas works was built on what is now the Ham Car Park, together with a large gasometer for storing the gas. So that coal could be easily delivered by rail, a more modern plant was built alongside Sidmouth Station. The Ham gas works then ceased production. Finally, after WW2 a new gas main was laid into Sidmouth from Exeter.

By 1900, the Alma Bridge was becoming unsafe and after discussions, Sidmouth Council commissioned the notable local architect, RW Sampson, to design a replacement bridge which was more substantial. The Council had, in 1893, first considered a scheme for the general improvement of the area, including the purchase of the Ham Meadow, building a new footbridge and provision of a new sloping path up the Hanger to replace the old steep steps, but progress was slow and funds not forthcoming.

Mr JG Radford, a local solicitor, who lived at 'Sidmount' then acquired the Ham Meadow and presented it to the town for the benefit of public recreation, but was dismayed a few years later at its poor state of upkeep resulting from damage caused by the installation of the new drains and sewers. The Council, therefore, agreed to its reinstatement, and unemployed fishermen were offered work raising the level of the Ham Meadow. It was then re-seeded, seats were provided and an attempt was made to screen the gas works with trees.

With the Ham Meadow now safely in public ownership, the Council turned its attention to the construction of a new Alma Bridge and applied for a loan of £150 from the Local Government Board to allow a new zig-zag path to be cut into the Hanger to provide an easier sloping ascent to the Cliff Path – the whole project being complete by 1902. The only complaint thereafter being that the view of the gasworks site (where the swimming pool and the car park are now located) and some very old and dilapidated cottages in Eastern Town spoilt the vista.

At the end of World War Two, the site of the old gas works was purchased by Sidmouth UDC, all the buildings were demolished and the site used to provide car parking for the shopping area. After an abortive attempt to build a supermarket on part of the site, finally a much sought after swimming pool was built.

At high tide, the lower part of Sidmouth town centre lies at sea level, and in storm conditions can be easily flooded by sea spray thrown over the promenade or by heavy rains. This is because the sea level is too high to allow the flood water to flow through the storm drains back into the sea. To prevent this happening, a huge hole was dug in the Ham lawn and an enormous concrete tank constructed to hold flood water until it can be discharged back into the sea at low tide. With the lawn relaid, few even know of this tank's existence.

With ongoing coastal erosion, the old railway tunnel has disappeared and Pennington Point at the river mouth is fast falling away, allowing the sea to sweep into the river. What is left of the Alma Bridge is now at considerable risk and due to deterioration of the parapets and walkway, much of it has had to be removed and a temporary structure now disfigures what was once an attractive brick and timber bridge. There are plans to build a replacement bridge further upriver and a new path cut into the Hanger. Meantime, it may seem strange that it bears a Blue Plaque, but in the interim it still commemorates the bridge's designer, the Sidmouth architect, RW Sampson, whose buildings, both hotels and private houses, played such a part in Sidmouth's development.

Julia Creeke

2 AURORA *now the back portion of Kennaway House*

Aurora became a separate residence in 1906. In the mid-1930s it was the summer holiday home of JRR Tolkien, who wrote part of *The Lord of the Rings* here.

Aurora started life as the rear part of what is now Kennaway House, which was built in 1805 by Captain Thomas Phillipps. (See chapter on Kennaway House for a full history). The next owners were the Kennaways who vacated the house on completion of their new home at Escot. The house had several owners during the 19th century, but had been up for sale for some years when Mr R Hatton-Wood purchased it in memory of his wife, to become Church House. To help finance this institution, he purchased Barton Cottage in 1906 and divided off the rear portion of Kennaway House to

Aurora, originally the rear part of Kennaway House, hived off in 1906 (SVA)

JRR Tolkien

By all accounts Tolkien found Sidmouth restful and inspirational. According to biographers, he loved to spend a quiet evening in a pub nearby mulling over his work with a pint and probably smoking his pipe. There he observed a character in another shadowed corner and, in a flash of inspiration, he realised that 'Strider', once a Hobbit called 'Trotter', had become Aragorn.

In WW2, Tolkien's son, Michael, was appointed to Coastal Defence in Sidmouth in 1941 and so during the War, Edith Tolkien continued to visit Sidmouth. Years later in 1971, staying in the Belmont Hotel, Tolkien wrote a letter to his son Christopher:

May was such a wonderful month and we came in for a "spring explosion" of glory, with Devon passing from brown to brilliant yellow green and all the flowers of spring leaping out of dead bracken or old grass... an added comfort was the fact that Sidmouth seemed practically unchanged, even the shops, many still having the same names (such as Frisby, Trump and Potbury).

form a separate residence which was named Aurora. It was intended that the rents of these two properties would help finance Church House.

The finances of Church House were always rather precarious and, on a number of occasions, the Trustees sold off parts of the property: Nortongarth garden in 1926, Barton House in 1932, Barton Cottage in 1936, and finally Aurora in 1960 for the sum of £3,433. This was long after a celebrated literary figure, Professor JRR Tolkien, rented it for family summer holidays.

JRR Tolkien, Professor of Anglo-Saxon at Oxford University, and visionary writer, loved Sidmouth and between the years of 1934 and 1938, the family spent their summer holiday here. Tolkien would drive down with the luggage, and his wife, Edith, would travel down with the children on the train, arriving at the now closed Sidmouth Station, to stay at Aurora in Coburg Road.

In the summer of 1938 Tolkien, after a long period of writer's block, wrote part of *Lord of the Rings* in Sidmouth on what turned out to be their last family holiday at Aurora, as WW2 broke out the following year. There is a quote to this effect in his biography: 'In August the family went on holiday to the seaside town of Sidmouth. Here Tolkien had a rush of creativity and took the story to The Prancing Pony, where the Hobbits first meet Aragorn.'

The Hobbit was first published in September 1937 and was such a huge success that Tolkien's publisher urged him to write a sequel which began as *The New Hobbit*, but ended up some fifteen years later being published as *The Lord of the Rings*. In 1954, *The Fellowship of the Ring* first hit the bookshelves. *The Hobbit* and *Lord of the Rings* changed the face of fantasy literature forever, and have since passed into literary legend, remaining best sellers ever since their publications, and attracting a worldwide fan base of billions. All aided by Peter Jackson's

First single volume edition 1968

phenomenally successful film trilogy based on *The Lord of the Rings*.

We can be proud of this attractive little town, as one of the greatest fantasy heroes was conceived here by one of the greatest authors of fantasy literature of all time and who favoured Sidmouth as the place to spend his holidays.

Vicki Angus Campbell

③ BANWELL HOUSE *Miss Barnard's Lace Shop*

Lace was sold at this shop from 1780 until the 1960s. Royal customers included Queen Victoria. However, production of the lace was underpinned by hardship and child exploitation.

Mary Nicholls was the first owner of the business, and she both made and sold lace on the premises.

How and when lace-making first came to East Devon remains unanswered. Lace-making began in Italy in mediaeval times and spread from there into Europe. Perhaps it came to Devon with Hugenot refugees, or from Flanders with Protestant refugees or was carried to Devon from elsewhere in England. However, Honiton parish records of 1573 record 'Point Makers' – another name for those involved in lace-making. Later, in 1617, James Rodge of Honiton, Bone Lace Seller, left £100 to the poor (the equivalent to about £12,000 today) meaning that his business must have been prosperous.

A short hop from Honiton over Gittisham Hill would have brought the skill of lace-making to Sidmouth where, in 1698, a petition to prevent the importation of foreign-made lace, records 302 lace-makers in Sidmouth (a figure which must have included Sidford) and a further 321 in Sidbury.

Honiton lace was the generic name applied to a very fine bobbin lace made in a small coastal area of East Devon. Called Honiton lace, because originally the lace from the individual makers was collected in Honiton, which was on the London turnpike road, to be sold to the travelling lace dealers who took it back to the large cities where it was sold to wealthy citizens, wealth being measured by the value of the lace you wore. The skill to make the finest Honiton lace was originally passed down in families and its superb quality would rival the finest continental lace, particularly Brussels, with which it was often compared.

Mrs Nicholls's lace business must have prospered and she taught her daughter, Caroline, the skills. Caroline continued the business on her mother's death, making a flounce for Princess Victoria in 1830. Caroline married Stephen Hayman, a lace dealer, in 1838, and together they built a very successful business and were still listed in the town's 1879 trade directory. The shop also sold pins, bobbins and thread to the lace-makers, but provided the patterns free. Many of the patterns were the designs of Miss Marryat, daughter of the famous novelist, Captain Marryat. The Captain had a sister, Fanny Burney Palliser, who visited Sidmouth from time to time and, in 1885, wrote an early history of lace-making. She was also involved in encouraging the Sidmouth lace-makers to use new patterns.

In 1864, following an exhibition in Bristol, Caroline Hayman was requested by Queen Victoria to make two flounces in the honeysuckle pattern with matching narrow lace to trim a dress. Peter Orlando Hutchinson recorded the order in his diary for 1865:

I had in my hand and examined some lace flowers made for the Princess Christian's wedding. There were eleven yards [10m] of half a yard [46cm] wide and narrower lace for the dress trimming. The cost was £300 [approximately £15,000 at today's value]. Supplied by Mrs. Caroline Hayman.

Barnard's lace shop – Banwell House. Left Caroline Nicholls Hayman; right Mary Nicholls Barnard (née Hayman) circa 1870s (Sidmouth Museum)

The beauty and costliness of lace and the skill which went into its making belies the world of hardship which lay behind it. Sadly, it was most frequently a world of poverty, low wages, poor conditions, long hours and child labour. It was very much a cottage industry, often employing several family members in making lace to supply lace factors, or individual shops to whom they were affiliated, and who clung tenaciously to their individual makers. Often the thread was weighed before being supplied to the makers and the finished lace sprigs weighed on return to ensure no work had been done on the side and sold elsewhere. On completion of their work, they might be paid in cash, but more often payment was made in goods from the general shops kept by their employers, or sometimes in a mixture of cash and goods. Frequently, the prices charged for these goods were above that of the same goods bought in local shops. It was a much hated system and the cause of continual complaints from the lace-makers and letters from their supporters to the local press.

In 1841, a report was made for the Government by the Childrens' Employment Commissioner and from this we learn from the evidence of Mary Anne Rogers, who was the principal of the Lace School in Sidmouth, that she worked for Mr Hayman 'who gives his women [lace-makers] half money and half goods, according to the value of the work, and to the children all goods, the parents receiving the goods on their behalf'. From this it appears that the Haymans were party to this unpopular method of payment. Not only that but they also employed child labour.

Mary Anne Rogers recorded that as a child 'she learned Trolly work at 7 years old, this was a lace edging and easier than the head work or sprigs and flowers'. Evidence given to the Commissioner by Mrs Amelia Clark of Sidbury gives an idea of the harsh conditions to be found in these lace schools which had grown up to teach the skills of lace-making and to provide the children of poor families with the most rudimentary of education, such that when they left, some could read only the shortest words and only slowly, and were hardly able to write, whilst others could 'read, write and sum' by the age of 15. As to the conditions at the Sidbury school, which appears typical, there were:

...eighteen scholars when all are well, but some are generally absent because they are not well. Takes them from 6-7 years old. Their mothers put them to it a deal too early, but are driven to do so. Girls generally stay about 8-9 years i.e. till about 16 and not beyond 17 and are then as good work-women as their mothers. At first 2-3 hours a day is enough unless the child is very quick, as it is trying work to teach them. In the first year they get about 5 hours work each day and after 3 years work from about 7am to 6pm in summer and in winter from 8am to 8pm with an hour for dinner and half an hour for tea and they never stay later. [Summer hours were shorter because children had to help in the fields and with agricultural work]. Though sometimes to oblige they will be allowed to take their lace pillows home at night if the lace is much wanted. Though it be against all the rules, some bring breakfast with them, as it is so long for them to sit without eating and they get very cold.

For the first 3 years the children pay 6d [2p] a week and 4d thereafter. For the first 6 months she takes their work, but it is of scarcely any value. The other girls and families take their own work to the shops and receive payment by way of goods. They might earn 3-4 shillings [15-20p] a week after four years at the school. 3s 6d [17p] would be a very good week's work, but the earnings depend upon the patterns being worked as well as the quality of the work. When they leave after 7 years they are skilled lace-makers and may easily earn the same as their mothers.

The Reverend Edmund Butcher, the early chronicler of life in the Sid Valley, railed against the lace trade and its practices:

It is a melancholy consideration that so much comfort and health are sacrificed in producing these costly and beautiful patterns, which after all are unnecessary articles of female decoration. The sedentary nature of this employment and the early age at which multitudes of children are confined to it, make a terrible havoc of their life and health. The sallow complexions, rickety frames and debility which numbers of these young women exhibit are sad and decisive proof of the pernicious nature of their employment. The confinement of children is by far too rigid; ten hours a day is the time for which they are commonly kept at work and even then, if they have not completed their task, they are frequently not released, but further deprived of the little pittance of time in which they should have to regain the use of their cramped limbs.

That Mrs Hayman did not really approve of the situation then pertaining with regards to the employment of children is shown by her statement in 1865:

Formerly children used to have to go as apprentices for 7 years and went at 5-6 years old and after their 7 years went 6 months to learn finishing. There are now five public schools in the town open on payment of 1 penny a week. All children ought to be obliged by law to go to school.

It was, in fact, the Education Act of 1870 which was to start the decline of the lace-making trade when compulsory elementary education was introduced. It gradually, and in many cases rather reluctantly, was adopted and became the norm. Thereafter, the art of lace-making had to be learnt in other ways and lace schools quickly faded away.

Honiton lace was a pillow lace using initially fine linen, and later cotton thread, wound onto bobbins. The patterns made of paper and known as prickings were mounted on the pillow and

Miss Hannah Barnard working at a lace pillow (Sidmouth Museum)

the design marked out by fine pins. Honiton was a piece lace, made as individual sprigs which were then assembled into a design and linked by fillings whose designs were numerous. Thus a lace collar might be comprised of sprigs or motifs made by a number of individual makers linked by fillings.

In smoky cottage interiors it was difficult to keep the work clean, which was essential, and fires were frowned upon. If necessary a fire pot was used, a stoneware pot in which hot ashes were placed and which would hold their heat for hours. These were either placed by the lace-maker's chair or often under their skirts. Good light too was beneficial and so daylight was sought, often leading to lace-makers working outside in the open. In the evening, a lace-maker's lamp was employed. This was a glass globe about the size of a large orange and filled with water. Placed in front of a candle, it would focus the light on the lace-maker's pillow and illuminate the work.

Mary Nicholls Hayman, who married Frank Barnard in 1877, took over the lace business from her mother, Caroline, but ran it for only a few years. Her two daughters, Lucy and Hannah, were both lace-makers, but it was Hannah Barnard who was to be the fourth and final member of her family to run the little lace shop at Banwell House in Old Fore Street. The shop window was adorned with the royal arms of the Duchess of Kent, mother of Queen Victoria, for whom her great-grandmother, Mrs Nicholls, had made a special pattern for the Duchess and the young Princess Victoria.

As late as 1932, Miss Hannah Barnard was still supplying Honiton lace to royalty when the Duke of Connaught placed an order for some lace and personally visited the shop. For the wedding of a later Duchess of Kent in 1934, the ladies of the Sid Valley commissioned Miss Barnard to make a set of twelve place mats and one large mat for which the ladies all subscribed.

Miss Barnard lived above the shop and was well known in Sidmouth where she had a lot of friends and acquaintances. She was on friendly terms with the family who ran the Anchor Inn next door and would sometimes come in, bringing her lace pillow, and work away on a commission. If the children happened to be busy doing a jigsaw, she would sit with them working her bobbins and occasionally look over her glasses, delicately pick up a piece of the puzzle and place it in the growing picture before continuing her work.

Although her home had a bathroom, it seemed the working of the hot water system left something to be desired and she

would ask for her large tin bath to be carried into a back room of the Anchor Inn and filled with hot water and there she would happily take her bath. Many too could remember her sitting on a stool outside her shop working at her lace pillow as was the custom of generations of lace-makers before her, who would gather in twos and threes outside their cottages to work at their lace, even in winter, because there the light was better than in the dimly lit cottage interiors.

In 1960, Miss Barnard was visited by a BBC film crew to record one of the last professional lace-makers at work. In 1963 she left Sidmouth, moving to the Midlands. The Congregational Church where she had been a deacon held a special service to mark her departure and made a presentation. In 1953, Miss Barnard had said she believed that as an industry the art of Honiton Lace was dying as young people had neither the time, patience, nor skill of their forebears to make it. Henceforth it would have to be kept alive as a craft, and the skills were needed so that it could be taught at vocational classes. The little shop closed after one family's 180 years spent in the Honiton Lace Trade, a trade which is now almost forgotten in Sidmouth.

Sidmouth Museum has a particularly fine collection of Honiton lace; this is now shown in a reconstruction of Miss Hannah Barnard's Lace Shop in the Museum at Hope Cottage.

A sample of Sidmouth's wedding gift to the Duchess of Kent, made by Miss Barnard, 1934 (Sidmouth Museum)

Julia Creeke

BEACH HOUSE *once Blossom House*

Originally a plain Georgian house dating from before 1776, it was renovated in Gothic fashion following storm damage in 1824.

This was the first residential property to be built on the seafront. It appears in late 18th century watercolours and in a print of 1776 as a plain Georgian brick house with a double-hipped roof, standing alone looking out to sea over a rather rough gravel road. The town had always turned its back on the sea, the thatched cottages huddled behind the shingle embankment, and it was not until Sidmouth became a fashionable resort and visitors began to frequent the town that lodging houses with sea views were in demand. Beach House was possibly the first of these.

From the Reverend Edmund Butcher's earliest writings we learn that, by 1803, a billiard table had been installed on the ground floor and a reading room on the first. This 'Marine Library' was being run by John Wallis (junior) whose father was a London bookseller, who specialised in children's books and games, dealing from premises in St. Paul's Churchyard.

The Library became a popular place frequented by visitors, and the focus of activities on the Mall, as the gravel walk and carriageway had become known. Over the next few years buildings sprang up on both sides: to the west in 1809 a new and enlarged Library replaced the old thatched open-fronted Shed (shelter) with a new building comprising a library/shop and a new shelter on the ground floor with a billiard room above. To the east, Temple House dated from about 1805 and was then occupied by a Miss Maguire. From 1872 to 1970 it was leased to The London and South-Western Bank

When the great gale of 22 November 1824 struck, this part of the seafront suffered greatly; not a building was left undamaged. The sea rushed up the beach and over the shingle embankment and tore at the fabric of the buildings. There was no distinction between the beach, Esplanade or private gardens. Shingle was not only piled against walls, but the ground floor rooms of houses were full of shingle too; there was not a window intact and many doors were broken down. Even three months later, the whole Esplanade from end to end was still one expanse of shingle. All the garden railings and fences were gone – washed away – and what had been pretty gardens in front of the houses were ruined. Much of the town's labour force was employed clearing away the mess and it was not until the spring that things began to return to normal. There was hardship since many of the fishing boats had been damaged and most of the beach was gone.

Major repairs were essential and it seems likely that the opportunity was taken to give the rather plain Georgian façade a face-lift and turn the house into the delightful Sidmouth Gothic confection that we know today. The work was certainly carried out in the mid 1820s and it was then that the house was re-named Blossom House.

There was more trouble from the sea in December 1876, when a succession of gales and very high tides caused the sea to flood the town, damaging many of the seafront houses and contaminating old wells. Fortunately, they already had fresh

Beach House Gothicised circa 1826 (SVA)

piped water from elsewhere. Blossom House, located so close to the sea, did not escape, and windows were broken, shingle got into the downstairs rooms and the ground floor flooded.

Mrs King, who owned the house in 1884, changed the name from Blossom House to Beach House. For a time it was a guest house and then a private house. In 1989, the façade underwent a major restoration, partly funded by English Heritage. Unfortunately, it subsequently suffered further flooding in storms, necessitating yet more repairs. Nevertheless, with its pretty front elevation, it remains an important feature of Sidmouth's seafront.

Julia Creeke

5 THE BEDFORD HOTEL

A Regency building, becoming home to Wallis's Marine Library when it moved from further east along the Esplanade. It was reduced to a shell in the Great Storm of 1824, and first became a hotel in 1835.

In 1813, Wallis's Marine Library moved to these new premises at the corner of the Esplanade and what is now Station Road, then only a footpath. These premises may have been recently built or converted from an existing building, although 20 years before there was but one building on the seafront and a few years earlier none at all. It was close to the western extremity of the Mall or 'Beach', as the Esplanade was then called.

Wallis's Marine Library as it appeared in 1815 when Sidmouth's Long Print was first published (Sidmouth Museum)

The Library verandah, which had a canopied roof, was furnished with benches, and all kinds of trinkets, publications and prints were displayed for sale in its windows. Telescopes were on hire, and Lord Gwydir and Lord Charles Bentick had witnessed the entrance into Torbay of HMS *Bellerophon* with Napoleon on board. Immediately there was a rush to charter a sailing vessel for a trip to Torbay, such was the curiosity of many to try and catch a glimpse of Napoleon. Ten years later, and to the delight of spectators crowded on the verandah, a flotilla came within three miles of the shore, when Lord Bentick went out as Ambassador to Sicily, travelling in HMS *Calidonica* of 120 guns accompanied by three 74s (ships with 74 cannons) and several transports.

John Wallis (senior) is first recorded as a bookseller and map dealer in London at 16 Ludgate Street, where from 1775 he traded as the Map Warehouse and where John (junior) started to innovate with publication of children's books. In 1813, John (junior) left the London business and John Wallis (senior) took into partnership Edward, his eldest son. John Wallis (senior) died in 1817. John Wallis (junior) had been in business in Sidmouth since 1803 where he had opened 'the Marine Library'. Once established in Sidmouth, he began to publish a succession of topographical views of the town, culminating in the commissioning from Hubert Cornish, a talented artist and brother of George Cornish of Salcombe Hill House, of the famous long view of Sidmouth. In this, Hubert Cornish sets Wallis's Library very prominently in the centre. The original watercolour is now in Sidmouth Museum. The subsequent print in three sections gives a unique perspective of Sidmouth's seafront in 1815. The publication of this print cost Wallis £900, a huge sum in those days and probably now equivalent to £45,000.

A little pen and ink drawing bearing the date 1818 shows that Wallis's Library must have prospered in the three years since the publication of the Long Print as he had already extended the building, almost doubling it in size. A contemporary account says: 'It is now a very neat pile of a building with battlements and a flagstaff, upon which the Union is hoisted to celebrate the anniversary of each principal victory during the late war [Napoleonic] as well as upon royal

Wallis's Royal Marine Library after alterations in 1818 (Sidmouth Museum)

birthdays. It has a verandah under which is a retreat from the sun furnished with seats'.

On 24 December 1819, their Royal Highnesses the Duke and Duchess of Kent arrived in Sidmouth with their suite. In a letter from Kensington Palace subsequent to the presentation of a copy of the long print to the Duke at the York Hotel the previous October, John Wallis was honoured with his appointment as bookseller to their Royal Highnesses.

Sidmouth was subjected to a gale of great ferocity on 22nd November 1824 and a report in the *Taunton Courier* paints a vivid picture of events at the Library:

> The sea broke over the building, burst open the doors under the verandah, stove in the doors and 2 windows next to Fort Field, every wave rolling through the billiard room the front of which was entirely dashed in. The table weighing upwards of ½ ton was lifted up and carried against the chimney piece which was broken to pieces. The pianoforte, tables etc and every article in the Library were by the volume of the waves swept into the Reading Room at the further end.

John Wallis, his two youngest sons, a library assistant and a maid were in an upstairs room and the story is continued by William Wallis, John Wallis's son, then aged 14. He was a long-time friend of Peter Orlando Hutchinson who, three months after the storm, had come to live in Sidmouth with his parents and later recorded his friend's account:

> The house was being battered by the full fury of the wind and waves, with the water rushing right through, the doors and windows broken in and the cellars filled with shingle, everything on the ground floor was under water. John Wallis fearing that the walls would not stand much longer was faced with the choice of seeing his family crushed under falling masonry or drowned and decided that they must try and escape somehow. The back of the building abutted the narrow alleys of Western Town and by good fortune a boat had drifted up against the back wall and one by one the members of the family were lowered down into it and thus escaped. Next morning both inside and outside the Library was total devastation, almost all the carriageway had gone, there was shingle everywhere and downstairs the building was a gutted shell at the mercy of the next gale.

In the mid 1820s, as part of the repairs after the gale, the Library was refurbished and a camera obscura, a fashionable novelty and precursor of the camera, was installed in the western corner of the Library. This showed Sidmouth's surroundings in great detail in miniature: admittance to this popular attraction was priced at one shilling (5p) each person. In spite of the price it proved extremely popular. He also republished the long panorama print showing the refurbished Library.

The re-modelled Library was a combination of club, reading room and fancy goods emporium, and known as the 'Sidmouth Subscription Room', but colloquially it was always referred to as 'The Lounge', a place of retreat for promenaders, especially in bad weather.

However, a rating assessment of 1833 indicates that John Wallis was no longer in business at the Royal Marine Library and that a William Barrett was now owner of the Library, house, premises and the adjoining Bedford House. By 1835, there was an advert for the Bedford Hotel soliciting custom. William Barrett was a man of many parts. He was born in 1781 and seems to have had a variety of occupations starting with commercial traveller, later a lodging house keeper, but ending as a wine merchant, in between which he was a property developer, being responsible for the development of Elysian Fields. He lived for much of his life at Bedford House, with his

Millen's Bedford Hotel circa 1902 (Sidmouth Museum)

Just before Good Friday 1898, Sidmouth's bakers announced they would not be baking hot cross buns on that morning. John Millen, owner of the Bedford Hotel, together with some friends, asked Mr Wheaton, a Newton Poppleford baker, to bake 2,000 hot cross buns so Sidmouth's children could each have a hot cross bun. The distribution of a bun and an orange to each child took place on Bedford Lawn opposite the hotel. Thus began a Sidmouth tradition that has continued to this day. The annual Good Friday hot cross bun distribution still takes place in the same place, although the Lawn has, in the intervening years, become the seafront car park.

Some of the worst damage to the Esplanade occurred in the gales of 1924 opposite the Bedford Hotel where a huge hole opened up. Before repairs could be effected, it was made even worse by a subsequent gale. Finally it stretched across the road almost to the front wall of the hotel. When the new Sidmouth sea wall was completed in 1926, a triumphal arch was built across Station Road at the junction with the Esplanade, and Colonel Wilfred Ashley MP, Minister of Transport, performed the ceremonial re-opening the Esplanade, watched by a big crowd.

wife, Susannah, and four children. In 1841 he ended up in Exeter Jail for non payment of the Church Rate on untenanted houses in Elysian Fields. At the time, he had transferred ownership of the Bedford Hotel to his daughter Anna. He was discharged from jail in 1842 and continued to live at Bedford House and was described in a local directory as late as 1857 as lodging house keeper. The original Library was now the 'Subscription Reading Room' but its frontage was still little changed from its days as Wallis's Marine Library.

Colonel John Grey was living at Bedford House at the time of his death in December 1842. Colonel Grey had joined the Light Dragoons in 1805 and received steady promotion. He had fought at Quatre Bras and was present with Wellington at Waterloo where he was wounded. In 1825 he took command of the Royal Scots Greys, remaining so until 1839 when he retired to Sidmouth, first to Clifton Cottage and then to Bedford House.

By 1879, the property had become Millen's Bedford Hotel. It was described as an exceedingly comfortable hotel with old world charm, ably and genially managed by its proprietor who prided himself on the excellence of his cuisine. For some years prior to 1895, a men's club had been established in the adjoining building to the east, but when this moved to new purpose-built premises next door to the Marine Baths, the vacated building was incorporated into the hotel.

The hotel made history when it became one of the three earliest premises in the town to be lit by electricity supplied from a generator that the enterprising Bill Dagworthy had installed at the rear of his garage a few doors further up Station Road. Remnants of Wallis's original Library building are still visible in the canopied loggia and the first floor crenellations.

The area now occupied by the seafront car park was once the Bedford Lawn and belonged to Bedford House which had been built behind the Library in the 1820s and which became part of the hotel. What is now Station Road then ended at The Three Cornered Plot (The Triangle) and a simple path led down across the Lawn to the Esplanade. Station Road was extended down to the Esplanade at a later date, cutting off the Hotel from the Lawn, which was finally put up for sale. It was bought by Bill Dagworthy for a car park and from there he ran his coach excursions and the bus service up and down Salcombe and Peak Hills, using unique vehicles known locally as a 'Toast Rack'. One still survives owned by Bill Dagworthy's grandson.

Julia Creeke

6 BELMONT HOTEL and GATEWAY

Originally 'Belmount', a fine Regency house with a large walled garden. It was home to a number of notable personalities. Much altered and extended, it became a hotel in 1921.

In the late 18th century there still remained a remnant of the mediaeval strip cultivation alongside the eastern side of a narrow goyle bounded by the Woolbrook. In 1810 there was evidently already a house on the land for the Reverend Edmund Butcher, in his book *Beauties of Sidmouth* published that year, writes that 'the lodging houses including 'Belmount' which stands upon a level with the 'Fortfield'.'

This house was one of the six that were built by Emmanuel Baruh Lousada of Peak House who was to become the second largest landowner in Sidmouth after the Lord of the Manor. These houses were situated on the periphery of the Peak Estate or on land not far away and included both 'Rosemount' and 'Belmont'. (For the full history of Peak House, see separate chapter).

For a short time, Major-General Baynes occupied the house. He left England for Canada joining the Nova Scotia Fencible Infantry and then the Glengarry Light Infantry in the War of 1812, when hostilities broke out between the United States and the British colony of Canada. These local troops were raised to complement the British Garrison in times of war. Colonel Baynes rose to the rank of Major-General before retiring when the Glengarrys were disbanded in 1816. The following year, his mother moved into Woolbrook Glen (now the Royal Glen).

In 1813, the particulars of the sale of Sidmouth Manor state that Sir Joseph Scott, Bart, is renting the dwelling house and shrubbery, comprising just over one acre, for £21 p.a. In 1817, the Reverend Butcher again refers to the house and the many improvements and additions which Sir Joseph had made to it, making it into a stylish double-fronted house with verandahs and bow windows. The old crenellated wall and arched gateway still stands fronting the Esplanade, and may date back to the time, early in the Napoleonic Wars, when a regiment of militia was garrisoned on the Fortfield.

Sir Joseph Scott, Bart (1752-1828) was seated at Barr Hall, Staffordshire, and was active in public life, being High Sheriff of Staffordshire in 1779 and MP for Worcester 1802-06. His association with Sidmouth, where he took an active part in the development of the town as a member of various committees, went back at least to 1812. In February of that year, he chaired a Committee Meeting at the London Hotel concerning estimates for the building of a harbour. He was also a member of the Committee which, in the same year, established Sidmouth School which provided free education for poor children. His wife died in 1822 and Sir Joseph, now an old man, gave up 'Belmont'.

The SVA purchased, in Worcester, a pair of oil paintings by Henry Haseler, the Sidmouth artist, dating from c. 1821, one of which is a view of 'Belmont House'. They now hang in Sidmouth Museum and provide a rare glimpse of what the house and its surroundings were like in the early 1820s.

Sir Joseph Scott was succeeded by an illustrious occupant. A contemporary guide book tells that 'The Marquess Wellesley

Belmont House, published by J Wallis 1817 (Sidmouth Museum)

Belmont Gate, a relic from the Napoleonic Wars when militia were encamped on the Fort Field (SVA)

and suite occupied the house during the two seasons he honoured Sidmouth with his company'. The Marquess was the elder brother of the Duke of Wellington, and had been Governor General of India 1798-1805. He also served as Foreign Secretary and later as Lord Lieutenant of Ireland.

Occupying 'Belmont' in 1833, and already with Sidmouth connections, was Moses Guttares who had married the niece of Emmanuel Baruh Lousada (on his wife's side), who had built Peak House and died in 1834. This family of Sephardic Jews married their kinsmen and were all closely connected by family ties. They were descended from Portuguese/Spanish people of Jewish faith who had fled the Inquisition and had made fortunes in trade with the West Indies.

For the next 30 years little is known about the house, but in all probability it was let. In 1869 Mr William Hine-Haycock bought the lease and came to live at Belmont with his wife and family. Born in 1831, he was educated at King Edward's School, Birmingham. In 1853 he was admitted as a solicitor practising in London until ill health forced his premature retirement. He was a member of the MCC for 37 years and finding Sidmouth Cricket Club's future very uncertain, he and Mr Thornton, who resided at Knowle, set about rejuvenating the Club. He was a genial and kindly man and much missed when he and his wife returned to live in London in 1884. The family's association with Sidmouth continued at Core Hill House until the late 1960s when they sold the house, moving to Dartmouth.

Just to the east of the gate of Belmont was an old platform, probably part of the foundation of the armoury associated with the former Fort, which was demolished after the Napoleonic Wars. This platform had been in use as part of a substantial clothes line but, in August 1866, this construction, laden with washing collapsed in a gale on top of the unfortunate housekeeper at Belmont, Lucy Scotford, killing her

instantly, whilst she was attempting to rescue the washing. The *Sidmouth Observer* reported the inquest held at the Bedford Hotel, at which it was stated that she had, since the age of 20, been employed for 30 years at Belmont.

Peter Orlando Hutchinson relates in his diary of September 1882 that he had visited Mr Hine Haycock who showed him four ancient coins which had been dug up whilst the lawn in front of Belmont was being altered. Two were Saxon, one of the reign of Henry III and the fourth of Elizabeth I dated 1575.

In December 1896, Belmont became home to Mr and Mrs RH Hatton-Wood, an elderly couple of 77 and 74 respectively. Born in 1819 in Cheshire, Richard Henry Hatton-Wood was, through marriage, a man of very considerable wealth. He had been Deputy Lord-Lieutenant of Warwickshire and High Sheriff of Merioneth. He and his wife were life-long benefactors to the communities in which they lived. They founded the Hospital of St Cross, Rugby, and gave the Museum and Library to the town. In Sidmouth, their benefactions were considerable, including land that was to become Blackmore Fields and also the Drill Hall. The Parish Church was also to benefit by the gift of the font cover, a stained glass window and the steps leading up from Church Street but, in addition, there was a vast number of benefactions to individuals of which few were aware.

Following a disastrous fire in January 1902 which destroyed the north side of New Street in Sidmouth and very nearly engulfed much of the lower town, the need for a new and more up-to-date fire engine was apparent. The West of England Fire Insurance Co. had, since the 1860s, maintained an engine and fire brigade in Sidmouth, but this old engine was ineffective, and the steam appliance sent from Exeter took two hours to reach Sidmouth owing to the horses having to pull it up Four Elms Hill. The Town Council held a debate but felt unable to raise the money. On hearing this, Mr Hatton-Wood offered to finance the purchase of a Merryweather Steam Fire Engine and this was presented to the town at a ceremony on the Ham.

Mrs Hatton-Wood's health was the reason for their coming to live in Sidmouth, and since doing so she had always been concerned that the Parish Church lacked any social facility of its own. When Mrs Hatton-Wood died in October 1905, the *Sidmouth Observer* reported that she had left the substantial sum of over £83,000. In her memory, Mr Hatton-Wood purchased Fort House, the old home of the Kennaway family, renaming it 'Church House' (now 'Kennaway House') and gave it to the town as the facility which his wife had intended.

Mr Wood died in his 90th year in 1908. After the Lord of the Manor, he was the largest property owner in Sidmouth and was very fond of the old houses. Those with thatch were of particular interest and he bought more than one for the purpose of restoring it rather than allow it to be demolished and replaced with something modern and less picturesque. He was a fine judge of wine and the quality of his cellar of port was famous well beyond Sidmouth. He collected rare books and manuscripts and owned an original copy of the Edward VI Prayer Book which, as a staunch churchman, was his pride and joy.

About 1920, Belmont was purchased by the Fitzgerald family and further extended and opened as a hotel in 1921. Soon after the outbreak of WW2, Sidmouth became 'RAF Sidmouth'. It was not like other enclosed Stations and almost all Sidmouth hotels were requisitioned to house the Medical Training Depot. The Belmont Hotel became the Airmens' Mess. The only part of the original Regency house still clearly visible is the first floor balcony with its bowed French windows. When the Fitzgeralds

The house with addition to the east when it first became a hotel (Sidmouth Museum)

retired, the hotel was purchased by the Brend family of Barnstaple and is now part of the Brend Group of hotels.

Julia Creeke

7 BLACKMORE HALL *(site of)*

A substantial Regency house built in about 1814, noted for the beauty and seclusion of its gardens. Over the years it had a number of prominent residents – and a notorious one. The house was demolished in 1955, and its gardens retained as a public park.

A larger area known as Blackmore Fields originally belonged to the Manor of Sidmouth. Detailed archival research by the Arts Society Sidmouth found that in 1813 the Reverend Philip Story purchased around two acres (0.8 ha) from this larger estate for £2,500 and built Blackmore Hall, possibly as a holiday home for him and his family. He was a wealthy landowner from Lockington in Leicestershire, where he was Lord of the Manor and owner of Lockington Hall.

The Blackmore Hall estate was in essence a gated enclosure surrounded by walls, with the entrance gates located in Blackmore Drive. The separate triangle of land below what later became the health centre was left outside the enclosed gardens initially, but was enclosed later.

The house was built in a plain Regency style, arranged over two storeys, with a pitched roof and dormer windows. The portion containing the main reception rooms and principal

Blackmore Hall, circa 1920 (courtesy of Geoffrey Leader)

bedrooms was set forward, fronting on to the gardens, whilst a spacious 'service wing' was set back behind, stretching across to Church Lane. To the rear there was a coach house, stables and outbuildings.

The overall footprint of the house and immediate outbuildings was large – it encompassed what is now the car park for the library and health centre, the site of the recently re-designated St John Ambulance Centre car park and a portion of the Methodist church hall.

There are no known photographs of the interior, but a document held by the Devon Heritage Centre from 1913 provides a glimpse. It describes the ground floor in terms of a spacious inner hall with a 'handsome Principal Staircase,' a 'lofty and well proportioned Drawing Room' with French windows opening onto the verandah, a dining room, also opening onto the verandah, and a large Morning Room.

On the first floor there were four principal bedrooms and four secondary ones.

The service wing was 'well shut-off from the reception rooms' and the 'domestic offices' included 'kitchen, scullery, larders, housemaid's and butler's pantries, servants' hall, housekeeper's room, boot room...a secondary staircase, a coal cellar...and very good wine cellarage.'

The gardens were enclosed within high walls of brick, stone and pebbles, most of which survive intact today. The main garden was divided entirely across the middle by a chevron-shaped brick wall, portions of which also still survive. The land closest to the house was planted for visual enjoyment, whilst the plot beyond the dividing wall was the kitchen garden.

A view across Blackmore Fields towards Blackmore Hall, 1848, painted by PO Hutchinson (Devon Heritage Centre)

Following the death of Reverend Story in 1819, the house was purchased by Sir John Kennaway, the owner of nearby Fort House (now Kennaway House). It is thought unlikely, however, that he ever lived at Blackmore Hall, choosing instead to let it out. His descendents sold the estate in 1845 to Esther Cornish, a relative of the prominent Salcombe Regis family. She lived at Blackmore Hall until her death in January 1861.

The next owners, the Strahans, arrived as outcasts from London society following one of the most notorious banking scandals of the 19th century. It wasn't the biggest bank failure of the age, nor were the financial malpractices involved the worst, but the bankruptcy struck hard at the Establishment. The banking house of Strahan, Paul and Bates, founded in 1660, had been particularly favoured by the aristocracy and senior clergy.

William Strahan (1807-1886) – born William Snow, he took his mother's maiden name later – came from the bank's founding family and married Elizabeth Ann, daughter of General Sir George Bulteel Fisher. William and Elizabeth lived at Hill Street, Mayfair, in a house with nine servants. He had been an accomplished sportsman at Eton and Cambridge, and later played cricket for Surrey and the MCC. In 1829 he not only rowed in the first ever University Boat Race, as the Cambridge captain, but it was he who was tasked to write to Oxford laying down the challenge.

His downfall came in 1855 when he and his two partners tried, and failed, to trade the bank out of a solvency crisis by using assets belonging to their clients. They were arrested for fraud, placed in Newgate Prison and tried at the Old Bailey. The prosecution was led by the Attorney General. Found guilty, they each received a sentence later described by the *Daily Telegraph* as 'cruelly severe' – transportation for 14 years.

In the event, they were not transported and William Strahan served only four years, in Millbank Prison. He and Elizabeth then arrived at Blackmore Hall in February or March 1861 with six children and four servants. For people wanting to retreat a long way from London to a civilised locality, and to a house with grounds shielded from the public's gaze, Blackmore Hall must have seemed ideal.

It was probably the Strahans who carried out modifications to the original layout of the gardens that came to light later in a detailed survey carried out by Sidmouth architect RW Sampson in 1913 (copy held by the Devon Heritage Centre). This indicated that the kitchen garden had been relocated to

Sir Aubrey Strahan FRS

the triangle of land below what is today the Health Centre, to be replaced in part by a badminton court and croquet lawn. On the lawn immediately in front of the house was a tennis court.

William and Elizabeth Strahan remained at Blackmore Hall for at least eleven years and perhaps up to fifteen. They then went to live in Italy, where they both eventually died.

One of the six children accompanying the Strahans when they came to Blackmore Hall was 8 year-old Aubrey. After Eton and Cambridge, he later became Sir Aubrey Strahan FRS, President of the Geological Society and Director of the Geological Survey. It is possible that his interest in geology was ignited by coming to live on the Jurassic Coast. For example, Peter Orlando Hutchinson records in his diary for 1872 that 19 year-old Aubrey had purchased for two shillings and six pence (12p) a large fossil tooth found on the beach.

The next owners were Edward Fisher, a retired solicitor from Leicestershire (no relation to Mrs Strahan) and his wife Emeline. Then, in the mid-1880s, came George Scott, who was retired from the Bombay Civil Service, and his wife Augusta. Mrs Scott stayed on after her husband died in 1902 and, in 1905, she purchased the fields adjoining Blackmore Hall to ensure they were not built on.

Colonel The Hon. John Pleydell-Bouverie in the grounds, circa 1920 (courtesy of Geoffrey Leader)

After Augusta Scott's death in 1913, her daughter sold the house to Sidmouth Urban District Council (SUDC) for £4,250, which in turn sold it in 1914 for £2,500 to Colonel The Honourable John Pleydell-Bouverie and his wife Grace Harriet. This onward sale was on the condition that SUDC would have first refusal whenever the house came up for sale again. Significantly, SUDC retained ownership of the Blackmore Fields, later to be bowling greens and tennis courts.

The Hon. John Pleydell-Bouverie was born in 1846, the fourth son of the Earl of Radnor. He became an officer in the 17th Lancers, a prestigious cavalry regiment famous for its role in the Charge of the Light Brigade. He served with them in the Zulu war of 1879 in South Africa, fighting in the decisive battle at Ulundi. The 17th Lancers were then sent to India and were stationed there for the whole of the 1880s. India was not a new experience for Mrs Pleydell-Bouverie as she had been born there, in 1860, the daughter of General Robert Mallaby of the Bombay Staff Corps.

Colonel Pleydell-Bouverie died in 1925 and his wife continued to live at Blackmore Hall until 1952, when she sold the house back to SUDC for £3,000. She moved across to Devonia in Coburg Terrace and died there in 1953.

A poignant reminder of the time spent at Blackmore Hall by the Scotts and Pleydell-Bouveries is the row of 10 small headstones against the wall abutting the churchyard – a pets' cemetery, probably for dogs (e.g. Joey, Snowy and Winkie).

As soon as SUDC re-purchased the property, it set about clearing and replanting the gardens, creating new entrances and paths, and installing seats. Advice was sought from the head gardener to Lord Derby, who visited in July 1952 to discuss the layout. The gardens were then formally opened as a public park on 18 July 1953 and named 'Coronation Gardens' in honour of HM Queen Elizabeth II.

In July 1955, SUDC decided to demolish Blackmore Hall, this being judged as the only viable option given the extremely poor condition of the building. Demolition was completed by February 1956 and the site has been used as a car park ever

The Hon. Grace Harriet Pleydell-Bouverie (courtesy of Geoffrey Leader)

since (although this has recently been sold). Small areas were sold-off for the building of the Methodist Church Hall and the then St John Ambulance Centre.

However, a fragment of the house survives today – the stone plinth and tiled floor of the verandah. This is now used as the platform for a row of benches.

Blackmore Gardens became popular as a public open space from the outset, valued both as a place for quiet recreation and a venue for public events. Most recently, the children's activities in the annual Sidmouth Folk Week have been centred there.

John McCarthy

BYES TOLL HOUSE

Built in about 1817 to collect tolls to maintain the adjacent Waterloo Bridge over the River Sid and its approach thoroughfare, Salcombe Road. The bridge provided much improved eastern access to the town.

It is now hard to imagine a Sidmouth without Salcombe Road, such a busy thoroughfare has it become. In the early 19th century, the whole of the area opposite the main Postal Depot and Radway Cinema was fields stretching down to the Sid, bisected about two thirds of the way down by the Mill Leat which was drawn off above the weir and flowed down in a channel to the mill. This ran through what was once Parsons Builder's Yard and foundry, but is now covered by a development of retirement housing: the old leat completely filled in, and its former line now obliterated.

As Sidmouth grew, there was more development on the east bank of the river and lower slopes of Salcombe Hill, but carriage access to the town was still via the Mill Ford and, if the river was in a spate and the Ford impassable, it meant a long detour via the bridge at Sidford. As a number of influential residents had estates on which they had newly built houses on the east bank of the Sid, in the Parish of Salcombe Regis, it was not surprising that there was agitation for the river to be bridged near the town.

It seems that the County was prepared to provide some money to build the bridge and a subscription list was opened for the purpose of raising additional money to make a new road to connect with the upper part of High Street. The road was cut from a field which belonged to Joseph Hook. It seems likely that George Cornish of Salcombe Hill House, Lord of the Manor of Salcombe Regis, had contributed some money towards the cost of the bridge, since Vaughan Cornish writes in a footnote to his book *A Family of Devon* that the new bridge 'was of one handsome stone arch. The first stone was laid on Michaelmas Day 1820 by Cornelia Cornish (George Cornish's younger daughter) aged fourteen'. It was named Waterloo Bridge in honour of Wellington's great victory in 1815.

At this time, the roads were still controlled by the many Turnpike Trusts which then existed, few of which made any profit and as little money as possible was thus spent on the roads, many of which were in a dreadful state. It seems that traffic had always used the Mill Ford free of tolls, but passage over the new bridge and road had to be paid for and many preferred to use the old route. A neat toll house in the then fashionable Greek revival style was designed and built alongside the bridge and a toll gate placed across the road on the eastern side.

As the condition of the roads grew progressively worse, so calls for the abolition of the Turnpike Trusts grew more vociferous and eventually they were abolished by Act of Parliament. The toll house and gate were thus redundant and the little house was let as a dwelling.

The toll gate is said to have been made by an ironmaster at Honiton and is almost identical to the gate which is still exists in its original position outside Honiton on the Axminster Road. From old photos, it appears that the Sidmouth gate never hung on handsome iron gate posts with acorn finials such as supported the Honiton gate, but on much more modest wooden ones. To the north of the Toll House was an area once fields, but by this time known as 'The Lawn'.

It would seem that the toll gate had had a previous life as originally it was located at Stephen's Cross (at the foot of Trow Hill). It was then moved down to the road across Waterloo Bridge when that was completed and finally, when all tolls were withdrawn, it became the front gate of the house 'Egypt' in Millford Road, before finally being returned and re-hung at the entrance to the Byes. It managed to escape destruction at the beginning of WW2, when the Byes railings were removed to be melted down, the iron reused in armaments. After the end of the War, the gate was replaced at the entrance to the Byes, hung on two pieces of R.S.J.

By the late 1970s, the whole area of the Byes entrance was in a sorry state and so the Sid Vale Association, with the blessing of the District Council, undertook the building of a new flint boundary wall and gate posts. The old gate was taken down and restored and then re-hung on flint gate posts, typical of many in the district and, more recently, a pillar bearing details of the many Listed Buildings in the vicinity has been erected just inside the gate. The adjacent bank inside the wall is now planted with spring bulbs which give a fine show.

The whole of the grassy area alongside the River Sid is known locally as 'The Byes' and it is often asked what the word 'byes' means. The most likely derivation is from the old meaning of 'bye land' or land left unploughed, or unploughable, around the edges of the mediaeval fields. The land close to the river bank was probably left unploughed because it would have flooded when the river was in spate and crops would be washed out of the ground.

Over the years, a footpath developed through this land, passing by the wonderfully named 'Roly-poly' Field, which led to

Looking east along Salcombe Road with the Toll House on the left; the gateposts can be seen (Sidmouth Museum)

the ancient hamlet of Seed or Sid, situated part way along Sid Road. It was the oldest and most populous part of the Parish of Salcombe Regis. As Sidmouth grew, this stretch of open farm land remained undeveloped because the Sid had a habit of flooding in heavy rains. In the 1920s, an area was purchased by Miss Annie Leigh Browne, the sister of Lady Lockyer and wife of the eminent astronomer, Sir Norman Lockyer, and named 'Sid Meadow'. Miss Annie Leigh Browne lived at 'Hills' in Sid Road, which overlooked the area. She donated the land on her death to the National Trust to hold for public enjoyment. Subsequently, further areas have been given to the Sid Vale Association and parts incorporated into the Byes. There is a local tradition that in the vicinity of the Roly-poly Field there existed, about a century ago, a small house which straddled the river – it is long gone and all that remains is a length of masonry wall.

Over the years, the River Sid has repeatedly flooded at times of heavy rains. One of the worst was in 1963 when, following a summer storm, the deluge was such that the river came right up to the top of Waterloo Bridge and an abandoned car was washed over the top of the bridge and out to sea. The river later washed a tree under Millford Foot Bridge, jamming it there. Debris built up causing the river to divert its course down Eastern Town, flooding the whole area and parts of the lower town. A repeat of this is now prevented by a gate which automatically closes the road as the river rises.

The little Toll House has suffered numerous floodings over the years, some very serious with the occupants having to be rescued. Attempts have been made to try and stave off this flood risk, but the Council finally had to concede defeat and the house is now only occasionally occupied. The whole area alongside the River Sid, as far as Sidford, is now known as 'The Byes'.

Julia Creeke

9 CEDAR SHADE (formerly Belle Vue)

A late Georgian house which, in 1834, was for a year the home of the poet Elizabeth Barrett (Browning). In the 20th century it became a hotel, named Cedar Shade.

Although it is sometimes said that Cedar Shade was once a farm house, there is no mention of it or any other house on the site in any early 19th century literature on Sidmouth, and it is not until 1826, in a print of that year, that there is a representation of 'Belle Vue' (the original name of the house). It seems likely, therefore, that the present house came into being about 1820, and enjoyed a slightly elevated site with an open view over the Blackmore Fields to the Church.

Having lived for some months with his large family, including Elizabeth, at 8 Fortfield Terrace, Mr Edward Moulton-Barrett was gratified to see the great improvement in the health of his daughter, Elizabeth. It was also apparent that the rest of his young family were enjoying their time at Sidmouth. With the lease about to expire and unable to find another desirable residence, he was forced to take another house, possibly

Cedar Shade, then called Bellevue as it appeared in 1826 from a painting by George Rowe (Sidmouth Museum)

Norton Garth, not far from No. 8, and the family moved there. Elizabeth hated it, writing to a friend:

> We are still in this ruinous house, without any practical function the walls are too frail even for me to have any desire to spend the winter within them. One wind we have had the privilege of hearing already – down came the tiles while we were at dinner. We have had one chimney pulled down to prevent it tumbling down.

There were instructions too from the bricklayers not to lean on the windows 'for fear the windows should follow the chimney'. Just where this house was located is uncertain.

Mr Moulton-Barrett continued to search for a house but as Elizabeth wrote in a letter: 'as he said the other day, "if I can't find a house that will fit us I must go", but I hope he may find one – and as near the sea as this one'. Then writing to Lady Margaret Cocks on 15 November 1833, she says: 'Papa was so puzzled as to what house would fit us, that he had all but resolved to remove us to Bristol Hot Wells'. Elizabeth apparently got into trouble for not wishing to leave Sidmouth and expressed her 'pleasure at Papa finding a pretty villa or rather cottage with thatch and a verandah and a garden about a quarter of a mile from the sea and with a genuine Devonshire lane with hedgerow elms bordering our garden'. This house was 'Belle Vue'.

The family settled into Belle Vue for the last part of their residence in Sidmouth and, in September 1834, Elizabeth wrote happily: 'We are living in a thatched cottage with a green lawn, bounded by a Devonshire lane' (the lane was the present All Saints' Road). The family found much to enjoy in Sidmouth and in May 1835 a group of them set off at ten in the morning by the steam packet for Torquay. The family would have enjoyed the trip but for 'the devastating sea sickness'. 'The packet returned us to Exmouth about six in the evening – there we had tea and came home upon wheels at nine in the evening'. In the summer of 1835, Mr Barrett decided that the time

Elizabeth Barrett Browning in a drawing by Field Talfourd (National Portrait Gallery)

had come to move again and in December the house was sold. The family reluctantly left Sidmouth for Gloucester Place, London, where they remained until 1838 when they moved on yet again to the famous address in Wimpole Street. Eleven years after she left Sidmouth, Elizabeth married the poet, Robert Browning, at St Marylebone Parish Church, to the fury of her father who, despite Elizabeth's numerous attempts at reconciliation, disowned her for the rest of his life.

It was whilst at Sidmouth that Elizabeth became friends with the widowed Reverend George Barrett Hunter, the Nonconformist Minister at the Marsh Chapel (previously situated on part of the present Western Ham Car Park). The Reverend Hunter had a six year-old daughter, Mary, and was an eloquent preacher and a man of considerable personality. Under his influence, Elizabeth wrote hymns and poems and he became such a frequent visitor at Belle Vue that he was accepted almost as a member of the family and accompanied them on many of their expeditions to such places as Dawlish and Torquay. She in turn followed him to various chapels in the area where he was invited to preach. Her aunt, Arabella, who was living with the family, resolutely refused to 'like' life at Sidmouth, but Elizabeth's younger brothers loved it: there was fishing on the Sid and Otter, and always the shore to be explored.

When Mr Barrett made the decision to leave Sidmouth and as their departure drew near, it became increasingly apparent that the Reverend Hunter was not just a good friend, but very much in love with Elizabeth. But it did not seem to be reciprocated on her part and, although he continued to correspond with her and see her from time to time, his attentions were always gently rebuffed and their relationship came to an acrimonious end in 1845 when Robert Browning entered her life. Thereafter she refused to see him alone. He died in an asylum in 1856.

Sometime after the Barretts' departure, Belle Vue was extended and the lovely hexagonal conservatory added. The early vicars of All Saints' Church (completed in 1837), lived in 'Cedar Shade'. The first to do so, the Reverend Joseph Bradney, was a subscriber to the building of the Church. When he died in 1865, the house had been for some years in the possession of John Leekey, and he changed the name to 'Oaklands'.

It next became the home of Mr and Mrs William Toller: she was the only child of Commander John Carslake's younger brother, Henry Joseph and his wife Hester, who lived at 'Spring Garden'. William Toller was born in 1806 and had served in the old East India Service; he had become a JP for Devon and a respected member of the Sidmouth community. His wife, whose family were classed amongst the local gentry, outlived her husband by 17 years and their daughter continued to live there until about 1940.

The house later became a comfortable and popular hotel – Cedar Shade – but when it was put up for sale in the 1980s, it was bought by the WRVS and turned into a retirement home. The delightful conservatory was by then in a poor state, but with grant aid was carefully restored. Some years later, finding the operation of the retirement home uneconomic, it was closed and the house put up for sale. It was finally bought by developers who converted it into flats and built a number of individual houses along the eastern side of the drive.

Julia Creeke

After extension with the octagonal conservatory: taken when the Tollers lived there (Sidmouth Museum)

10 HIGH STREET *(previously Chick's Lace Shop)*

An early Victorian house, used for nearly 50 years by the Chick family for assembling and selling lace. Local lace was known generically as Honiton Lace, because it was placed into the national market there.

Samuel Chick I was born in Axminster in 1776, the son of a small time farmer. In 1804 he married Abigail Tucher of Buckland St. Mary and they settled in Branscombe to farm on a succession of properties, prospering so that they were able finally to settle at Berry Barton.

Abigail had developed an interest in the art of lace-making, for which the village was well known, which led her to become a dealer, collecting the individual sprigs from the local makers and then selling them on elsewhere. In due course she began to collect them and supervise their making up into articles, and finally marketing the finished lacework herself. She made journeys to places of fashion, like Brighton, to sell her lace. The *Brighton Herald* of 1833 printed a note from Abigail thanking her customers for their support during her recent stay in the town. She then informs them that she has just received a new consignment of laces of every description: 'The whole of the best manufacture and after the first fashion'. Gradually the business thrived. With thoughts of retirement, Abigail divided her business between her two eldest children, Samuel II and Harriet.

Around 1830, Samuel II had been sent to Weymouth to learn the trade of clockmaker: as he had been lame since childhood, farming was considered out of the question. In 1823, aged 25, he married his first cousin, Harriet Staple, at Radipole, Dorset. It was in Weymouth, probably to help family finances, that Harriet began to sell her mother-in-law's laces although, in 1848 Local

Harriet Chick with her son Samuel (courtesy of the Tomlinson family)

Directories, Samuel is listed as 'Honiton Lace Dealer'. In 1849, the family left Weymouth to set up in business in Sidmouth, the move being accomplished by sea. Abigail and Samuel I, now retired, had also moved to Sidmouth and were settled at Castle House on the corner of High Street and Blackmore Drive.

Samuel II and Harriet together with their family settled into their new home at No. 3 High Street (now No. 10), one of two adjoining early Victorian 3-storey brick-faced houses at the lower end of the east side of High Street. The ground floor opened straight onto the pavement, and there was a rear wing which housed the lace workshop, reached by an outside stair from the yard, which opened onto Russell Street via a tiny garden. There was also a small shop where the lace workers received part of their pay in goods, a system common in many trades in the 18th and 19th centuries and which was the cause of much discontent. It is hard to realise that in the 1850s, the only sanitation was a combined ash pit and privy and no town centre house had any proper sanitation until the coming of the main sewer in 1875.

The lace-makers collected their raw materials and patterns for pricking on to their pillows and brought in the finished sprigs and pieces, which were then joined, made up and finished in the workroom before being despatched to London, where Harriet and Samuel II's son, Samuel III, had established himself as a lace merchant. He had married Emma Hooley, a Macclesfield girl, whom he met whilst she was visiting relations in Newton Poppleford. Since leaving school, he had been working for Debenhams in Cheltenham to learn the drapery business, but at the age of 21 he was sent to London to establish a wholesale warehouse for Honiton lace at 6 Newman Street, north of Oxford Street. He and Emma lived above the business. Lace was despatched from there to customers all over England. As Samuel III's London business grew, there was a constant problem of getting supplies quickly from Sidmouth or special orders completed on time. His greatest competitor was his uncle, John Tucker of Branscombe, who was also a lace dealer with a firm hold on the lace-makers of Branscombe and Beer. Unfortunately, as a result of a long-standing family animosity, Samuel and John did not meet, nor do business together. By the 1870s, Samuel's business was in decline and he began to take on the sale of foreign laces, travelling on the continent with his draper friend

*Chick's Lace Shop, with awning and clock
(courtesy of the Tomlinson family)*

Mr Biddle, to purchase lace. He sold some very fine pieces to the Victoria & Albert Museum in South Kensington.

In the mid 19th century, a skilled lace-maker could earn 1/- to 1/6 (5-7p) a day and, if there were several workers in a household, it could considerably augment the family income; the average wage for a labourer being about 10/- (50p) a week. The Chicks were not the only suppliers of lace in the town, but, unlike the others, did not depend on private orders, selling their lace wholesale to the fashion trade as 'Honiton Lace'. The problem was that their lace workers did not get paid their wages entirely in cash, but in kind from the shop which most lace dealers kept on their premises. There was a general complaint amongst lace workers that if they had cash they could buy the same items for less from local shops. Items needed to sustain a family could generally be bought up to 2p (old money) cheaper elsewhere. In any case the wage, for highly skilled work, was paltry and there was a further complaint that the dealers got the lion's share of the profits on sale, yet they couldn't do without the makers who had to work long hours in poor conditions for little reward. The lace dealers who employed them guarded their work force jealously and did everything in their power to stop them moving on to work for others or selling lace on their own account to private customers. It was not a happy situation.

The lace seems to have gained the generic term 'Honiton', because in earlier times the lace made elsewhere in East Devon had been collected there prior to being sold to the travelling lace dealers; Honiton being on the main London turnpike road. Lace had been made by makers living in Honiton since the 17th century and a petition of 1698 listed 1,341 persons in Honiton engaged in lacework of one sort or another, and a further 2,116 working in East Devon towns and villages. The lace made in Honiton was augmented by lace from Beer, Branscombe, Sidbury, Sidmouth, Colyton, Ottery and Gittisham, but sold under the title 'Honiton lace' which gained a reputation for being some of the finest English-made lace.

Lace from the area had been supplied to several members of the Royal Family, including Queen Victoria's wedding flounce, which was made in Beer. The high point of demand for lace was in the mid 19th century but gradually with changing fashion its use declined until by the late 19th century only a relatively small amount was being made; demand having fallen away in the last ten years of Harriet's life. Gone were the days when literally thousands of women worked at their lace pillows in almost every village in East Devon and their children either learnt from their grandmothers and mothers or attended lace schools where, to begin with, they learnt to make simple edgings and motifs, at the same time gaining a little basic education by repeating things like tables parrot fashion. The Education Act of 1870 made elementary schooling compulsory and caused a further decline in skilled lace-makers.

*A Honiton lace collar made by Chick's lace-makers,
circa 1910 (Sidmouth Museum)*

As the 19th century progressed, the lace, all too often by past standards, had become debased and of poor design, the cotton thread often thick and clumsy. In the 1720s an ounce of the finest linen lace thread cost the equivalent of an ounce of gold and that was before the lace was worked, the resulting lace being so valuable that it was transferred from dress to dress. Early in the 19th century, cotton thread replaced linen and this could be spun even finer to be worked into the net inserts. As demand increased, so short cuts were looked for, such as use of machine-made net on which the handmade sprigs were mounted, or tape which was worked into patterns and connected with infilling. But there were still many superb lace-makers in the area capable of producing the finest work when this was required.

By the end of the 19th century, Samuel III was involved in several other business ventures and had become a prosperous trader. In 1911, he was responsible for selecting and sending to Toronto, Canada, fifty items of antique lace for the newly founded Royal Ontario Museum. He believed that this collection, which still bears his name, was the finest and most representative with which he had been associated. It still remains in the Museum collection to this day.

Samuel Chick III retired to live at Branscombe for part of each year, where he involved himself in local matters. He died in December 1925 at Chestergate Park, one of his London homes, leaving an estate valued at £155,313 (nowadays equivalent to £4.75 million). His unmarried brother, Edward, a fine amateur photographer, lived with Harriet and was friends with Peter Orlando Hutchinson who used to visit the house on occasion. Harriet, however, died in 1892 and Edward outlived her by only five years. Thereafter, the Sidmouth house was sold by the family with much sadness for many of the younger generation had enjoyed happy summers at Sidmouth since their childhood. Another member of the family, Dame Harriette Chick (1875-1977), lived for many years in the house Samuel Chick III had built for himself on the east side of Branscombe. Harriette was an outstanding microbiologist and nutrition scientist, becoming Director of the Lister Institute, London, and President of the Nutrition Society from 1956 to 1959.

Julia Creeke

---

11 12 13 14 15 CLIFTON PLACE

including Clifton House, Connaught House, Rock Cottage, The Beacon and Clifton Cottage

A picturesque group of five houses, built between 1805 and 1840, each with a fascinating story to tell.

Clifton Place grew up on a narrow triangle of land at the western end of Sidmouth Beach. On the earliest Sidmouth map drawn in 1789 at the time of Thomas Jenkins's acquisition of the Manor, the land is shown as a remnant of the mediaeval field system.

About five years later, the first house, 'Rock Cottage' was built (it still bears its original name). It was a plain thatched Georgian house with a verandah on the seaward side and in 1818 was owned by Mr Joseph Sparks and let as a lodging house. As Sidmouth's popularity grew so did the need for suitable accommodation for the visiting gentry, and houses to be rented out were built on many sites close to the sea.

Much of the land on which Nos. 1-5 Clifton Place were built was first conveyed away from the Manor in 1790. However, it was about this time, following the inheritance of the Manor after the death of Thomas Jenkins, that numbers 2 and 3 were built. Originally two cottages, No. 2 was accessed from the sea side and No. 3 from the road. No. 2 was occupied by the Manor Agent and eventually No. 3 was added in. In 1900, its rent was 10 shillings (50p) per week. It remained in the possession of the Manor for 150 years, even after Heugh Balfour, the last Lord of the Manor, died. It then passed to his daughter and grand-daughter and was finally sold in the late 1970s.

Clifton Place from the beach, 2018 (Diana Colville)

About 1805, Mr Heffer purchased some land for £20 and it was on this plot, immediately below Rock Cottage, that he built a house, to which, about 1810, he added another very similar in style, the two being known as 'Heffer's Row' – now 'Connaught House' (No. 5) and 'Clifton House' (No. 4). Samuel Heffer was a local fisherman who had become prosperous, but the family still worked their boats from the beach below their houses, drying their nets by hanging them over the low cliff outside.

These houses Samuel Heffer rented out, either as a whole or as rooms, and in 1809 Thomas Stapleton (1766-1831), 6th Baron le Despenser (and also the 16th Lord le Despenser), began construction of 'Knowle Cottage', which he described as 'a cottage upon a large scale'. He had probably been influenced in his choice of Sidmouth because it was fast becoming a fashionable resort for the wealthy. While construction of Knowle Cottage, an enormous thatched property of 40 rooms, progressed and wishing to be close at hand, Lord le Despenser in 1810 took a lease from Mr Heffer of No. 5 Cifton Place. In addition, Lord le Despenser took a lease of No. 1 Fortfield Terrace for his wife and her household.

Thomas Stapleton, Lord le Despenser, should not be confused with his Despenser relation, Sir Francis Dashwood, of West Wycombe Park, who had become notorious because of his association with the Hell Fire Club. Thomas Stapleton was said by contemporaries to be a private man who eschewed all political divisions, but his reputation was nonetheless colourful. He was a rich, capricious and difficult man who could indulge his pleasures as he chose. His wealth derived from West Indian Plantations and, in 1781, he succeeded his father as 6th Baron of the Leeward Islands, a title inherited

from an ancestor who had been Governor of Nevis. In 1791, he married Elizabeth Eliot of Antigua and together they had two sons and six daughters. His reputation soon caught up with him in Sidmouth, and it was said that 'he stayed up all night and laid in bed all day'.

Lord le Despenser's seat was at Mereworth Castle in Kent which had come to him by descent. Mereworth was one of the surviving three great Palladian classical houses to be built in England which followed very closely the design of Palladio's Villa Rotunda, near Vicenza, Italy. Mereworth was built in 1723 to the designs of the architect Colin Campbell. The design of this most classical of classical houses if compared with what Lord le Despenser was now building at Sidmouth – a huge

From a painting in 1810. The fishermens' cottages on the beach were washed away in 1824. The three houses higher up are (from the furthest) Rock Cottage, the first of Mr Heffer's houses, and No. 2 Clifton. Artist unknown (private collection)

Clifton Place in a photo in 1863 by Francis Bedford (courtesy of Margaret Harker)

thatched, fanciful rustic cottage – the differences could not have been more stark.

Whilst Knowle was under construction, he would from time to time visit the site and if the slightest thing displeased him about the work he would order it all undone, to the dismay of the workmen. So the building work often progressed incredibly slowly and he became extremely unpopular with his work force. (There is more about Knowle in the relevant chapter). He was never to occupy 'Knowle' having for unknown reasons lost interest in its completion; Knowle having to be finished under the direction of Sir John Soane's office. Lord le Despenser continued to occupy Mereworth until his death in 1831.

Heffer's Row when still in possession of the family, about 1870

Below Clifton Place there were cottages on the beach long occupied by fishermen, but when the great gale of November 1824 struck, it was of such ferocity that their occupants had to escape by climbing up the cliff to safety. As the waves swept up the beach, one occupant, said to be a Mrs Partington, attempted to sweep the water from her door with a broom. With the storm abated, nothing was left of the cottages. The story of Mrs Partington and her broom may or may not be true, but it was used by the Reverend Sidney Smith, Anglican cleric and wit, in a speech at Taunton in support of the Great Reform Act.

Ten years later, a sea wall had to be built to protect Nos. 2 and 3, Clifton Place. In 1836, after another onslaught which damaged Rock Cottage, further seawall construction took place until, in 1842, the last section of cliff below Heffer's Row was faced, a plaque on the wall recording its completion. These walls are all private property and their upkeep is the responsibility of house owners. Over the years, there were problems and, in the 1920s, several holes appeared after storms and were plugged with old railway sleepers. In the early 1980s, a succession of fierce storms and very low levels of beach shingle resulted in serious damage to the wall of the Beacon and also to Rock Cottage. Major civil engineering work was undertaken to insert a massive concrete footing along the base of all the walls fronting Clifton Beach. This footing is now covered by the Clifton Walkway completed in 2001.

The risk of fire at Clifton Place, always the great hazard of thatched roofs, grew with the advent of road-going traction engines, which stoked up and then belching forth smoke and sparks, attempted to ascend the lower part of Peak Hill. In 1908, Rock Cottage was gutted by fire and the following year Clifton Cottage, then the property of Mr Jemmett who resided next door at 'Sea View', suffered the same fate. Nos. 4 and 5 had been knocked together in the 1920s to make a hotel. In 1944, No. 5 was burnt out and No. 4 badly damaged, the fire said to have been caused by a mirror left in the sun on an eiderdown in one of the attic bedrooms, causing the curtains to catch fire, which in turn set the thatched roof alight. Some of the lower walls survived together with the bay window and front door. No. 4, whose thatch had been removed to prevent the fire spreading, became so waterlogged that even the joists warped.

No. 5 was rebuilt and renamed Connaught House, and for 20 years was the holiday home of Mr and Mrs Hickman. Mr Hickman was a director of Harrods. Mr and Mrs Browett and his sister moved in bringing with them the most magnificent collection of antique Meissen porcelain. In due course, Mr Browett gave the majority of his collection to the Victoria and Albert Museum where it still remains. Miss Browett eventually went to live in a house in Convent Road. Thieves broke in, tied this now elderly lady to a chair, and made off with silver and china. Running out of fuel late at night on the way back to Exeter, they were found by the police who helped by providing them with petrol, but never thought to question what they were doing out so late nor what was in the back of the van. Miss Browett was released, severely shaken, the next day, but neither stolen items nor thieves were ever found.

In the late 1960s, No. 4 had another interesting owner, Miss Sabina Lamb. She had been brought up in Constantinople where her father, Sir Harry Harting Lamb, was Chief Dragoman to the British Embassy at the Ottoman Court, where he acted as translator and advised on diplomatic etiquette and PR. It was a role only given to diplomats with long service in the region and fluent in the language: in fact Sir Harry spoke four Balkan languages fluently. Miss Lamb was an acknowledged authority on English parish churches and claimed to have visited and photographed every one. She used to give formal dinner parties for the teenaged children of her friends. The young people were expected to come dressed appropriately and the idea was that they learnt etiquette and how to behave at such events. Surprisingly, the young people greatly enjoyed these occasions.

Clifton Cottage had been built about 1820 as a charming small summer, or garden house, for Peak House then owned by Emmanuel Baruh Lousada. Of Jewish heritage, his family was of aristocratic Spanish/Portuguese descent. His grandfather had emigrated to the West Indies where one branch of the family lived for 150 years in great style on their Jamaican estates. Emmanuel Baruh Lousada (1744-1832) was a wealthy City merchant and trader, who, wishing to establish his position in English society, sought to become a landowner, and was one of the first of his faith to do so. In 1793 he purchased an initial 25 acres (10 ha) of land on the lower slopes of Peak Hill (further land purchases rapidly followed), where he built an elegant Georgian house. The family were to remain associated with Sidmouth for almost 100 years, but, throughout that time, through lack of heirs, the estate never passed from father to son, always from uncle to nephew.

About 1822 Clifton Cottage was leased by Mr Lousada to Henry Haseler, the artist and local drawing master, whose pictures are a unique first-hand record of Regency Sidmouth, and can be seen in the town's museum. The little house was

Clifton House (arrowed) in 1934 when, with its upper neighbour, it became Clifton Guest House (private collection)

disposed of by the Lousada family and much extended in the 19th century. It had to be almost rebuilt after the disastrous fire of 1909 and the house today, in spite of its Regency appearance, is largely Edwardian. In the 1840s, for a short time, it was lived in by Colonel John Grey, who had retired from command of the Royal Scots Greys, a post he had held since 1825. He had fought at Waterloo where he was injured. He died at Bedford House, Sidmouth in 1842.

The Beacon, first called Beacon Place, was built about 1840 as two back-to-back cottages in a style which is a mixture of Sidmouth Gothic and Swiss Chalet, for the picturesque scenery of the Alps was admired by the Victorians. For many years, the two houses were always let, but in about 1911 they were made into one house, which for a short time was owned by a Mrs Chubb of New York, who was a member of the safe and

Connaught House from Peak Hill Road (SVA)

Clifton Cottage in 1826, from an old print after the painting by George Rowe (Sidmouth Museum)

lock-making family. In the First World War, it became a 'Second Line' Voluntary Aid Hospital with twelve beds, where army patients could be sent for convalescent care.

Rock Cottage was rebuilt after the fire in 1908 by architect RW Sampson who became known nationally for the quality of his council house designs which set new standards in public housing. His style was traditional, but Rock Cottage, an excellent example of 20th century 'cottage orné', is probably his most distinctive design. Initially owned by the Wood family it passed to Florence Watson and, in 1937, to Henry Coates.

In 1942 the house was bought as a holiday home by Sir Francis, an expert in merchant law, and Lady Isabella Tudsbery, who owned the Scottish estate of Champfleurie in the Royal Burgh of Linlithgow in West Lothian. They owned Rock Cottage for 24 years and, during this period, members of the Wills tobacco family also made use of the property. In 1944, the Tudsberys established what became the Thistle Foundation in Craigmillar, Edinburgh, to provide homes for disabled ex-servicemen that would, in the words of Sir Francis, enable them 'to live in homes of their own, surrounded by their own families, by their own friends, and by their own belongings.'

Their only son, Robin, was an officer in the Royal Horse Guards and, for nine months in 1943, was given the role of guarding the Royal Family during WW2. When he left this service, the Princesses Elizabeth and Margaret gave him a tea party. He was then posted abroad and, aged 25 years, was killed by a roadside bomb on 30 April 1945: especially poignant as hostilities in Europe ended four days later. His parents built a chapel named after Robin which is sited at the centre of the Thistle Foundation, and this was dedicated by the newly-crowned Queen in August 1953, accompanied by her mother and sister. The Queen returned in 2013 to commemorate its 60th anniversary.

In 1966 Rock Cottage was sold by the Tudsberys to Russell and Patricia Vernon. They, like the Tudsberys, stayed for 24 years and then gifted the house to the National Trust in 1990. After letting it for a time however, the Trust found it surplus to their acquisition policy and sold it back into private ownership.

During WW2 a heavily sandbagged pill box was built at the foot of Peak Hill Road and a mock barn, complete with timbered walls, was constructed on the road just below No. 1 Clifton Place and armed with a machine gun. Both were manned by the Home Guard. The barn was later dismantled, but at regular intervals the machine gun was set up in the garden of No. 2 Clifton Place and fired out over the sea for practice. The noise in the house was apparently terrifying. Fortunately its services were never required. However, a large 400lb (180kg) bomb, dropped by a marauding German aircraft, fell harmlessly into the sea, where it exploded, the blast causing some damage ashore, although all the Clifton houses survived the war undamaged.

The sundial on the seaward elevation of Connaught House, inscribed with the appropriate legend for a location overlooking the sea – 'TIME AND TIDE WAIT FOR NO MAN' – dates from the year 2000 and records the passing of the Millennium, whilst the house had reached its first half century. There can be few places where a group of thatched houses occupy such a picturesque setting so close to the sea.

Julia Creeke

Rock Cottage and The Beacon beyond from Peak Hill Road (SVA)

16 THE CLOCK TOWER and JACOB'S LADDER

This pseudo-castle was built in the 19th century as the boathouse for nearby Cliff Cottage. The first Jacob's Ladder was built in about 1871 and has been replaced several times.

For centuries, lime had been important in the rural economy for making lime mortar, limewash and plaster, but during the 18th century the pioneering agriculturalists found that the application of lime in small quantities to soil which was well manured, as part of a crop rotation, considerably increased the crop yield, by improving soil quality and releasing plant nutrients. The demand for agricultural lime burgeoned and more and more lime kilns were constructed for the burning of limestone. In coastal areas, since limestone was heavy, these tended to be near the sea, so that the limestone could be brought by boat and off loaded close to the kiln.

Such a lime kiln was constructed above Jacob's Ladder Beach and the stone was shipped in by boat, to be dumped on the beach and brought up to the kiln by donkeys, using a sloping path cut into the face of the cliff. The limestone came chiefly from the Torbay area, particularly from around Babbacombe, where the cliffs were quarried – the flat rock platforms at the base of the cliffs used as jetties from which to load the stone

onto the ships are still clearly visible all round the Babbacombe and Brixham areas, particularly near Anstey's Cove. One of the suppliers of limestone for the Sidmouth kiln was Mr Yates, who had for many years been in partnership with Lord Rolle of Bicton, as a ship-owner trading in limestone for the local coastal kilns, until the business failed. In 1821 he became Minister at the Old Meeting.

The lime kiln was a dumpy, square, crenellated tower which resembled a small coastal fortification and, although it continued in regular use, erosion of the cliffs was becoming an increasing problem for access. In 1847, the Sidmouth Improvement Committee (the predecessor of the Sid Vale Association) resolved to make good the pathway from the kiln to the beach because much of it had fallen away. In 1852 the problem recurred. The local population was unused to being denied access to the western beaches and, in 1853, it was decided, rather than keep trying to repair the path, to cut steps into the face of the cliff alongside the lime kiln. Permission to carry out the work was sought from Mr Lousada of Peak House, who owned the land.

It was now not easy for the donkeys to reach the beach to bring up the limestone, and the kiln gradually became

Path in cliff, painted by PO Hutchinson, 1851 (Devon Heritage Centre)

Almost vertical first ladder, painted by PO Hutchinson, 1871 (Devon Heritage Centre)

Sloping Jacob's Ladder painted by PO Hutchinson, 1878 (Devon Heritage Centre)

redundant. The owners of Cliff Cottage now had a very substantial and semi-derelict structure adjoining their garden, and about 1870 much of the old path and kiln finally fell down.

By the late 19th century, a pseudo castle had been built on what remained of the old lime kiln for use as a boat house for Sea View, as Cliff Cottage was now called. Boats were lifted up and lowered down on davits. The boat house was topped by a lookout and clock which struck the hours. To the east, stone steps descending to the shore had been built to provide private access to the beach for the residents of Sea View, but on the western side a new long wooden ladder had to be made as the old steps had finally fallen in. This ladder was rapidly dubbed 'Jacob's Ladder' by the locals, but the long, straight, steep ladder was difficult to ascend and the ladies hated it. It was soon replaced with another much more substantial staircase, very similar to today's version, which is the third replacement. Peter Orlando Hutchinson's three water colours, 1851, 1871 and 1878, clearly show the changes.

The Clock Tower became part of Connaught Gardens when the Sidmouth UDC purchased Sea View in June 1930. When

Clock Tower today (SVA)

war came in 1939, Jacob's Ladder was dismantled and up went coastal defences. The Clock Tower was taken over for the duration of the War by 389 Coast Battery Royal Artillery who were equipped with two 138mm guns. The lookout at the top of the Clock tower was used as a round-the-clock observation post, and a pill box was constructed close to the entrance from the road.

When peace came, Jacob's Ladder had to be rebuilt and, in the late 1950s, the chineway down to the beach was finally cut. A huge pile of rock was bulldozed down onto the beach to the horror of local residents, but within a winter it was all swept away by the sea. In the 1950s, a walkway was built from the concrete apron at the bottom of Jacob's Ladder, under the cliff, to the main beach. The concrete apron was badly damaged in the storms of the winter of 1974 and had to be repaired at a cost of £35,000 and, later, the Clock Tower was strengthened and repaired and the clock made operational, striking the hours on a small external bell with no great resonance, but a distinctive plaintive tone. There had been further damage to the apron in subsequent storms and in 1996 rock armour was placed against the undercliff walk. The pseudo-castle, after languishing unused for many years, was finally converted into a café which has proved a popular facility for both visitors and locals.

Julia Creeke

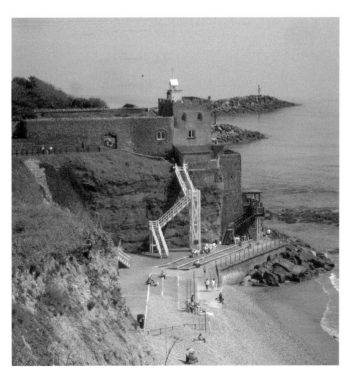

Jacob's Ladder today (SVA)

Former home to Arabella Buckley (b.1840 – d.1929), who was an author internationally renowned for making science subjects more accessible for children.

Mrs Arabella Fisher lived in this house from 1921 until her death at the age of 88 in February 1929. She had come to live in Sidmouth, at Beatlands, following the death of her husband in 1895, but she moved to Oxford when, in the words of her friend Lilias Cowan, 'the march of civilisation on Salcombe Hill became too alarming.' However, after Oxford and a brief period in London she returned to the peace and quiet of Sidmouth.

In her lifetime, Mrs Fisher was better known as Arabella Buckley. She was the author of sixteen science books which were internationally renowned. They were translated into German, Japanese, Polish and Swedish. She had an American as well as a British publisher and paperback editions of her works are still available online today.

The majority of her books were written for children but her first book, published in 1876, was for adults. *A Short History of Natural Science* aimed to 'give a modest amount of scientific information which everyone ought to possess, while at the same time ... form a useful groundwork for those who wish afterwards to study any special branch of science'.

Miss Arabella Buckley in her bath-chair on the seafront (Sidmouth Museum)

She had entered the world of science at the age of 24 when she became secretary to Sir Charles Lyell who was the foremost geologist of his day. She was the daughter of the vicar of St Mary's Paddington, and although we know her brothers were educated at Merchant Taylor's and Cambridge, we know nothing of her early education. However, she went on to have a formidable on-the-job education. Charles Lyell was a close friend of Charles Darwin and Thomas Huxley and in 1858 he was instrumental in the publication of the papers of Darwin and Alfred Russel Wallace on natural selection. Arabella, dealing with all his correspondence, was at the centre of the London scientific scene and in contact with the most eminent scientists of the time.

Alfred Russel Wallace later described her as 'My most intimate and confidential friend'. When later in life he was in financial difficulties, she asked Darwin to persuade the Prime Minister to grant him a pension. It is particularly interesting that as rational scientists they were both spiritualists and members of the Society of Psychical Research.

After Lyell's death in 1875 she edited scientific books and went on the lecture circuit. Educating the public in scientific matters became her life. In 1879 she gave a series of ten lectures at Dr Chaning Pearce's Geological Museum in Brixham. She lectured in school halls and institutes throughout London and beyond. In 1882 she was at the Edinburgh Philosophical Institute and in December 1901 she lectured at Leighton Buzzard. These lectures formed the basis of her books.

The first she wrote for children was *The Fairy Land of Science* which dealt with the forces of nature which she deemed more magical that the old fairy tales. The next two, *Life and her Children* and *Winners of Life's Race*, tackled the hot topic of the day which was evolution.

No. 3 Coburg Terrace (right) detail from a watercolour by PO Hutchinson 1848 (Devon Heritage Centre)

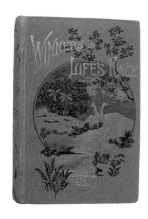

One of Arabella Buckley's children's books.

In 1884 she married Dr Fisher, who was a widower 20 years her senior. He had been living in New Zealand but by 1891 they were living in Torrington, Devon, where she was lecturing 'Devonshire lads' and turning these lectures into books. Some of the chapters in her books had previously appeared in shorter form in American magazines and her *Moral Teachings of Science*, published in 1892, started out as a series of lectures for Chautauqua, which was an Adult Education movement in America.

Why she came to Sidmouth after her husband's death is unknown. She entered into town life and continued to educate the public in scientific matters. Between 1900 and 1904 she gave University Extension Lectures in Sidmouth and was instrumental in starting a library and reading room. It was during this time that her six natural history books for the Cassell's *Eyes and No Eyes* series were published.

By 1929 she was almost blind and was wheeled around town in her bath chair by a companion, but was still very interested in the world around her. After her death, a group of friends appealed for money for a memorial to her and a bronze plaque was commissioned and set up on the south wall of the parish church, where it can be seen today.

Maureen Thurlow

18 4 COBURG TERRACE and THE OLD CHANCEL

Sidmouth's best known figure from the Victorian era, Peter Orlando Hutchinson, moved to No 4 with his parents in 1824. From 1859 to 1890 he built the Old Chancel as his home, using fragments from Sidmouth parish church and other historic buildings.

The row of four houses called 'Coburg Terrace' had been built about 1820 on behalf of Sir John Kennaway, whose residence was close by at 'Fort House' (now Kennaway House – see separate chapter). Sir John had married Charlotte, the daughter of James Amyatt MP and when her father died in 1813 she inherited property in Sidmouth. The Terrace was given the name 'Coburg' in honour of the Duke of Kent who died at Sidmouth in 1820, who had estates at Amorbach in Coburg and whose wife, the Duchess, was the daughter of the Duke of Saxe-Coburg Saalfeld.

Into 4 Coburg Terrace in January 1825, moved Dr and Mrs Andrew Hutchinson and their family, which included their second son, a rather frail child called Peter Orlando (POH) (their eldest son Young Bingham was in the Navy), his sister,

the cat and a canary. It was a strange twist of fate that brought the family to Sidmouth, for 46 years earlier Peter's great grandfather, Governor Thomas Hutchinson of Massachusetts, on his way westwards, had paid a brief visit to the town in order to see two friends from America, who were lodged in

4 Coburg Terrace (nearest house), watercolour by PO Hutchinson 1848 (Devon Heritage Centre)

the town; alas they were both away. All three men, committed Royalists, had fled the American War of Independence and were living in England.

Governor Hutchinson, as a Royalist and after much harassment, had in 1774 felt compelled to leave America as the outbreak of the War of Independence loomed, and seek refuge in England, where he settled in Croydon. He was frequently at Court, where, as England seemed increasingly likely to be expelled from America, his experience and knowledge was often sought. Whilst in England he determined to see more of the country and knowing that both Judge Curwen and the Reverend Isaac Smith, exiles from America like himself were settled at Sidmouth, he stopped over with the intention of seeing them.

Unlike his friends, Governor Hutchinson was never to return to America, and died in Croydon in 1780, dispossessed of his very considerable American estates. The previous year he had written sadly:

The changes of the last 4 or 5 years appear a dream or other delusion. From the possession of one of the best houses in Boston, the pleasantest house and farm at Milton, free from debt and an affluent income, and prospect of being able to make a handsome provision for each of my children, I have not a foot of land at my command and personal estate of about £7,000 only, depending on the bounty of government for a pension'.

The next year he heard on 30th June 'that one Brown of New York had purchased my estate at Milton for £38,000 lawful paper money'. The poor Governor was heartbroken: he was never to return to America and died the following year aged 69.

POH's childhood was marred by long spells of illness, probably a disease of the hip, and he was lame throughout his life. He embarked on a series of walking tours to acquaint himself with the regions of England – he was already an accomplished artist and illustrated his tours in watercolour as well as keeping a diary. 1837 saw him embark for America to visit his American relations and see the places where his ancestors had lived.

POH had a lifelong fascination with guns and, as a teenager, he and another boy were severely reprimanded for causing an explosion in one of the Fort guns still situated then on the Fort Field. In 1854 he was given a brass gun captured from pirates nine years previously by his cousin Lieutenant John Roberton.

He mounted this on a gun carriage and used to parade it round town, taking it to the beach for target practice: he even took it uninvited to a parade of visiting Yeomanry on Peak Hill.

Dr Andrew Hutchinson, who died in 1846, had left Peter £500 and his 134 acres of land in South Australia, which had been bought for £100 and which Peter subsequently sold for £1,000. In 1855, when to his great sadness his mother died, he inherited 4 Coburg Terrace, which had been bought from the Kennaways, and £3,000 which he invested in the Great Western Railway. He now let No. 4 and with a secure income went to Paris for a year, which he enjoyed but, being a confirmed low churchman, railed against the popery of French church services.

PO Hutchinson aged 38, a self-portrait (Devon Heritage Centre)

On his return to Sidmouth he was almost immediately involved in the controversy that erupted over whether Sidmouth Parish Church should be rebuilt, or the old church repaired and refurbished. POH and other low churchmen were outraged at this wanton desecration of a building which had been in use for 600 years and the preservationists now took issue with those wanting to give Sidmouth a fine new Church. A new west window had been solicited from Queen Victoria as a memorial to her father, the late Duke of Kent, who had died whilst staying in the town, but it was now intended to place the new organ in front of it, entirely obscuring it.

POH decided to prevent the Queen becoming further embroiled in this unseemly controversy and, backed by the Earl of Buckinghamshire of Richmond Lodge (now Sidholme), he took a petition to Osborne House. In his dress uniform of the Volunteer Artillery and carrying his sword, he presented himself and was assured the petition would be considered. On his return he found himself at the centre of an even worse storm yet, in spite of this, POH remained a staunch churchgoer and in 1859, unchallenged, he signed a contract to buy and re-erect the Old Chancel of Sidmouth Church on the eastern section of his garden at 4 Coburg Terrace. Thus began the project which was to occupy him for the next 30 years.

At first he re-erected the Old Chancel, slightly smaller, but little altered, commenting in his diary for 15 December 1863: 'Ever since I erected the Old Chancel I have been contemplating adding to it in the same antique style and thereby converting the whole affair into a residence'. He therefore journeyed to Awliscombe where he bought the old window from the south transept which was being replaced, and used it for the Oak Room, busying himself with carving and painting the room's interior decoration.

He now contemplated an entrance hall and some upper rooms to make the place habitable 'though not to complete the whole design'. He and his housekeeper, Mrs Webber, moved in on 31 October 1866 but alas the house was so cold, damp and dusty that the stress of living in such conditions caused her death. The final work started in 1889 as he received payment for the publication of the two volumes of the *Diary and Letters of Governor Hutchinson*, which he had edited and which were published in both Britain and America. At last on 18 January 1890 he wrote 'the building work is finished at last', although work continued inside the Old Chancel right up to the end of his diary.

This diary was to occupy him throughout his life and in it he

The Old Chancel, early stage of conversion, circa 1864 (Sidmouth Museum)

recorded everything of note, illustrating many of them in watercolour. He made frequent journeys to various places to visit sites of archaeological, historical or geological interest and details of these visits were all recorded. He went often to Dawlish, Chudleigh and Uffculme to visit relations and explored the environs of these locations, all of which were recorded and illustrated in the diaries. He made frequent forays into the area around the Sid Valley, often accompanied by his friend Mr Heineken – POH missed him greatly when he died. Everything of note in Sidmouth found a place in the diary pages. In spite of his lameness, POH must have walked untold miles in his lifetime on these expeditions.

Unfortunately, on two occasions he committed the diaries of earlier years to the fire, declaring that he had never read them and no one else would. He said there was much in them that was childish, and so what good was it keeping them. The diaries that remain are all post Christmas 1846. This has denied posterity of learning more of his early life and travels, but at least his later diaries all survive. (Copies are in Sidmouth Museum and are available to visitors). He would have been amazed to see the recent interest in his diaries and seeing them published in two handsome volumes.

POH was a man of wide interests as can be seen from the diaries. As well as being a very adequate artist and musician, history, archaeology, geology, the study of fossils, ancient buildings and military matters were all subjects of particular interest to him. Through his diaries he has also provided later generations with a wonderful commentary on the life and events of 19th century Sidmouth and its citizens. He could remember and recount going with his father to a reception held by the Grand Duchess Hélène of Russia at 8 Fortfield Terrace and seeing her Russian entourage in their uniforms and commenting that she spoke good English.

Alongside all the building work on the Old Chancel and everything else, he kept up a full social life, being welcome in many local houses and visiting his friends regularly and joining them for picnics and musical evenings. He also worked on his amazing five volume *History of Sidmouth* which he wrote in manuscript and for which he had been collecting material since about 1849. He considered publication in 1870, but the cost of £200 he felt beyond his means and doubted finding subscribers to cover the cost. Volume one he completed in 1872 and the fifth volume in 1880, when he was 70. He bequeathed them with his other papers to Exeter Museum.

POH still kept his diary and there were amusing episodes

such as when Sanger's circus came to town and encamped on Blackmore Fields. Amongst the animals, the circus included nine elephants. Peter recorded the event thus:

Soon after breakfast a man came to the door in a fluster and said I had better come out. Upon this I went out and there I saw nine elephants walking about the field and many men busy erecting tents for the performance. The weather was fine and it was a pretty sight to see so many huge creatures ambling about the field. There were two or three elephants by the railings pulling away at the thorn bushes, brambles and weeds in my hedge and putting all this rubbish, thorns and all, into their mouths and masticating it. When the procession went round the town, all nine elephants were yoked in tandem or in single file to one of their large carriages.

He was now an old man, and the deaths of several of his close friends left him very isolated and his own health was not very good. He went out little, particularly in the winter, although he still wrote, and interior painting of the Old Chancel continued. The Reverend HG Clements, who had been Vicar of Sidmouth since 1865, was a regular visitor to the old man and he conducted Peter's funeral service, having got to know him well over the years. The Reverend Clements read a paper on POH to the Devonshire Association in July 1903, which recalled his

life, interests and literary achievements. Mr Clements often spoke of the spartan conditions in which Peter lived at the Old Chancel and of his love for his cat and pet birds, and of his resigned acceptance of the infirmities of old age, saying in conclusion 'how typical an antiquary in face and figure, in character and demeanour Mr Hutchinson was. His handwriting was a copy of the antique, carefully and slowly executed, his diction and utterance were equally deliberate.' The Reverend Clements regretted 'how rapidly and completely he seems to have passed out of recollection' and so it remained until recent years. Only those who wished to elicit some information on Sidmouth's past consulted his history and fewer still knew of his evocative watercolours which 'paint a picture' of the Sidmouth he knew and loved. Recently, the *History* has been a source of much information for writings on the town, including this book. His diaries have been indexed and published in extract by the late Catherine Linehan and, more recently, a much fuller version by Jeremy Butler. The Old Chancel is now a Grade I listed building – this would have pleased POH, but he would also have been much amused that people are often completely taken in by its architecture and assume it to be very ancient. What no one can doubt is that Peter Orlando Hutchinson was a representative of that quintessential figure 'the English eccentric' – cultured, inquisitive and gifted.

Julia Creeke

---

19 CONNAUGHT GARDENS

Cliff Cottage was a thatched late-Georgian house with extensive gardens, demolished in 1932. It was once the home of Constance Kent, who achieved notoriety as a convicted murderess. The gardens were opened as a public park by the Duke of Connaught in 1934.

The original house on this site was not so much a cottage as a pretty detached marine villa with thatched roof and canopied verandahs with lattice supports and trellis work. It

was built in 1821 by Emmanuel Baruh Lousada (junior) on land owned by his uncle Emmanuel Baruh Lousada (senior) of Peak House on an exposed grassy knoll at the foot of Cliff Fields. The area was all in the ownership of Mr Lousada (senior), who was a wealthy merchant of Jewish heritage. By the time he settled in Sidmouth, it is doubtful if he was actively practising his Jewish faith; Sidmouth was fairly remote and he hoped that by taking an active part in local life and supporting local causes, his ancestry would be forgotten and his quite

Cliff Cottage, 1826, from a painting by George Rowe (Sidmouth Museum)

considerable landholding overlooked, and thus it proved. (A full history of Peak House is given in a separate chapter.)

The site of the original drive up to the villa is marked by a change in colour and texture of the stonework which is still visible in the boundary wall opposite Manor Road. The house overlooked a large lawn (now the main lawn of Connaught Gardens) and enjoyed a fine view of the eastern cliffs.

In 1834, Constance Emily Kent was born in the house to parents whose relationship was already an unhappy one. Mrs Kent began to suffer frequent bouts of insanity, often being locked in her room. These bouts of insanity are now thought to have been caused by syphilis acquired from her husband. This was yet another tragedy since three of the children died and were buried in Sidmouth Churchyard and two more were to die young. There was the inevitable local rumour and gossip and, to save his family this unwanted attention, they moved away in about 1838, first to Somerset then to Wiltshire, where Mrs Kent died due to a bowel obstruction.

Later, Mr Kent married the children's governess, and in due time a son was born to the second Mrs Kent, but the older children became increasingly resentful and the infant was found dead with its throat cut in an outside privy in the grounds of their Wiltshire home. The police were unable to solve the crime although their main suspect was the daughter Constance. Five years later, aged 21, Constance Emily confessed to his murder and was convicted and sentenced to death but, being a minor at the time of the crime, the sentence was commuted to 20 years imprisonment. (See Further Reading for books which describe the full story.)

The sentence was served in several jails where she assisted in the hospitals and, having learnt the art of ceramics, she became skilled in the laying of mosaics, decorating the Chapel at Portland Prison and, after her release, worked on the mosaics in the Crypt of St Paul's Cathedral. Her youngest brother, William, had settled in Australia and so as to be near him she emigrated under an assumed name, arriving in Melbourne in the midst of the typhoid epidemic of 1890. She joined relief workers at Prince Alfred Hospital and continued working in various institutions until the First World War when, aged 80, she joined the Australian Army Nursing Service. She was still working in her 90s and much respected in Australian nursing circles. She died in 1944 aged 100.

Her Sidmouth birthplace had undergone many changes and was called Sea View: the thatch had been replaced with slates, the house extended, and the garden had been walled and shelter belts of trees planted, so that it had grown to fine maturity, but the house's sombre reputation persisted. Part of the garden was surrounded by high black palings atop the stone walls which added to the sense of mystery. Mr Jemmett, who was one of the last owners of Sea View, was an elderly, eccentric and irascible man, and the butt of much torment by the local youth.

Eventually about 1930 the house, in a very dilapidated state, was put up for sale and Sidmouth Urban District Council debated its possible acquisition, but concluded they did not have the money. Finally Mr Dagworthy purchased it to save the property being lost to the town. After much further discussion, the Council agreed in 1932 to buy it, in order to preserve its fine garden for public enjoyment. The house was found to be in such poor state that it was demolished, and now all that remains is the terrace overlooking the main lawn.

The Duke of Connaught, the third son of Queen Victoria, who was wintering in Sidmouth, and after whom the gardens were named, performed the opening ceremony in

Constance Emily Kent, circa 1858

Duke of Connaught (left), with Equerry,
on the Esplanade (Sidmouth Museum)

Connaught Gardens

November 1934. The event is recorded on a plaque on the rear wall of the terrace. In the 1980s part of the garden of Clifton Cottage was sold to the Council for inclusion in the Gardens and now forms the area behind the Band Stand.

The Gardens are one of Sidmouth's most attractive features and enjoyed by locals and visitors alike. From June to September, the Town Band plays concerts on Sunday evenings and, over the years, the Gardens have helped Sidmouth to win many awards in the Britain in Bloom Competition.

Julia Creeke

20 COTMATON OLD HALL *(site of)*

Originally a Tudor house, rebuilt in the 17th century and destroyed by fire in 1934. It was inherited in 1810 by John Carslake, who had served on HMS Victory at the Battle of Trafalgar, and who married Thomazine Leigh of the prominent Salcombe Regis family.

The name 'Cotmaton' is ancient, for in 1260 when the Otterton Cartulary was written, Robert de Cotmetton is recorded as holding land at Woolbrook. This probably refers to an area around the small stream which flows down Bickwell Valley and out to the sea at Clifton. For centuries this stream was known as the Woolbrook (Saxon for little stream).

By 1426 the Harlewines were settled on their lands at Ascerton and were to be associated with Sidmouth for more than 200 years. In due time they were to own extensive lands at Cotmaton where, in the early 16th century during the building of Cotmaton Hall, the date 1520 was recorded carved into a stone. During the 17th century the family spread to other parts of Devon and assumed greater prominence, so that by the middle of the century, the Sidmouth properties were in decline and the Ascerton estate was split into several portions; the Cotmaton estate being sold to the Duke family of Otterton.

In 1695, Robert Duke sold his Sidmouth estate to Henry Carslake of Branscombe, who settled at Cotmaton Hall. In the

Cotmaton Old Hall, from a print after the painting by George Rowe (Sidmouth Museum)

Sidmouth Parish accounts of 1697, there is an entry: 'M Henry Carslake for 180 rede for ye fort £1.12.0d.' (£1.60). Presumably this was for thatching the roof of an associated building.

Henry Carslake was born in 1642, the second son of Henry Carslake of Sidbury and his wife Grace. In 1696, aged 54, he married Dorothy Leigh and his only son, Henry (the third of the name) was born in 1698, but sadly his wife died following the birth and, just three years later, with the death of Henry (the second), his small son was left an orphan to inherit his father's estates.

At the age of 32, Henry Carslake (the third) married Elizabeth Bampfield, the wedding taking place at Seaton Church in 1730. This young lady was of good pedigree, but she also brought with her an inheritance from her great uncle and that included part of the Ascerton lands; Henry purchasing a further portion. The couple had eight children, but Elizabeth died in 1744.

Their eldest son, another Henry, an officer in the Guards, died, unmarried, of smallpox in Plymouth in January 1760, just two years after inheriting Cotmaton from his father who had died in 1757. William, the second son, now inherited his elder brother's property at Cotmaton. William's wife Elizabeth

inherited her father's property at Bulstone and William, with financial problems besetting him, seems to have gone to live there, allowing the third of the brothers, John Bampfield Carslake (always known in the family as 'Uncle John'), to buy out the Cotmaton property.

Cotmaton Hall was a long thatched house typical of many in Devon dating from Jacobean times, although parts were much older, and one room was always referred to as 'the Justice's Room'. However, on acquiring the estate, he seems to have added a new Georgian section onto the front of the old house. The lands stretched up the slopes of Peak Hill to beyond the present Cotlands and to the south to join the Sea Fields. 'Uncle' John, who was a bachelor, lived at the Hall with his sister, Elizabeth, who was often referred to as the 'Beauty of Devon'. At one time Sir Isaac Heard, the Garter King of Arms, wished to marry her, but she broke off the engagement, and in spite of numerous offers of marriage she remained single. She was painted by Sir Joshua Reynolds, her portrait hanging on the staircase of Cotmaton Hall was remembered as being particularly handsome, but it was destroyed in about 1870 when the warehouse in Clifton, Bristol, where her great nephew's goods were in store, caught fire.

'Uncle' John Carslake, in 1809, built a new house on the estate at right angles to the old, to which he moved, leaving his sister, Elizabeth, occupying the Old Hall. This new house was known as 'New Cotmaton' and was a plain three-storey building overlooking a broad lawn with a beautiful view of the sea and hills. In 1815, 'Uncle' John Carslake died leaving a complicated Will which, in the first instance, left everything to his sister Elizabeth who was living at Old Cotmaton Hall. On the death of Elizabeth, which came only a year later, further provisions of the Will came into force, whereby his nephew, John Carslake (at the time a prisoner of war in France), became the ultimate possessor of the freehold of the estate but, in the meantime, as well as John, other family members had an interest in the Will and New Cotmaton House was required to be let to provide an income for at least one of them. Thus it would be many years before John was free to do what he pleased with his inheritance.

The terms of this Will are part of the reason why, for many years, John Carslake was always short of money, particularly in the early years of his marriage, and even in later life, money remained a concern. It is also why he and his wife for many years led such a peripatetic life, moving from one house to another to find cheaper accommodation, and from one place to another, as is manifest in the diary his wife kept for much of her married life.

John was born in Colyton in 1785, the sixth child and eldest son of Bampfield Carslake, a surgeon, and his wife Elizabeth Crago, and the fourth of the Carslake brothers. John joined the Navy as a First Class Volunteer aboard the *Royal George*, bearing the flag of Lord Bridport, and by 1800 was a Midshipman. He spent a period in the West Indies on board *Courageux* under Captain John Oakes Hardy, but when hostilities with France resumed in 1803 he joined HMS *Victory* under Lord Nelson. He was involved in extinguishing a serious fire in the ship's cockpit. The *Victory,* after a spell in the Mediterranean, left Gibraltar for the West Indies in pursuit of the combined French and Spanish Fleets.

John Carslake's meritorious conduct aboard HMS *Victory* at Trafalgar resulted in his being mentioned to Lord Collingwood, who promoted him the following day to a Lieutenancy in the *Bellisle,* and in this ship he returned to England. In December 1805, he rejoined the *St George* attached to the Channel Fleet

Commander John Carslake in middle age

where he distinguished himself by jumping overboard in choppy seas to save a seaman and the First Lieutenant, Mr Caulfield. He had been aboard the *St George* for over 18 months but, before she sailed again and in consequence of his heroic actions, he was sent to Chatham to join HMS *Proserpine* as First Lieutenant.

Proserpine was still fitting out and

Captain Charles Otter had not yet arrived to take up his command. Their first orders were to proceed to Gothenburg to bring home Lord Leveson Gower, Ambassador to St Petersburg. Thence, to keep watch on the port of Toulon where, on 28 February 1809, *Proserpine* was attacked by two much larger French frigates and after sustained resistance was forced to surrender and her officers and crew taken prisoner.

John Carslake was transferred to V'leascut Prison, Verdun, where the recurring problem of sending and receiving mail became one of his major preoccupations. The letters give some idea of conditions at Verdun, where there was even a certain amount of freedom and a marked improvement 'since the arrival of Mr Otter, time certainly flies more agreeably'. Later he and his fellow prisoner, Bingham, were paroled and allowed to live in two tiny cottages and, although he never tried to escape, John Carslake was always willing to assist others to do so and would give them small amounts of money saved from his meagre candle allowance, which he achieved by going to bed very early, thus saving on candles.

The conditions of imprisonment of Captain Otter were of a very different order and commensurate with his rank, and John told his sister Betty in a letter dated October 21st:

To have two select friends, one of which is my old acquaintance Bingham who accompanies me twice a week on a visit in the country where the Captain resides. We leave town soon enough to join him at breakfast after which we employ ourselves in fishing till nearly dinner time, which generally occasions a pretty sharp appetite. In this agreeable manner the times passes so swiftly that we sometimes forget that we have nearly three miles to walk before the closing of the gates and so much have we overrated our walking abilities that twice we have been shut out. The Gens d'Armes who are posted there are generally very civil and we escape punishment on condition of future punctuality.

Their captivity was to last nearly six years but, after the Battle of Paris and Napoleon's enforced retirement to Elba, release finally came and in May 1814 John Carslake returned to England.

In early June he called on the Leighs of Slade House, Weston (between Salcombe Regis and Branscombe and now part of the Donkey Sanctuary), who were visiting London and met Thomasine, a distant cousin and youngest of the three Leigh sisters. (The spelling of the name Thomasine/Tomazine has varied in source documents; several spellings are used in this book). She noted in her diary 'he had tea with us: I like him'. Thereafter he went often to see them, breakfasting with them and going on outings. On 12th June, the Leighs left London for Devon and thereafter there are frequent mentions in Thomasine's diary of John Carslake visiting Slade but she also had two other admirers, both students at Oxford and friends of the poet John Keats, one of whom, Bailey, was in love with her, but was rebuffed.

John Carslake was unable to propose to Thomasine, even if he wished to, for his finances, after so long in captivity, were in a parlous state and, therefore, after a year's leave he returned to sea and remained so until the November following, when the ship paid off and, although he did not know it at the time, he was never to go to sea again. It had been the custom in the Navy to grant promotion on release to all those captured honourably, but for a small minority released at the end of the Napoleonic Wars, this automatic promotion was denied. This was John's fate, and he felt the slight keenly and campaigned for most of his life to rectify it, writing even to Admiral Hardy, under whom he had at one time served, as well as others of influence, but it was not until 1852, then aged 65, that he was officially retired Commander.

About the time *Tartarus* paid off, 'Uncle' John Carslake died leaving his nephew John the ultimate freehold of all his property at Cotmaton. Shortly afterwards 'Aunt Elizabeth' also died but, under the terms of Uncle John's Will, John could only derive an income from the lands as both houses had to be let. In April 1817, Thomasine was engaged to him and the wedding took place on 30th September at Salcombe Regis Church. It was a simple service and, as was the custom of the time, the principal bridesmaid, who was the bride's sister, Mary Leigh, accompanied the couple on the wedding tour, after which they settled down to live at 'an unspecified house in Salcombe' where their first child was born. He was named John Hawkey Bingham and christened at the Old Meeting. Hawkey and Bingham were the names of two of John's companions during his long imprisonment at Verdun.

Towards the end of 1819, the couple moved to a house overlooking the beach at Sidmouth – 3 Marine Terrace – to be near a doctor and here their second son was born. In December, she saw the Duchess of Kent and the baby Victoria, and a few weeks later witnessed the Duke of Kent's funeral procession. In June 1821, John attended a Grand Coronation Dinner at the London Hotel.

For most of their married life John and Thomasine never settled in one house for long and, having returned to their house at Salcombe, they went to 'Hills' on Sid Road. It was there, later in 1821, that the Customs men arrived and hunted the house for concealed spirits (it was known that the house was sometimes used for this purpose), but nothing was found. The next year, a daughter was born and named Tomazine after her mother. There had been a constant round of social events, but in July 1823 Thomasine recorded in the diary she kept throughout her life: 'Nothing but parties out and at home. Ah this was not happiness.'

There was yet another move in October 1823 to 'Cotlands'. Thomasine had laid the foundation stone of the house which John intended as a spacious family home. It stood on a slight eminence and had a beautiful view over the valley to Salcombe Hill and the sea. The Carslake family were to live there intermittently for short periods before they went back to 'Hills' and finally to 'Asherton'. Asherton was a small house which was built by his Uncle John on the Cotmaton property, and since the old name of Asherton was gradually being forgotten it was bestowed on this new house.

Disasters and accidents also find a place in Thomasine's diary and in 1824 she recorded: 'Dreadful storms all night. Walked to Sidmouth to see the wreckage. Beach all gone. Chit Rock and the cottages all washed away'. (This was the great gale of 22 November 1824). In July 1829, there were three wrecks with five drowned. There were several instances of John being hurt by falls from his horse. He had already damaged his back in his naval days when he fell from the rigging of his ship and it would cause him increasing pain as he grew older, until he was in constant pain.

John Carslake's finances were always a worry to him and of the four houses on the Cotmaton Estate at least three were always let. Cotmaton Hall was then occupied by Henry Stewart to whom it had been let. This gentleman made some improvements, the most obvious and notable being the addition of two large ground floor bow windows to the plain Georgian front, which had been 'tacked' on to the old thatched house, probably in about 1790.

The Carslakes left Sidmouth and spent some time living in Exeter and in Somerset, but returned in 1844 to live at Cotmaton Old Hall which was unoccupied. Asherton was let to Dr Jeffery, the man who took part with Dr Hodge, in the attempted body snatching of a young boy very recently interred in Salcombe Regis Churchyard, but foiled by a posse of armed villagers. The two doctors and their accomplices fled without the body, but peppered with shot, leaving behind their tools. One of these found its way to the village blacksmith and was fashioned into a new bolt for the Lych Gate at the entrance to the churchyard.

There were further house moves, and the marriages of their eldest son and daughter are recorded, as is the launching of the first steam ship built in Sidmouth. Towards the end of his life, John Carslake lived more and more at Cotmaton Hall, making many improvements during the 1850s, which Thomasine noted in the diary she still kept. Even the death of their old cat is recorded – its body was sent to be stuffed.

John Carslake had served for many years as a JP and, on one occasion, John Rattenbury of Beer, the most renowned smuggler in East Devon, came to see him at Cotmaton, to beg that he might intervene to obtain the release of young Rattenbury whom his father declared had been wrongfully 'taken up' for smuggling.

In early September 1846, a notice of a Public Meeting appeared stating:

A meeting of the inhabitants and those interested in the prosperity of Sidmouth will be held in the Town Hall on Wednesday, next, for the purpose of proposing Plans for the general improvement of the Place and the greater accommodation of visitors, also for securing to the Public the existing walks on the Cliffs and Salcombe Hill with the paths leading thereto – the Chair will be taken at 2 o'clock – Sidmouth, 9 September 1846.

This was the first meeting of what became known as the Sidmouth Improvement Committee, the forerunner of the present day Sid Vale Association. At that initial meeting, John Carslake was elected to the Chair. Discussions centred around the issue of footpaths and the attempts of the various landowners to enclose, thus blocking old rights of way.

John Carslake died at Clifton, Bristol, at the home of his son

The house and its lovely gardens when the Carslakes lived there
(Sidmouth Museum)

in August 1865, just short of his 79th birthday, and was buried in the Churchyard of Sidmouth Parish Church. Thomasine died in 1883, aged 86, at her daughter's home in London.

The houses at Cotmaton were sold in due course. Cotmaton House (New Cotmaton) became the home of Mr Tindall who was both an author and artist. He came to Sidmouth in the mid 1890s and in 1907 published *Sketching Notes*, which drew on his skill as a water-colourist. In the 1914-18 War, he became quite a celebrity when, at nearly 70, he joined the Volunteers in the Town Guard. This was a very sad time for him as is recorded on the War Memorial tablets in Sidmouth Church – he lost both a son and a daughter. Between 1922 and 1931, almost every day, he walked down to the beach and recorded 'careful observations of the foreshore'. These were subsequently typed and bound in volumes which are archived in Sidmouth Museum. He was an active member of the Devonshire Association and was highly regarded by all who knew him and much mourned when he died aged 87 in 1933. The house had a spell as a guest house and is now an Abbeyfield house, whilst Cotmaton Hall, after being the home of General Elton for many years was destroyed by fire in 1935.

Julia Creeke

The home during the final period of his life of the author and playwright RF Delderfield (b.1912 – d.1972).

In his day, RF Delderfield was one of the most famous writers in the English-speaking world, with a large and dedicated fan base. After establishing his reputation as a playwright, he became a prolific novelist and, in due course, fifteen of his plays or novels became films or television series. He lived at different locations around Sidmouth before finally moving to Dove Cottage, where he died.

Although his mainstream novels were quintessentially English, traversing Devon villages or suburban life in south London, his obituary in the New York Times speculated that he was more popular in the USA than in the UK. His agent claimed that he had sold millions of books in America. Moreover, a major collection of his manuscripts and papers from the period 1931-1970 is now held by the University of Boston in Massachusetts.

Born in London, Ronald Frederick Delderfield moved to Devon in 1923, aged eleven, when his father bought the *Exmouth Chronicle* and became its editor. This was an unusual career move by his father, a Bermondsey-born meat trader at Smithfield Market, who was the first Liberal elected to Bermondsey Council.

After attending schools in Devon, most of which would later feature one way or another in his novels, RF Delderfield completed a course at Exeter Commercial College, learning shorthand, typing and bookkeeping. It was at this time, aged sixteen, that he decided that he wanted to be an author and started to write plays and stories.

In 1929, he joined the reporting staff of the *Exmouth Chronicle*, ultimately succeeding his father as editor. In his autobiography *For My Own Amusement* he describes an everyday life of attending Magistrates' courts, council meetings, local events, amateur dramatics, visiting the bereaved, writing obituaries and cycling after fire engines.

In 1936, he married May Evans and in due course they adopted two children, Veronica and Paul. The marriage would be enduring.

His first phase of professional writing concentrated on plays. His debut play in London, *Spark at Judea*, was performed at the Ambassador's Theatre in November 1937. Unlike his later plays this was not a comedy: it speculated on the inner conflicts likely to have been experienced by Pontius Pilate. It was a strong start and the play was still being performed on BBC radio over twenty years later.

After serving in the RAF in a clerical role during World War Two, he returned to Devon to live at Knowle, Budleigh Salterton, to continue his literary career. He also helped May run an antiques business at Newton Poppleford, saying he did this 'so that I keep in touch with ordinary types of people – my public.'

His play *Worm's Eyes View,* a comedy, opened at the Whitehall Theatre in December 1945 and ran in the West End for over five years. It was also made into a film in 1951 starring Diana Dors and Ronald Shiner.

It was during this post-war period that he was introduced to horse-riding by Budleigh's GP, Dr Tom Evans, a passionate horseman and hunter. He told Delderfield that 'every day spent out of the saddle is a

Dove Cottage (SVA)

day wasted'. Delderfield said that when he went to see Evans with unclassified illnesses, he invariably prescribed hunting, and when he first went out with the hunt, the most terrifying thing was to see lady riders charging about side-saddle.

By 1949, he had begun to write novels as well as plays, and then in 1956 he decided to concentrate solely on a career as a novelist. There began a sweep of popular history sagas, mainly set in the inter-war years in his native south London, and his adopted Devon.

He wrote what have been described as leisurely panoramic novels, in an easy style, always underpinned by solid research, and frequently drawing on his own life experiences. These included *God is an Englishman*, *Theirs was the Kingdom* and *Give Us This Day*. In essence, the novels portrayed what might be called ordinary decent people, aspiring to get on, whilst remaining true to themselves. He showed little patience with the entrenched class barriers of that time.

Summing it up, he said, 'I set out to tell a straightforward story of undistinguished British people – the only kind of people I really know.'

Given that, it is perhaps surprising that he also had a keen interest in Napoleonic themes, and published a number of works on the subject. The lack of commercial success in this sphere did not discourage him. Tellingly, when he appeared on the BBC Radio programme *Desert Island Discs* in 1962, one of the recordings he chose to take with him was the French National Anthem, *La Marseillaise,* played by the orchestra of La Garde Republicaine. He also said that the only book he would take to the desert island would be *The French Revolution* by Robert Carlyle. More predictably, however, he said the only luxury he would take would be a typewriter and paper.

He came to the wider Sidmouth area in the late 1950s, first to live at Lower Coombe, Tipton St John. He then moved to Peak Cottage, at the top of Peak Hill above Sidmouth. Next, in 1967, he moved to the nearby Gazebo, after building extensions on two sides of what had originally been a cliff top oval summer house belonging to Peak Cottage.

RF Delderfield was famous not just for the content of his writing but for the prodigious rate at which he worked. His period in Sidmouth was certainly very productive, and he once said that he wrote 4,000 words a day, 365 days a year. It is claimed that, at a push, he could accelerate up to 10,000 words a day, which, if true, is astonishing. At the Gazebo, he

RF Delderfield

deliberately let the hedges grow up high in front of his study windows so the views would not distract his writing.

He had a strict regime for writing, finishing at four o'clock in the afternoon. Reportedly, if he finished a novel at three o'clock, he would then start the next one, keeping going until four. To start the day he would walk or drive down to the Esplanade for an early morning swim in the sea, and once said that this routine helped him be so productive.

He was a familiar figure around Sidmouth, a large tall man, short-sighted and usually smoking a cigarette. He was always good natured and approachable, happy to chat with anyone he met.

Finally, he and May moved to Dove Cottage on Manor Road, where he died in 1972 from lymphoma, aged 60.

RF Delderfield's reputation was further enhanced after his death by television dramas based on his best known novels, *A Horseman Riding By* and *To Serve Them All My Days*, which were set in Devon. In all, the BBC made five series based on his books. However, commentators today often headline the fact that the first Carry On film – *Carry On Sergeant* – was inspired by his play *The Bull Boys*. He deserves to be remembered for more than that.

He was outlived by his older brother Eric Delderfield (1909-1995), who himself was an accomplished and widely published author, writing mainly on west country themes. Eric continued to live in Exmouth throughout his life, after the parental move down from London in 1923.

May Delderfield continued to live at Dove Cottage until her death in 1988.

John McCarthy

Home during the final years of his life of Lawson Wood (b.1878 – d.1957), the celebrated graphic designer, painter and illustrator.

In January 1954, Lawson Wood, the comic artist and watercolourist, bought Downlands, a 1920s property on Salcombe Hill. On buying the house, he added a studio which enjoyed delightful views out over the Sid Valley and the sea to Berry Head, then clearly visible.

Lawson Wood was born in 1878 in Highgate to a very artistic family. His grandfather LJ Wood was a well known Victorian architectural watercolourist and his father Pinhorn Wood a talented landscape painter in watercolour.

Wood went to the Slade School of Art and also attended Calderon's School of animal painting which foreshadowed his later work and his abiding love of animals. At the age of 18, he joined Arthur Pearson as an illustrator and worked for them for six years. It was here that he met his wife, Charlotte Forge, who also worked for Pearson and in 1902 they were married. His work was very popular and at the age of 24 he risked all and became a freelance illustrator. Commissions came from many well known publications like *The Strand Magazine*, *The Illustrated London News*, *Punch* and even *The Boy's Own Paper*. As his fame spread, he was elected to the Royal Institute of Painters in Watercolours and exhibited at the Royal Academy regularly.

Lawson Wood at Downlands (Sidmouth Museum)

In 1915 he volunteered for the War effort and served as an officer in the Kite Balloon Wing of the Royal Flying Corp. With no way of detecting the approach of enemy aircraft except by sound, the idea was to fly tethered hydrogen balloons with observers who could scan the horizon through binoculars and could then report back to the ground if an attack was detected. With the ballons filled with hydrogen, it was extremely dangerous work and after the War Lawson Wood was decorated by the French for his work at Vimy Ridge. Throughout WWI, he continued to draw and paint and his patriotic designs were published in large numbers.

After the War, his work reached the height of his fame with the much loved caricatures of quirky dinosaurs and stone age humans. There followed comic policemen and small boys, animals and birds performing absurd antics and eventually Gran'pop, the famous ginger ape whose annuals were popular throughout the English-speaking world and were an essay in comic absurdities. Just before WW2, plans were well advanced for Hollywood to produce an animated film featuring all these characters, but the outbreak of war put an end to the plans and after the War no more was heard of it.

Wood always liked to achieve accuracy of detail in his animals and to ensure this he regularly visited London Zoo and a small menagerie in Eastbourne, the Wannock Tea Garden. In 1934, he was awarded a Fellowship of the Royal Zoological Society for his work with animals and their welfare and he even set up his own small sanctuary for aged animals.

His bird, animal and human designs were produced as a line of wooden toys in a small factory which he set up, and were christened 'Lawson Woodies'. They sold well in more prestigious outlets and are now keenly sought by collectors.

As the years passed, Lawson Wood became something of a recluse. In the 1920s, he had discovered a mediaeval house in Sussex which he fell in love with, but its situation was far from ideal so Wood had it dismantled brick by brick and timber by timber, and moved the whole house to a site in Kent which he considered idyllic. He enjoyed living there but, as the years went by and Kent became more heavily developed as suburbia spread outwards, he found it less and less to his liking. It was also too close to London so that there was a constant stream of visitors and publishers wanting to see him, which prevented him working. He finally decided he wanted to move away to somewhere more remote where he could lead a more reclusive life and continue with his work. The search led him eventually to Sidmouth and 'Downlands' on Salcombe Hill Road.

The house had a fine view towards High Peak and the sea. He continued to draw, paint and illustrate in his new studio

until his death from bowel cancer in October 1957, aged 79. Since WW2 his art had fallen out of favour with the public. He had become increasingly reclusive and few in Sidmouth knew of his presence.

Lawson Wood's original work is collected now and fetches high prices at auction. Sidmouth Museum is fortunate in holding a considerable collection of his artwork and 'woodies'.

Downlands was acquired in the early 1960s by Ronald Wilson and his wife. He had spent some years working in

Lawson Wood in his studio, painting by Phoebe Sholto Douglas, 1936 (courtesy of Sunderland Museum and Wintergarden)

Canada and, now retired, found Sidmouth a congenial place to live. He was an active member of the Sid Vale Association and was responsible for 'engineering' the gift to Sidmouth Museum of the original nine foot (2.74m) long watercolour, painted by Hubert Cornish circa 1814, which shows Sidmouth seafront in Regency times when the town had become a very fashionable resort. Ronald Wilson wrote a number of articles about the town's history and also a popular small booklet entitled 'Salcombe Regis Sketches' (now long out of print).

A Lawson Wood comic watercolour (Sidmouth Museum)

Knowing that the house in which he lived had been the home of Lawson Wood, Ronald sought and finally purchased a smallish watercolour by him of a rather desperate looking pelican staring at a goldfish swimming in a narrow necked jar, which he hung in Wood's old studio in recognition of the many hours he must have spent painting in the room.

Julia Creeke

 ## 23 THE FORT HOTEL *(originally Fort Cottage)*

Originally, there was a thatched cottage here immediately adjacent to the Fort, a 17th century gunnery emplacement. During the 1930s, the building, now converted into a hotel, was the home of the painter-poet David Jones (b.1895 – d.1974).

During the 1930s, a number of distinguished literary figures came to Sidmouth for 'holiday' visits, including George Bernard Shaw, JRR Tolkien, Vera Brittain and her friend Winifred Holtby. In contrast, David Jones, artist, engraver and poet, stayed in the Fort Hotel for five years between 1935 and 1940. Although his brilliance was known to, amongst others, TS Eliot, it is only in recent years that this extraordinary polymath, David Jones, is now considered the greatest painter-poet since William Blake.

The Fort Hotel was on the site of Fort Cottage which in turn had been two small cottages adjacent to the 'fort'. (See next chapter for a fuller description of Fort Field.)

Fort Cottage in 1815, detail from Sidmouth's Long Print (Sidmouth Museum)

The Fort had been intermittently present since the 17th century and consisted, in varying degrees, of local militia and gunnery overlooking the sea at times of threatened coastal invasion. During practise firing, it was certainly inconveniently close to nearby dwellings and Peter Orlando Hutchinson wrote of 'two small cottages and a potato plot and I have been told that one of the tenants left because the firing of the guns broke all the windows.'

At the time of the Napoleonic wars, there was now a single large cottage and its appearance is clearly shown in the 'Long Picture' water colour (1814) (now in Sidmouth Museum) and in subsequent engravings. It was a substantial, plain but attractive house with a thatched roof. Windows in the southern-facing thatch and high in the eastern wall indicate living space in the attic. Its fine garden is commented upon by the local historian, Anna Sutton, who recalled it from her childhood in the late 19th century.

Throughout the 19th and early 20th centuries, Fort Cottage was available for both short term and, more commonly, long term leases as indeed were most properties on the front. The names of tenants were recorded in the *Sidmouth Journal*. Charlotte Mary Shore (1800-1883) née Cornish, was the daughter of George and Sarah Cornish and lived there after she was widowed. Between 1882 and 1901, Matilda Cridland offered furnished apartments to rent. One of her most distinguished tenants was Samuel Read who was a fine water colourist and architectural artist and was on the staff of the *Illustrated London News* for 30 years. He died in Fort Cottage in 1883 and is buried in Sidmouth cemetery.

By 1921, the property belonged to the successful local business man, WA Dagworthy, who owned the first car in the town. He planned to convert the cottage into a pavilion with stage and dressing rooms, as well as a tea room and roof garden. The local architect RW Sampson drew up the plans but, although a balcony was added to the front and a wing added which contained two flats, the overall ambitious scheme was abandoned. He did, however, convert the ground floor into the Fort Café.

In 1934, Mr Dagworthy sold the building to Reginald Griffin, who converted the property into the Fort Hotel. An additional storey over the centre of the building was added. A local newspaper report commented that 'the outer walls are the only remains of the old cottage.' A third storey on the east wing of the hotel was constructed later. On the ground floor the dining room faced towards the sea. On the first floor there was a large lounge and sun parlour. The bedrooms extended over two floors. The tariff for full board weekly stay was 3½ to 5½ guineas (£3.70 to £5.80) a week. The hotel was unlicensed.

It was during this period that David Jones (1895-1974) stayed in Sidmouth. He was born in Brockley, south-east of London and became a student at the Camberwell Art School. The First World War intervened and in 1915 David Jones signed-up with the Royal Welch Fusiliers. His famous poem *In Parenthesis* is a poetic account of both his own experiences and those of his comrades-at-arms. He was at both the battles of the Somme and Passchendaele, and had more active duty than any other poet or painter. Although wounded on the Somme in 1916, he returned to the frontline after recuperating back in Britain. He also caught trench-fever and had to spend several months in a hospital behind the lines in France. Not unexpectedly, he never recovered psychologically from his war experiences.

Fort Hotel in the 1930s. Artist unknown.

Private David Jones

When the war was over, Jones went back to study at the Westminster School of Art where he met, amongst others, the artist Eric Gill. In 1922, he joined Eric Gill's Guild of St Joseph and St Dominic at Ditchling, Sussex. He became a Catholic and went to live in Wales and then Caldey Island with the Anglican Benedictine monks. Over the next few years his health deteriorated and almost in desperation, in 1934, his friends took him on a trip to the British Protectorate of Palestine, as it was then known, to visit the holy sites. This was to have a profound effect on both him and his work. In 1935, his friends helped to pay for him to stay at the Fort Hotel in Sidmouth where he remained until 1940.

His stay, or perhaps convalescence, in Sidmouth seemed to help him considerably. He painted some pictures, completed his book *In Parenthesis* for publication and began to write what would eventually become his later long poem *The Anathémata*. His preserved correspondence, including letters he wrote while staying in Sidmouth, is published in *Dai Greatcoat*.

David Jones' poem *In Parenthesis* is written as a narrative. There are seven parts which describe different aspects of soldiers' training and life in the trenches. The narrative thread is strong, although, sometimes, unfamiliar vocabulary and sentence structure fragment the storyline. The horrors he witnessed, some of which are described in the poem, stayed with him so vividly that in 1935-1940, twenty years after the war, when he lived in Sidmouth, much of his poetic work was a continued reflection of the soldiers' suffering and the action on the battlefields in France. *In Parenthesis* was published by Faber in 1937 with one of his distinctive drawings on the front cover. In the Introduction, TS Eliot, described it as a 'work of genius'.

David Jones spent much of his time in Sidmouth reading, writing and painting. He often attended Mass and other services at The Convent of the Assumption in the Chapel dedicated to Our Lady, Help of Christians. This was an orphanage and school; it is now St John's School.

His paintings, drawings, woodcuts and lettering are more accessible than his poetry and several important pictures were painted in Sidmouth either from his bedroom window or from the roof of the Fort Hotel. The most well-known is *Sidmouth Cricket Match* (1937). It is full of movement with Fortfield Terrace in the background. There is artistic licence although dogs probably did run onto the field.

David Jones described the Fort Hotel as '*very* comfortable'. When a friend visited him there, 'He was somewhat surprised to find David chatting to elderly ladies and retired colonels in the hotel, but when there came a pause...David would whisper to Tom "Let's go for a wet" and they were off to the nearby pub for a pint'.

Jones would have been a respected ex-soldier and WWI veteran in the local community although few would have known or read his work. Shortly before his final departure he was operated on for appendicitis in the Victoria Cottage Hospital. In a letter of 16 May 1940, he wrote that the hospital with the 'white iron bedstead' reminded him of being in hospital in France in the war. He wrote to a friend: 'I had a wireless earphone thing over my bed in hospital, so for the first time in my life listened rather a lot to it'. His final painting from the Fort Hotel is dated 1940. It is of the Bedford Hotel and there is smoke coming from the chimney which indicates that it was probably drawn in the spring before he had appendicitis.

Jones continued to write poetry in Sidmouth including graphic and distressing passages describing the soldiers' last cries in no man's land. He stated in a letter, that he drafted more than 40 pages of poetry whilst at the Fort Hotel, some of which contains references to the town.

David Jones's life in Sidmouth was obviously a rich and fruitful episode in his life. It was here that he seems to have finally laid to rest the voices of the dying soldiers of the First World War and move on to explore material which became part of his later major work, *The Anathémata*. Sidmouth's unique and special Fort Hotel had a healing role and gave him the rest that he needed for his creativity to move forward.

It is puzzling that a figure praised by TS Eliot, WH Auden, Graham Greene and Seamus Heaney is so little known. It is for this reason that a recent biographer, Thomas Dilworth, wrote: 'If Beckett was the last great modernist, Jones was the lost great modernist.' He is, however, now receiving more attention, including numerous art exhibitions and a 2016 adaptation of *In Parenthesis* by Welsh National Opera. There is also the David Jones Society.

Between 1942 and 1944, the RAF requisitioned the building. After the war, it reverted to a café with flats, and is now known as The Fort.

Mary Coghill and Nigel Hyman

24 THE FORT FIELD and CRICKET PAVILION

A fort with five cannons was built on the southern edge of this site in 1628. It was de-commissioned after the Battle of Waterloo, and the land was leased in 1823 to a group of gentlemen for use as a cricket pitch. The first pavilion was erected in 1827.

In the mid 16th century there was no maritime law. Piracy along the Channel coast was rife, particularly in summer: there were Venetian galleys at Teignmouth, plus Spanish and Frenchmen and, most feared of all, Barbary pirates raiding from North Africa. As the Armada threatened, there were elaborate plans to fortify the coast, but nothing came of them.

The threat from the sea persisted and a recommendation from the Privy Council in 1628 suggested a fort be constructed. The principal threats were now Dutch and French. By the mid 17th century there are references to the Fort by name when there are payments for powder and shot in the accounts of the Parish Chest. The Fort was situated on a small rocky promontory overlooking the shore, just to the west of the present Fort flats and café. In 1794 it consisted of five pieces of ordnance, a small armoury a short distance off and a flag staff.

Gunnery practice for the Fort guns consisted of firing at Chit Rocks and particularly Chit Stack. Some direct hits loosened this so much it fell in the great gale of 1824. The Fort was manned

The Fort as it was in 1815 before being dismantled, painted by PO Hutchinson 1859 (Devon Heritage Centre)

by 80 members of the Sea Fencibles, a sort of maritime Home Guard, specially raised for coast defence at the time of the Napoleonic Wars. After the Battle of Waterloo, the cannons were removed and the armoury became dilapidated.

In William Day's map drawn in 1789, the Fort Field was still a large open field divided by its mediaeval pattern into strips which were being farmed. The demolition by fire of that part of Western Town situated on the area of the present Bedford Lawn Car Park resulted in much of it falling out of cultivation. It became a large grass field used for grazing and bisected from north to south by a gravel drive linking Fortfield Terrace to the seafront (Station Road did not then exist). At the time of the proposed sale of the Manor in 1813, Joseph Hooke was renting the 18 acres (7.3 ha) of the Fort Field for £100 p.a.

Early in the Napoleonic Wars, when the threat of invasion was very real, a Company of Volunteers was stationed in a tented camp on the field and there was constant drilling and manoeuvres.

After the defeat of Napoleon, a group of local gentlemen took a lease of the Fort Field in 1823 and set about making a cricket pitch, and it was soon a flourishing club. Many improvements had been effected and a contemporary guide book says:

> ... the turf has been wholly taken up and is newly laid and levelled, constantly rolled, swept and kept in perfect order. The Club meet from the month of May, every Tuesday throughout the season and play is continued all day. A marquee is pitched upon an elevated spot at the northern extremity of the Field where a cold dinner is provided for members and their friends, to the number of 30 persons, a small tent with attendants being pitched next to the marquee.

Playing members usually brought one of their own servants and, as there were often left-overs, a good meal could be part of the 'perks'. There was a gravel walk around the ground which was surrounded by painted railings 'to exclude improper company'. Subscriptions were 10/6 a year (52p) for a single person and £1.10 for a family (£1.50).

Between the years 1824 and 1827, a thatched Cricket House had been erected. In 1824, it is clear that a match between the

Gentlemen of Sidmouth and those of Exeter had taken place on the Fort Field, for in *Woolman's Exeter Gazette* of 21 August, there is a report of the return match at Quicke's Field. The game was scored in 'notches' and won by Sidmouth by eight notches, one incident requiring referral to the President of MCC for clarification. A report stated: 'Play lasted from 11 to 6 when the parties and their friends in all between 40 and 50 sat down to a handsome cold collation and spent the remainder of the evening in high glee'.

Things seem to have progressed very satisfactorily until the death of Captain James Clark of Sid Abbey, who for some years had been the lessee of the Fort Field from the Manor; cricket ceased to be played and the Club disbanded. The cricket house became dilapidated and before 1840 was 'pulled down and the material sold'. The Reverend Cresswell, Vicar of Salcombe Regis, complained:

The cricket pavilion (SVA)

> The Cricket Club, which for some years past offered that noble recreation to the inhabitants and was gradually instilling into the minds of the peasantry a love for something better in the way of amusement than dancing and wrestling is now come to an end.

We might infer from this contemporary quote that others beside the 'gentlemen' of Sidmouth were also beginning to play cricket.

In 1850, the Sidmouth Improvement Committee (forerunner of the Sid Vale Association) was paying rent for the Fort Field – £21 p.a. – to a Mr Radford, a local solicitor acting for the Manor. It was then sublet to Mr Hooke but conditions were imposed regarding the field's use. There were arguments too about the grazing of animals; cattle had been turned out on the Field instead of the obligatory sheep and had frightened a young lady.

In 1852 comes a mention of the Fort Field's return to its former use when Mr Drewery asked the Committee its terms for letting the field: 'To some gentlemen for the purpose of cricket practice'. In 1854, Mr Seal paid rent of four guineas (£4.20) for the season. In 1858, William Bishop was employed at a salary of £1 p.a. 'to watch over the Cricket Ground to prevent as much as possible boys and disorderly persons from frequenting it and stop the beating of carpets and other undesirable uses'. In the same year, there was talk of a cricket club being formed. There must have been progress in re-establishing the game, because in 1859 there were matches against both Exeter and Budleigh, the latter followed by a buffet supper and ball for 70 at the London Hotel.

Richard Napoleon Thornton purchased Knowle Cottage in 1867 and, possessed of a fortune of £400,000 left to him by his natural father, retired at the age of 33 to live in Sidmouth. He had played cricket for Oxford and all his family were keen on the game; WA Thornton scoring the first ever recorded century on the ground. The Fort Field under this patronage was brought into first class condition and cricket flourished, with the addition of events such as a match between the 1st and 2nd halves of the alphabet, and in August 1874 between an Invited XI and the Gentlemen of Devon, followed by a grand ball at Knowle Cottage to which the participants and local society were invited.

The improvement Committee was now finding the field a burden and surrendered the lease to the Manor from Lady Day 1870. Four years later, Richard Thornton took a 14-year lease on behalf of the club. The following year, 1875, a match was played in August between the Gentlemen of Devon and the Gentlemen of Somerset after which, at a meeting in the pavilion, it was decided to form the Somerset County Cricket Club. The next year Richard Thornton, aged only 44, died and there was great sorrow in the Club at his passing.

Sidmouth Cricket Club was now a flourishing institution, but the Cricket House was shabby and too small. The members set about rebuilding it as a pretty thatched pavilion, which with later extensions and alterations is the pavilion of today. It is one of very few thatched pavilions in the country.

Although well known touring sides now came regularly in summer, there were still some novel matches, such as in 1886. In that year, 32 Sidmouth fishermen took the field against a

Sidmouth Amateur XI: the result showed the fishermen were better with hook and line than cricket bat. An enjoyable dinner followed at the London Hotel and the occasion was pronounced a success.

A well-known personality who played at Sidmouth was the author, Sir Arthur Conan Doyle, who, in 1902 and 1903, came to Sidmouth as a member of an MCC XI and played in two-day matches. The first year, the match was on 27-28 August and the MCC XI won. Following the match he stayed with his family at the Royal York Hotel. On the second occasion, the match was on 14-15 August and was a draw. Before coming to Sidmouth, he had been staying in Beaminster, where it is said the barking of the local dogs gave him the idea for *The Hound of the Baskervilles*. This is incorrect because the book was actually published sometime before his visit. In 1926, two 'greats' of cricket played in Sidmouth in the same match – Sir Jack Hobbs and Frank Woolley – 2,000 people turned up at the Fort Field to watch them score centuries.

The accolade for the longest hit goes to Lloyd Baker who, from the Belmont end, drove a ball which, with a few bounces on the way, ended up against the wall of the Churchyard of the Parish Church. It is said that a ball hasn't yet been hit for six into the sea, although they do occasionally land on the beach: now, with the sea not always very far from the Promenade at high tide, this must be a distinct possibility. Other massive hits have cleared Fortfield Terrace and in 1931 a member of the Sidmouth Club, whose premises were in the first house of the Terrace, caught a ball hit by the Taunton batsman, R Illingworth, on the first floor balcony.

For years, the last surviving bathing machine did duty as the Score Box, but a ferocious gale one winter in the 1980s literally 'blew it apart'.

Tennis and croquet were added to cricket as sports played on the Fort Field and more recently hockey during the winter months. There is an excellent little booklet published by Sidmouth Cricket, Lawn Tennis and Croquet Club which brings the Club's history up to date. When HRH The Duchess of Kent visited in 1987 to celebrate the completion of the appeal which funded the purchase for The National Trust of almost 200 acres (81 ha) of cliffs and farm land on Salcombe and a further 19 acres (7.7 ha) on Peak Hill, the town went *en fête* on the Fort Field. There were all kinds of displays and demonstrations by local individuals and institutions. In the same year, the Royal Marines, together with their band, staged a splendid Beating the Retreat on the Field which attracted a large crowd estimated at over 2,000 people.

Cricket is played on the Field regularly during the summer months and it sometimes serves as a minor counties ground. A Bridge Club meets in the pavilion. The Field is also one of the emergency landing grounds in Sidmouth for the Air Ambulance.

Julia Creeke

FORTFIELD TERRACE

Fortfield Terrace, an incomplete crescent, is one of Sidmouth's most prominent landmarks and is an example of 18th century speculative development. Construction of only one pair of houses of the westward extension had begun when its architect, Michael Novosielski, died suddenly in Ramsgate in 1795 aged only 45.

CH Tatham in a letter to Henry Holland, the eminent Georgian architect, dated 10 July 1795 wrote:

Mr Jenkins informed me of Mr Novosielski's death by which he is the sufferer on account of a crescent of considerable magnitude contracted for by the deceased and now erecting at Sidmouth in Devonshire.

Mr Jenkins was Thomas Jenkins, a long time resident of Rome, who had bought the Manor of Sidmouth in 1787 from the Prideaux family for £15,600, the latter having been ordered by the Court of Chancery to sell to pay off debts. Thomas Jenkins considered the Manor as an investment for his retirement and, after owning it for ten years, wound up his affairs in Rome and in 1798 returned to England. He did not travel overland because of the unsettled conditions in France, due to the Revolution, and

The Terrace (SVA)

items of antique sculpture coming to Britain. He acquired *Neptune and Triton*, now in the V&A, for Sir Joshua Reynolds, and *Venus* for William Weddell of Newby Hall (this was sold and is now in Dubai). It was in Rome that he became acquainted with Novosielski, who was born there in 1750 of Polish parents.

Novosielski left Rome about 1771 and came to London where he became an assistant to the architect, James Wyatt. Fourteen years later he began working on his own account on a series of commissions in London, the most noteworthy being his reconstruction of the Opera House in the Haymarket, then the largest theatre in Europe after La Scala, Milan.

instead returned by sea, but he became ill during the voyage and died a few days after landing at Great Yarmouth, never having once set foot in his new Manor. He left a handwritten Will in Italian, bequeathing his estate to Captain Thomas Jenkins, a great nephew, who was in the Dragoons. But the way the Will was drawn up led over the years to numerous lawsuits.

Not all the land for the Terrace came with the purchase of the Manor, and in fact much of the land on which the Terrace was actually built was purchased from Emmanuel Baruh Lousada of Peak House, and another area from a couple living in Newton Poppleford.

Thomas Jenkins was born in Honiton, the son of William Jenkins who was probably a clergyman. His brother, also William, was Vicar of Upottery. Thomas left as a young man to seek his fortune elsewhere and by the 1760s had settled in Rome, where he restored and dealt in pictures and antiquities. After some years he had established a thriving business, complete with his own workshops in part of the Colosseum, supplying 'antiques' to the grand tourists: anything from cameos to sculpture could be provided, some were genuine antiquities (where necessary he would repair them), others were copies. He also procured commissions for the British artists visiting Rome. He was painted with his favourite niece, Anna Maria, by Angelica Kauffmann (the picture is now in the National Portrait Gallery). Thomas Jenkins never married but his prosperity was such that he also acted as a banker to the English community. He was responsible for at least two major

The houses in Fortfield Terrace were intended for renting to the aristocracy and gentry then just beginning to frequent Sidmouth as a fashionable resort. The wings were left brick-faced, whilst the central pair of houses were rendered. Around

1870, salt air had badly affected the brickwork and finally all the houses were rendered and the canopied balconies and French doors added. Thomas Jenkins lost no time in letting the completed houses and the early residents are recorded in archived documents, and from these it is known the houses were called 'The Crescent'. The two most westerly houses were under

The architect, Michael Novosielski, by Angelica Kauffmann, 1791 (National Gallery of Scotland)

construction and still unfinished and it fell to his nephew, the Reverend William Jenkins, who was Vicar of Sidmouth, to oversee the completion. He remained a Tenant at Will of five of the houses. He let the two most westerly houses before their final completion, so their tenants must have been subject to some inconvenience and noise. In 1813, at the time of the proposed sale of the Manor, five of the houses which were on short rentals brought in a total of £366 p.a.

The Terrace may possibly feature in Jane Austen's unfinished novel *Sanditon* written in 1808. Sadly, there is no proven connection between Sidmouth and Jane Austen, although in a letter of 8 January 1801 to Cassandra, she says 'Sidmouth is talked of this year as our abode.'

Thomas Jenkins and his niece Anna Maria, painted in Rome by Angelica Kauffmann, 1790 (National Portrait Gallery)

When Thomas Jenkins died, he left his estate, not to the Reverend William Jenkins his nephew, but under his Italian Will to his great nephew, also Thomas Jenkins. His father, William, was Vicar of Sidmouth, and also Chaplain to HRH The Duke of Cumberland and holder of the Rectory of Northleigh, near Honiton. He also held a number of the leases along the Terrace as a Tenant at Will. This great-nephew, Thomas Jenkins (junior), is described as 'late Captain in 11th Regiment of Light Dragoons' and was married to the sister of one of the great Regency dandies, Edward Hughes Ball Hughes, and was resident at Sidmonton House in the County of Southampton. Thomas was involved in numerous law suits involving the Jenkins Will and on a number of occasions tried to raise money from the Manor of Sidmouth by selling areas of land and several of the houses in The Crescent.

After 37 years of ownership, his debts caught up with him and things came to a head when he borrowed £45,000 from his brother-in-law, Ball Hughes. Failing to keep up with repayments, the Court of Chancery gave possession of the Manor to Ball Hughes who, finally with his fortunes in decline, sold his estate – 'Oatlands' in Surrey – and went to Paris where he lived until his death in 1862. In 1866, the whole of Sidmouth Manor was put up for sale and bought by GE Balfour of Manchester, father of Colonel John Edmond Heugh Balfour, and so Fortfield Terrrace became part of the Manor Estates.

The houses had a succession of tenants, some stayed only a short time, others spent their lives in one or more of the houses. One early resident was Joanna Fulford, a member of the Fulford family of Great Fulford at Dunsford near Exeter. Another was the two unmarried Copplestone sisters at No. 3. Their brother, Edward, was to become Professor of Poetry at Oxford and was instrumental in getting the poet, Percy Bysshe Shelley, expelled from the university for writing what was considered a subversive pamphlet. Edward later became Bishop of Llandaff and subsequently Dean of St Pauls in London. The sisters had lived with their father at Old Hayes (now Woodlands) previously. General Sir John Hart Dunne, who had brought the first Pekingese dog to England, presenting it to Queen Victoria, lived at No. 6 in the early 20th century. (See also the chapter on Sidmouth War Memorial Servicemen's Club.)

A resident of 5 Fortfield Terrace refused to complete her 1911 census form and defaced it instead with the words 'Votes for Women'. This lady, Rosina Mary Pott, was prominent in the Suffragette movement and it was she who provided bail for

Emmeline Pankhurst when she was arrested. She was married to a stockbroker and lived in Kensington, and she eventually came to live at Fortfield Terrrace. Her father was Edward Henry Corbould, an artist, who was also art tutor to Queen Victoria's children. Her action in refusing to complete the Census has gained national publicity in modern times and became a *cause célèbre*. Further chapters follow with histories to other Fortfield Terrace Houses and their occupants.

The houses had witnessed Sidmouth become a fashionable

resort and, with the exception of those that had been sold, were throughout the mid 19th century let to a succession of mostly minor titled people and gentry. Towards the end of the century, times had changed and, with their fortunes declining, all had become lodging houses. The Manor Estates bought back almost all the freehold houses, but, finding the upkeep of the Terrace burdensome, began to sell the houses and over the years all but two were converted into flats.

Julia Creeke

---

25 1 FORTFIELD TERRACE *Originally 1 and 2 were one house*

This was the first house to be completed on the terrace, a late 18th century speculative development that was intended to be a crescent but was permanently left unfinished after the deaths of the developer and architect. Caroline, Princess of Wales, stayed at No. 1 in 1806.

The first to hold the property as a Tenant at Will was the Reverend William Jenkins, the nephew of the developer of the terrace. The Reverend Jenkins, in an announcement in the *Exeter Flying Post* of 14 March 1797, had a Dispensation granted under the Great Seal to hold the Vicarage of Sidmouth. He also acquired another four houses under the same terms, obviously intending to let them for additional income but, since it was close to the Parish Church, it seems likely that perhaps he himself occupied No. 1, rather than the Vicarage (it is known that at a later date he let it).

In 1806, Lord Gwydir, then aged 52 and Deputy Lord Great Chamberlain to the household of the Prince Regent, having 'discovered' Sidmouth, began the refurbishment of 'Old Hayes' (now Woodlands – see separate chapter) as his seaside home and took a lease of 1 Fortfield Terrace whilst work progressed.

The Exeter Flying Post of 25 May 1806 reported that 'Her Royal Highness the Princess of Wales arrived here on a visit to that worthy and benevolent man, Lord Gwydir and family. His Lordship, we are happy to state, is rapidly recovering from the complaint that a few months ago threatened to deprive

society of one of its brightest ornaments.' After the Princess's relationship with the Prince Regent ended, she became an outcast in high society although some, like Lord Gwydir, privately had sympathy for her position. *The Exeter Flying Post* went on:

The Princess of Wales left Dawlish on 20th May and came to Sidmouth. On her arrival a Royal Salute was fired with guns at the Fort by the Volunteers. A flag was hoisted at the Fort and another on the Church Tower. The next day her Royal Highness, attended by Lord Gwydir, went and inspected the progress of the villa near the town in the cottage orné style which his lordship is building. In the evening Her Royal

Princess Caroline of Brunswick, wife of the Prince Regent, by Thomas Lawrence, 1798 (National Portrait Gallery)

Highness walked along the beach parade and expressed herself highly delighted with the romantic scenery and extensive sea views of this charming spot. On Thursday 22nd May her Royal Highness took leave of her noble host and hostess and the town on her way to Christchurch. She declined the honour of a salute from the Fort in consideration for the disposition of some visitors of distinction who were residing here for the recovery of their health.

Not long after Lord Gwydir vacated No. 1 to take up residence in his newly conceived cottage orné, No. 1 was let to Lord le Despenser for the accommodation of his wife and her household whilst he was building Knowle Cottage. Meanwhile his Lordship rented 5 Clifton Place from Mr Heffer. There ensued a period when the house was let to a succession of tenants.

In the 1841 Census, the Copplestone sisters, Caroline and Frances, aged 60 and 52 respectively, both unmarried, were living in the house with their two servants. They were the sisters of Edward Copplestone, an eminent cleric who became Bishop of Llandaff, and then in 1832, Dean of St Pauls. He had started his career as Rector of Offwell, near Honiton. The two sisters spent their lives in Sidmouth living, over the years, in three of the houses in the Terrace. By 1851, No. 1 had been divided into two houses, Nos. 1 and 1½, and an extension was built onto the eastern end of No. 1 to house the staircase; a new decorative porch was made and inside was the new front door. Meanwhile, the sisters were in occupation of No. 1½. They had spent at least part of their youth in Sidmouth, since their father, the Reverend John Bradford Copplestone, was living at 'Old Hayes' around 1800, but later went to live in Exeter when Lord Gwydir acquired the house. Edward Copplestone throughout his life paid visits to his sisters in Sidmouth and assisted them financially. Caroline, was the last surviving member of the Copplestone family to reside in Sidmouth. She died in October 1890 at the age of 92, and is commemorated by a plaque in Sidmouth Parish Church.

In 1851, an advert appeared stating that '1 Fort Terrace' was 'to be let unfurnished, the comfortable and desirable residence, with or without coach house and stables. Apply at

No. 1 at the eastern end of the terrace (Sidmouth Museum)

the house'. In 1861, a Dr Mackenzie of Cambridge and his wife and daughter were living at No. 1, but in 1863 ownership of Nos. 1 and 1½, like other houses in the Terrace, passed with the sale of the Manor to the Balfour family. By the end of the century it had become a lodging house with Mrs Phyllis Churchill as proprietor. In March 1897 there was a ferocious gale and the *Sidmouth Observer* reported:

Great damage done at No. 1 Fortfield Terrace – the occupants have had a miraculous escape from injury. The upper portion of the back part has been entirely demolished. The chimney fell this morning, sending the roof into the bedroom and taking the side of the house into the roadway.

Eventually, the Manor, finding the upkeep of the houses increasingly onerous, sold both Nos. 1 and 1½. No. 1½ was made into flats, whilst No. 1 is one of only two houses in Fortfield Terrace that remain private houses.

Julia Creeke

8 FORTFIELD TERRACE

This is the most prominent part on the terrace, and was originally designed as the centre-piece of a crescent. In 1831 the Grand Duchess Hélène of Russia, sister-in-law of the Tsar, rented No. 8 for herself and No. 7 for her entourage during her much celebrated visit to Sidmouth.

The Terrace's most celebrated resident arrived on 24 June 1831. She was the wife of the Grand Duke Michael (brother of the Czarina). The Grand Duchess was not Russian, but German, and had been born Princess Charlotte Marie of Württemberg in 1780. She spent her childhood in Paris and was not only attractive, but had developed a love of music and the arts. At sixteen, she was chosen to become the future wife of Grand Duke Michael. She learnt Russian prior to her marriage in 1824, became a member of the Orthodox Church, and changed her name to Helena Pavlovna. In spite of Russia's turbulent politics, she had a long and useful life, even nursing Russian soldiers wounded on the Crimean front – Russia's Florence Nightingale. She died in St Petersburg in 1873.

Following her marriage, the Grand Duchess had four children in quick succession and these repeated pregnancies had taken a toll on her health. The Royal family had relied on senior British doctors for some years and it was through connections in London and St Petersburg that it was decided that the Duchess would benefit from a stay by the sea. Sidmouth was chosen because it was fashionable, yet quiet and peaceful and the climate was good. In Russia, the visit could be publicly attributed to the need for Russian Royal Family to be represented at the Coronation of William IV due to take place in September 1831. It was also a goodwill visit as diplomatic relations with Great Britain were tense at the time.

Preparations for the visit had been afoot for some time with the Russian Consul-General heavily involved in arrangements. The visit was of sufficient significance to merit a piece in the *London Morning Post* of 26 May 1831, where it was stated that 7, 8, 9 and 10 Fortfield Terrace had been leased to accommodate the Grand Duchess and her immediate suite of forty and that improvements and re-decorating was taking place ready for their reception.

On 13 June, two carriages of servants arrived and two days later more carriages arrived with yet more servants, including a Russian band, and all these people were lodged in various parts of the town. Sidmothians had never played host to so many foreigners nor heard so much conversation in an unintelligible language. On 30 June 1831 the *Exeter Flying Post* reported the arrival of the Grand Duchess:

The Grand Duchess Elena Pavlovna with her daughter, by Karl Brullov, 1830 (State Russian Museum, St Petersburg)

This illustrious personage, her three daughters, and suite, amongst whom are the Countess Nesselrode, Madame de Tolstoy, Prince Gagarin, Dr Hurder, and Monsieur de Lobstor, First Secretary, arrived at Plymouth on Monday night.

The Grand Duchess Hélène had arrived after a 23 day voyage from St Petersburg in two ships of the Royal Russian Navy, a battleship and a frigate, but the ships had to be quarantined until clearance arrived from London on Thursday evening. The following day, the royal party disembarked and left in carriages for Sidmouth where they arrived in the evening. So began one of the town's most celebrated visits.

Altogether there were over 100 Russians located in the town. A royal salute was fired from the Preventive Station, a band played on the Fort Field, at the entrance to the Terrace a floral arch spanned the road opposite No. 1 and numerous Russian flags floated everywhere. A fine coloured print marks the visit.

The Grand Duchess was, from contemporary accounts, a lady of considerable charm with a good command of English, not uncommon as English governesses were often employed by aristocratic Russian households and there was a large English community in St Petersburg.

One of the best accounts of the visit is contained in this extract from the *London Morning Post* of 2 July 1931:

The principal lodging houses have undergone improvement. The places of public amusement and resort have been much

Russian band playing in the Assembly Rooms (private collection)

decorated and the inhabitants have united in the support of a brass band of twelve performers who will play three evenings a week until the close of October. The illustrious lady is of the most affable and engaging manner, quite easy of access, and is daily riding in her carriage, or on donkeys with the young princesses and may frequently be seen walking on the Esplanade as early as 9 or 10 o'clock in the morning. She is delighted with the situation and is delighted with the attentions which have been shown her, several of the nobility and gentry have called on her and have expressed a wish and intention of visiting them also.

She was accompanied during her stay by Counts Tolstoy and Gagarin and the Countess Nesselrode. The Grand Duchess occupied No. 8 and her close entourage No. 7 Fortfield Terrace.

She held a number of Receptions, inviting the local nobility and gentry, and conversed easily with those present. She liked to walk around the town accompanied only by a companion to see how the locals lived, often stepping inside to look around if she saw an open door. She enjoyed several sea trips along the coast, the farthest to Dawlish, her departure and return being marked by the firing of a salute from the Preventive Station on the seafront.

Meanwhile, her Russian House Band, resplendent in the uniforms of her household – long tunics tied with sashes and pantaloons tucked into high boots – when not required by their employer, played below the balcony of 8 Fortfield Terrace to an audience promenading on the Fort Field, or seated on benches.

The band were playing on 11 July when, at the London Hotel, there was a fashionable Ball for 140 distinguished guests with several of the Duchess's suite present including Prince Gargarin. The Ballroom was decorated with a profusion of flowers and the Russian Royal Arms, and the Ball went off with so much *éclat* that another was proposed which the Grand Duchess would attend. The Duchess was even to enjoy the company of her father, Prince Paul, brother of the King of Württemberg who had arrived to stay at Stone's Hotel (now the Royal York).

Probably the most delightful and surprising account of this memorable visit comes from the *London Morning Post* of 11 August:

The Grand Duchess Hélène on Monday embarked from this place in a steamer, which arrived the preceding day. At twelve o'clock a temporary platform was prepared from the water's edge to the promenade and covered with green baize and the inhabitants and visitors, to the number of 1,500 to 2,000, thronged the beach in anticipation of their illustrious guest's arrival. The Russian and English colours, quartered on one flag, were hoisted in the Fort Field and upwards of thirty pleasure boats stood off from the shore, many of them decorated with appropriate banners. At 2.30 pm the Officer of the Coast Guard hailed the approach of her Imperial Highness and one of the King's boats was rowed to the platform to convey the Grand Duchess and her immediate suite to the steamer, upon boarding which the English and Russian standards were simultaneously hoisted on the foremast and stern and a brass band played airs suitable to the occasion.

Sadly, the destination of the royal party is not recorded.

Her visit ended early on the morning of 24 August when, in a procession of seven coaches, the Grand Duchess left Sidmouth for Cheltenham as her doctors thought the waters there would be beneficial. From there she went to Windsor Castle to stay with King William IV and Queen Adelaide, finally going to Hastings on 11 October, before returning to Russia.

Only a year later, No. 8 was leased initially for two months by the widower, Edward Moulton Barrett, and he and his large family, including Elizabeth (later Browning) moved in. Mr Barrett was of creole descent, generations of his family having owned and lived on their Jamaican plantations. Financial problems, an insurrection by slaves and the impending abolition of slavery all combined to force him to sell Hope End, his Herefordshire estate, where the family had lived for more than 20 years. The health of Elizabeth was an added source of concern and he hoped a few months spent in Sidmouth might be beneficial.

The journey to Sidmouth from Herefordshire was about 140 miles and was achieved in two days with an overnight stop in Bath. The family's arrival at dusk was inauspicious: the arrangements for their arrival had gone awry – there was no one to welcome them, No. 8 was in total darkness and the house seemed very cramped after Hope End. Notwithstanding, within a few days they had taken an immediate liking to the town. For the first time in many months Elizabeth was able to dine with the family instead of in her room. She was able to enjoy expeditions along the shore and have donkey rides: Elizabeth declaring 'I don't know when I have been so long

Terrace with Imperial Russian Eagle in the pediment (SVA)

well'. Her translation of *Prometheus Bound* was probably accomplished at this time, taking just ten days.

Elizabeth wrote the following: 'We like very much what we have seen of the town. It is small and not superfluously clean, but of course the respectable houses are not a part of the town. Ours is the one Grand Duchess Helena had, not at all grand, but extremely comfortable'. Elizabeth, in a long letter, repeatedly refers to No. 8 as Rafarel House. The Rafarel family were of Italian origin and, although the house was still part of the Manor, at some stage the Rafarel family it seems, had acquired the remainder of the original lease of Elizabeth Spicer.

The family's stay at No. 8 was to last about a year and in May 1833 Elizabeth wrote to her friend Mrs Martin. The letter tells much about the joys of their stay in Sidmouth:

As for me I have been quite well all the spring, and almost all the winter. I don't know when I have been so long well as I have been lately; without a cough or anything else disagreeable. Indeed if I may place the influenza in a parenthesis, we have all been perfectly well, in spite of our boating and fishing and getting wet three times a day. There is good trout fishing at the Otter, and the noble river Sid, which if I liked to stand in it, might cover my ankles. And lately, Daisy and Sete and Occyta have studied the art of catching shrimps, and soak themselves up to their waists like professors. My love of water concentrates itself in the boat:

and this I enjoy very much, when the sea is blue and calm as the sky, which it has often been lately.

The family's stay in Sidmouth lasted over three years, but only the first part was spent at No. 8. They were to move onto two further properties (more about their stay is under Cedar Shade).

The glory days for No. 8 were, however, over and hence forward the house was to be occupied by various tenants until it was finally divided into flats. The double-headed eagle in the pediment above Nos. 7 and 8 is a replacement of the original put there in 1831 to commemorate the visit of the Grand Duchess.

Julia Creeke

---

27 9 FORTFIELD TERRACE

The former home of the Reverend Edmund Butcher (b.1757 – d.1822), a chronicler of Sidmouth and its environs, whose guide books were significant in promoting the town as a fashionable resort for the nobility and gentry.

This house was nearing completion when Thomas Jenkins died, and the pillared colonnade between Nos. 8 and 9 was still being built when the tenant, a Mr F Coleman, moved in. He leased the property as a 'Tenant for one Life' at an annual rent of one shilling (5p). Presumably this was the ground rent and, at the time of the 1813 Auction of the Terrace, Mr Coleman was still in occupation.

The Will of Thomas Jenkins, written in Italian whilst he was still living in Rome, left the Manor to his great nephew, Thomas Jenkins (junior) son of his nephew, William Jenkins, Vicar of Sidmouth. Thomas Jenkins (junior) had begun to raise large sums of money using the Manor as security or else selling off parts, all to fund a life of luxury, which in due course was to catch up with him. The Will itself caused disputes and lawsuits. He tried on three occasions to auction off Fortfield Terrace. Thomas (junior) was much influenced by his brother-in-law, Edward Hughes Ball Hughes, who had married his sister. Edward was a Regency man of fashion and a prodigious gambler, who had inherited an income of £40,000 a year and led an extravagant lifestyle. It was from him that Thomas Jenkins (junior) borrowed large sums of money. Eventually in 1834, unable to keep up the repayments, he had to dispose of the Manor by Court decree to Ball Hughes.

In 1819, the lease of No. 9 was assigned by the Reverend William Cockburn (see the Hunters Moon chapter) who had evidently occupied the house for a while as he first appears in Sidmouth as early as 1813. The lease was assigned to the Reverend Edmund Butcher in 'a bond for quiet enjoyment of a house in the Fort Field, Sidmouth'. The same year, the house was sold by the Manor to the Reverend Edmund Butcher, who also had the lease of No. 3 but lived in No. 9 with his wife Elizabeth, his son Edmund and his daughter Emma. The family were to occupy the house on and off for the next half century.

A Nonconformist minister, the Reverend Edmund Butcher, left London through ill health. He appears to have suffered from a chronic chest complaint which drove him to seek less polluted air and brought him to live in the Sid Valley, initially at Burscombe, Sidbury. In 1798, he was appointed Minister at the Old Meeting (see separate chapter). He

The Reverend Edmund Butcher (courtesy of the Trustees of the Old Dissenter Meeting)

was not what is called a popular preacher, but was well-liked and remained throughout the Regency period, only retiring when his health again failed.

He became an author and chronicler of Sidmouth, publishing several guide books, the first of which appeared in 1803, to be followed by another in 1810. This was in small format with a pull-out frontispiece. The next was his most famous guide, which has been used extensively as a source of information. This appeared in a subscribers' edition in 1817, entitled *Sidmouth Scenery, Views of the principal Cottages and Residences of the Nobility and Gentry at that admired watering place, Sidmouth* – a title typical of the flowery prose of the period. It was illustrated with 20 aquatints. There was a further edition in 1821, which included illustrations of several houses built since the First Edition. Versions of his guides continued to appear for many years after his death under the auspices of John Wallis at the Royal Marine Library.

His guide books have become an invaluable source of information concerning the early years of Sidmouth's development, when it was changing into a resort frequented by those of fashion and members of the aristocracy. They tell us much about the town and the people who resided there and where they lived, or who was visiting.

Edmund Butcher established a great rapport with Emmanuel Baruh Lousada of Peak House, one of Sidmouth's leading citizens, who gave him a piece of land opposite his own house and on it, between 1807 and 1812, the Reverend Butcher built 'Helens' in Cotmaton Road (although now much altered) for his own occupation. This was a most unusual friendship between a rich merchant of Jewish heritage and a Nonconformist Minister, but it appears Lousada appreciated the friendship and gifted his friend accordingly with a piece of land.

Butcher, later in 1819, acquired the lease of 9 Fortfield Terrace and then purchased it. From then on he lived there, beginning the Butcher family's 54 year association with the house. Documents seem to suggest that for at least part of 1820 he was living at the house with his wife, Elizabeth, and his 27 year-old son Edmund (junior) and 22 year-old daughter Emma. The same year, he suffered a stroke and after faithfully serving his congregation for over 20 years, he retired. He finally left Sidmouth with his family to live in Bath where he died in 1822, aged 65 years. He was buried in a cemetery at Lyncomb reserved to Unitarian Dissenters.

His son, also Edmund, became a doctor, Alderman of the City of Bristol and apparently, as the 1851 Census records, a

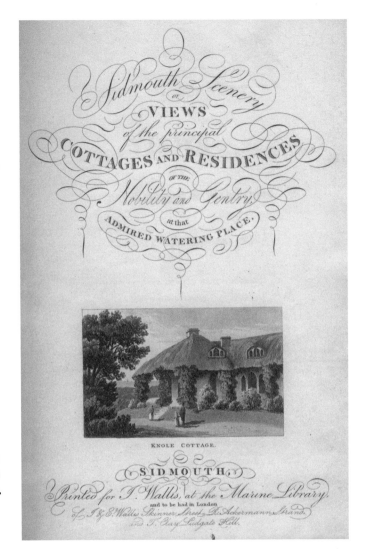

First page of Butcher's most famous guide book, 1817 (private collection)

sugar trader. He married Elizabeth Maria Landsdown, but she did not survive the birth of their second child, and the same year he married again. Finally he returned to No. 9 with his two surviving children. Subsequently, there appeared two adverts in *Harvey's Journal* of 1 April 1851 offering tuition to a few select young gentlemen in classics, mathematics, drawing and painting saying that he was an Associate of Bristol Fine Arts Academy.

The family left Sidmouth in 1853, but returned to 9 Fortfield Terrace in 1862, by which time Edmund was aged 70. Ten years later, but now alone, he is recorded in the 1871 Census as 'Lodging House Keeper', running the house with his cook and housekeeper but, in *Lethaby's Journal* of 1 August 1872, the following appeared: 'Died July 11 at 9 Fortfield Terrace, Edmund Butcher Esq., formerly of London and Bristol, but long resident in Sidmouth: son of the Reverend E Butcher, author of the *Beauties of Sidmouth* etc., the first Guide book of the town, aged 81 years'. So it came to pass that the Reverend Edmund Butcher's grandson sold the house on the Terrace, its new owners once again the Manor Estate.

The house then, like so many others in the Terrace, became a lodging house providing visitors to Sidmouth with accommodation. Gradually over the years the Manor Estate disposed of individual houses, the final ones on the death of the last Lord of the Manor, Colonel Balfour, in 1952. No. 9 has remained to this day one of only two houses in the Terrace which are still individual houses in private occupation and has not been divided into flats.

Julia Creeke

---

28 10 FORTFIELD TERRACE

Residence in the 1850s of the accomplished marine artist and innovative boat-builder, Robert Charles Leslie (b.1826 – d.1901). Since 1919, home to a notable local institution, the Sidmouth Club.

When the architect of the Terrace, Michael Novosielski, died in April 1795, building of the westward part of the Terrace was just started. Thomas Jenkins, the builder and owner of the Terrace, was still living in Rome and so could not take charge of seeing the western range completed. It seems likely that the task of overseeing completion of what was already under way fell to his nephew, William Jenkins, who was Vicar of Sidmouth.

In fact No. 10 was let by William Jenkins to a tenant whilst the workmen were still finishing it and adding the porch, but work on the remainder of the Terrace ceased. By early May 1798 its owner, Thomas Jenkins, was also dead, having only just landed in England. Fortfield Terrace was never to be completed as its owner and his architect envisaged, and remains so to this day. It was originally called 'The Crescent'.

In 1815, at the time of the attempted sale of Sidmouth Manor, No. 10 was leased for £65 p.a., the Tenant at Will being the Reverend William Jenkins, but all that was to change when he died in 1821. No. 10 seems to have been let to a succession of tenants until the early 1850s when the lease was taken by Robert Charles Leslie, a marine artist of some standing.

In 1851, after living in St John's Wood and Erith, Robert and Eliza Leslie moved to Sidmouth and occupied several houses, including Sid House and Old Cotmaton. When they left the latter in 1853, Tomasine Carslake, whose husband owned the property, made the following entry in her diary: 'the Leslies left Old Cotmaton today – Bah!' Her grand-daughter commented 'they were very dirty people and left the house in a great mess!' The Leslies were an artistic family and led rather a bohemian lifestyle which no doubt contributed. Eventually they moved into No. 10 Fortfield Terrace. Two

Robert Charles Leslie, marine artist and boat-builder (Frontispiece of A Waterbiography)

years earlier, Robert Leslie had married Eliza, a childhood friend, widowed and with an income, which enabled them to enjoy a lifestyle of their choice.

Robert Leslie's father, Charles Leslie, was an eminent Victorian marine painter who had many famous artists and authors as friends, including John Constable, Charles Dickens and William Thackeray. Robert, who was born in 1826, was also an able painter – in 1844 one of his pictures was exhibited at the Royal Academy – but he was brought up in a rather unconventional atmosphere, where the need for education was not uppermost and he spent most of his childhood on the banks of ponds and canals sailing homemade boats, declaring that his childhood had been 'one long holiday'. So it wasn't surprising that he had a passion for the sea and boats which directed the whole tenor of his subsequent life which was spent close to the sea.

He formed a great friendship with a Sidmouth fisherman who had inherited boat-building skills from his forebears. This man was Harry Conant and such was his trust in Leslie that he allowed him to borrow his boat *England's Rose* whenever he wasn't using it. Conant had begun his seafaring on board a small west country coaster employed in the coal trade, of which his father was skipper, and he was an accomplished sail-maker and rigger. Leslie often made trips along the coast in *England's Rose*. Eventually Leslie and Conant hand-built a gaff yawl called *Foam* which Leslie sailed widely and in which he competed in a Sidmouth regatta where the weather was so bad that the competitors couldn't see the marks nor each other. The small boats all eventually had to be beached for safety, which in the conditions was extremely hazardous, whilst the larger yachts retreated to the shelter of Exmouth.

Finally, Leslie and Conant embarked on a much more ambitious project to build a 45 ft (13.7m) yacht using their own skills and those of other local craftsmen, all the materials being locally produced down to the blacksmith's nails. Conant made the sails to Leslie's own plan, which was the then rare Bermudan rig. It took them two years to complete the project. Leslie called the boat *Rip Van Winkle* and in it he set sail with his wife and family plus a manservant, for a three month cruise to South West England.

This yacht was revolutionary and the forerunner of what we know today as a small family cruising yacht. Cruises under sail had for many years been the prerogative of the wealthy in sizeable yachts with professional crews, but Leslie set sail in a yacht which he could sail himself with an efficient and

manageable rig and, although the accommodation was fairly basic by today's standards and the cooking arrangements primitive, the family lived, cooked and ate on board. The children thoroughly enjoyed it, although Eliza, who didn't much care for the sea, would doubtless rather have been in her comfortable house back in Sidmouth.

Harry Conant, fisherman and shipwright (Sidmouth Museum)

Eventually it seems life had become too comfortable and predictable in Sidmouth, for Leslie and the family finally drifted away from Sidmouth in 1863, to end up in Southampton, where he continued his sailing exploits. Leslie documented his life in a biography which he entitled *A Waterbiography* illustrating it with some of his paintings and drawings.

When the Leslies left, the house seems to have been empty for some time – perhaps they left that too in a dreadful mess. Times had changed and fewer 'persons of quality' came to Sidmouth wanting to rent a house for extended periods, so that like most of the other houses in the Terrace, No. 10 seems to have degenerated into a lodging house for visitors wanting accommodation for a seaside holiday. It seems to have continued thus until in 1919, when Colonel Balfour, who owned the whole Terrace as Lord of the Manor, offered the Sidmouth Club (for men) a lease of the building.

The Club had been founded in 1890 by largely the same people who had formed Sidmouth Golf Club in 1889. They rented three rooms in the Bedford Hotel for billiards, reading, and a sitting room; membership could only be by invitation, and so was restricted very much to Sidmouth's 'great and good' and those in 'trade' were certainly excluded. The subscription was 3 guineas (£3.15) a year with a 50% reduction for any Curate with a living in the valley or in Salcombe Regis.

1896 saw the Club's first move to rooms in what is now the Kingswood Hotel, but was then the Sidmouth Baths Company. (Further information is in the Kingswood Hotel chapter). The members purchased a new billiard table by Burroughs & White which cost £106.18s.7d (£106.93) – it is probably the one still in use by members today. Billiards was the game of

The Rip van Winkle on her cradle, drawn by Robert Charles Leslie

gentlemen, who didn't normally play snooker. A telescope was also bought because the previous one had 'disappeared'. Ten years later there were plans drawn up by the Sidmouth architect, RW Sampson, to convert part of the Bath Company's coal store to a beer and wine cellar for the Club.

Although in 1918, WWI was drawing close to its end, the premises were requisitioned on behalf of the Red Cross for the treatment of wounded officers and the Club was left homeless. It was then that Colonel Balfour came to the Club's rescue and offered them a number of properties and the Club chose 10 Fortfield Terrace. The Club became the lessees in 1919 and has remained there to this day. RW Sampson was again asked to draw up plans for alterations in 1924. Three of his original drawings still survive and are on display in the Club.

In 1925, a challenge to a Billiards Match was received from the War Memorial Service Men's Club. The rules of the Sidmouth Club did not permit such a thing, nor the availability of the Club's facilities to people of the 'lower order'. After much heart-searching by members, the Club's Secretary was told to make the necessary arrangements for the match and that the opposing players and their friends be entertained at the Club. Things took a much more serious turn the following year, however, when Colonel Balfour offered to sell No. 10 to the Club for £1,350. At first the Club declined because it did not have sufficient funds, but the matter resurfaced in July when Colonel Balfour repeated his offer, but at a reduced figure of £1,000, and the Club unanimously accepted. It took many months before the purchase was finally made. In the meantime members of the Club decided to make the Officers of the Devonshire Regiment stationed in Exeter honorary members, and Colonel Charles JW Grant, a holder of the Victoria Cross, who lived in Sidmouth at Western Field in Manor Road, had recently become a member.

In the summer of 1931, HMS *Norfolk* arrived in Lyme Bay, and the Club decided to stand the Officers a dinner at a cost of £3.10.0 (£3.50) per head; there is no mention of the cost of wine. The Club also agreed to the playing of snooker on one of the two billiard tables. The rest of the decade seems to be taken up with routine matters.

Early in WW2, the Club was ordered to remove the brass plate on the door identifying the premises as 'The Sidmouth Club' and replace it with simply 'The Club' to confuse any invader or spy as to where they were. The chief problem during WW2 seems to be the shortage of alcohol, particularly whisky, so much so that it seems to have precluded making the Club available to RAF Officers stationed in the town. A subsidiary matter was an approach by Sidmouth Ladies Club for a Bridge Tournament, but this was rejected out of hand.

The Club's finances had always waxed and waned and the 1960s saw a drive to recruit new members, but the financial difficulties persisted, and in the mid 1970s the Club sold off the top two floors of No. 10 as a flat on a 999-year lease, and converted the basement into a garden flat. The proceeds from the sales ensured the Club's survival, so that in 1990 the Club could celebrate its centenary and continues to flourish to the present day.

Julia Creeke

Originally a large thatched villa, destroyed by fire. After reconstruction it was requisitioned in WW2 by the RAF, to become the first Dental Hygienist Training School in the UK.

The original blue plaque affixed at the entrance to Glenside was erected in collaboration with the RAF Institute of Dental Health and Training to commemorate the 50th anniversary of the School's foundation.

A large house known as Glenside was built in 1905 by Messrs RW and J Skinner. It was a very handsome and much admired thatched cottage built for Mr and Mrs FC Barnard; Mrs Barnard being the former proprietor of the Royal York Hotel. Regrettably, within two years it succumbed to fire, thought to be caused by a stray spark from the chimney.

At first the fire did not look at all serious, and while Mr FW Mitchell went for the fire brigade, a lot of willing helpers set to work to do what they could. Once notified, at about 6.15pm, Fire Superintendent Skinner immediately went with three other men with a reel of hose and appliances – and indeed he was there within four minutes. However, he had regrettably ordered that the 'fire rockets' not be fired, which would normally have been the signal for all firemen to respond to the emergency. When he arrived at the scene, and after an inspection that showed the seriousness of the situation, he immediately dispatched a man to have the rockets fired.

Glenside before the fire (Sidmouth Museum)

Moreover, when the hoses were deployed, the jets of water had no force and consequently they were of little effect. Fortunately, a large quantity of furniture was saved but amongst much left behind was a jewel case containing some £200 worth of jewellery. The case, charred almost to a cinder, was happily found the next day, with nearly two thirds of the contents undamaged.

There was a good deal of adverse comment, both regarding the inadequate water supply, and the apparent delay in getting the fire engine on scene. It is noteworthy that Sidmouth had been presented with a new steam fire engine as recently as 1902 by Mr Hatton-Wood of Belmont House, because of a disastrous fire in New Street in Sidmouth that threatened the whole of the central area of the town. The then Sidmouth engine, which was old, was so ineffectual that an engine from Exeter was sent for, but took two hours to get to the town owing to the horses having to pull it up Four Elms Hill. The fire was only extinguished due to a mammoth effort by the combined fire brigades and locals. Glenside was rebuilt in 1907, but this time with a tiled roof.

By the late 1930s, Sidmouth was a thriving seaside town and continued in this vein until World War Two was well underway. However, this was changing. Crude defences were erected along the Esplanade in 1940 to resist invasion, and not too far away, just beyond Salcombe Regis, a 'secret' radar station was being commissioned. Nevertheless, it wasn't until early in 1942 that the Air Ministry took an interest in Sidmouth regarding its valuable stock of hotels. It was recognised that this was a rich source of classrooms and domestic accommodation for RAF and WAAF personnel in training.

The first unit to arrive directly into the town on 4 May 1942, from Harrogate, was the RAF's Medical Training Depot. It included the Medical Officers' and Dental Clerk Orderlies' schools, which were allotted the Elizabeth Hotel. However, as the year progressed, many other hotels were needed for things such as male and female domestic accommodation for both permanent staff and students, a sick-quarters, an Administration HQ and an Equipment Section.

As early as 1941, it was recognised that, throughout the RAF, the Dental Branch was undermanned and that a backlog of

RAF Dental Branch badge

work was increasing in size. Mr Kelsey Fry (later Sir William Kelsey Fry), Civilian Consultant in Dental Surgery to the RAF, suggested alleviating the problem with the employment of dental hygienists to help prevent dental disease in aircrew. The training and employment of dental hygienists was already popular in the United States. In this country, such a move would contravene the Dentists Act. The Act was not binding on the Crown, however. Nonetheless, dental professionals were consulted, and said they would not oppose the idea in principle.

On 1 November 1942 Glenside was requisitioned and selected to be the Dental School. Shortly afterwards, the Dental Hygienist branch was formally adopted into the RAF, with the first course of instruction starting on 4 January 1943. The Dental School was the last unit to leave Sidmouth on 6 March 1945.

This introduction of dental hygienists to the dental workforce was considered such a success that, in 1949, training of civilian dental hygienists commenced at the Eastman Dental Clinic, London. They came to be well accepted by dentists, so that most dental schools now train dental hygienists. By 2018, some 7,000 dental hygienists were registered to practice in the UK.

After WW2, the building was converted into apartments and then, in 1980, became a care home for the elderly. The building was demolished in 2011 to make way for modern apartments.

Alastair Watson

30 GREENFIELD

Built in 1926, the home of Sir John Ambrose Fleming (b.1849 – d.1945), the world-renowned physicist, electrical engineer and inventor.

Until the late 19th century, Manor Road was no more than a track which from the south ran into the Western Fields, whose origins went back to mediaeval times when the entire area was part of the Manor of Sidmouth. Building in the late 18th and early 19th century had caused some of it to be sold off. Emmanuel Baruh Lousada of Peak House had purchased some fields, notably that which was to become the Archery Field (now Manor Road Car Park). Another area which was well wooded was part of the quite extensive grounds of Woolbrook Cottage (Royal Glen), but a considerable area still remained in the possession of the Manor. (There are separate chapters on Peak House and the Royal Glen.)

In the late 19th century, development of the area began with the building of three large villas, with distinctive flint facing, followed by 'Redlands' (demolished in the 1970s). The Victoria Hotel, opened in March 1904, was constructed at a cost of £30,000 and also occupied part of the old Western Fields, although some of the site was part of the grounds of the Royal Glen. Even though it was somewhat older, Westcliff Hall too had been built on part of the Western Fields and was a private house. By the late 1920s, the Royal Glen had lost its grounds along Manor Road and, by the 1930s, six houses occupied the frontage on the south side.

Sir John Ambrose Fleming was both the designer and builder of 'Greenfield' which was the first house built on the higher part of the south side – an aerial photograph from 1928 shows it in splendid isolation. He obviously got first choice in 1926 and went for the spot with the best view of the sea between the Victoria and Belmont Hotels. It was followed in 1928 by Western Field next door, which was built by Colonel and Mrs Grant on a massive plot.

Sir John Ambrose Fleming was a distinguished and eminent

Sir John Ambrose Fleming in 1904

scientist, electrical engineer and inventor, who in everyday life preferred to be called Ambrose, and retired to Sidmouth to Greenfield, where he and Lady Fleming lived for many years. He died in 1945, but Lady Fleming, who was many years younger, lived on at Greenfield until about 1978. Ambrose was a difficult and at times a rather unreasonable man. During WW2, when the newspapers were frequently late, and sometimes due to air raids never arrived at all, he would appear at Culverwells Newsagents to collect his and, finding them not there, would rage at anyone unlucky enough to be behind the counter.

He was born near Lancaster in 1849, son of James Fleming DD, a Scottish Congregational Minister, who subsequently moved with his growing family to north London.

Ambrose obtained a BSc degree in 1870, which enabled him to become an advanced student at the Royal College of Chemistry in South Kensington. After a further period as science master at Cheltenham College, he went up to Cambridge with an Exhibition and other scholarships, determined to study under the great James Clark Maxwell, who had become the first Cavendish Professor of Experimental Physics there, and he obtained his Natural Sciences Tripos in 1880.

He went to London in 1882 as consultant to the Edison Electrical Light Co. and, in 1885, was appointed the first Pendar Professor of Electrical Engineering at University College, London. He held this post until his retirement to Sidmouth in 1926 at the age of 77, when he moved into Greenfield, which was the name of the house in which he was born. He lived there with his two sisters, his first wife having died in 1917. In 1933 he married Miss Olive Franks of Bristol, a professional singer, well-known in the West Country particularly for her performances in oratorio.

Fleming lived at a time when the great scientific discoveries of the 19th century were beginning to be applied and commercialised. He was consulted over dangerous surges occurring in the famous 10,000 volt Ferranti electricity mains laid from the pioneer Deptford Power Station to London in 1890, and was able to suggest remedies. He advised on the design of small electricity power stations which were springing up all over the country, including Exeter.

In 1900, he also became consultant to the Marconi company and played a leading role in the first transatlantic radio transmission. He designed the world's first large radio transmitter, a complicated piece of equipment driven by a powerful electrical unit. Guglielmo Marconi designed the antennae. It was built at Poldhu, Cornwall, and on 12 December 1901 it was from there that the first test message was transmitted to St John's Newfoundland, where Marconi was waiting. Fleming was resentful through later life that Marconi claimed all the credit for the achievement, and this caused bad feeling between them. Fleming observed that Marconi was 'very ungenerous'.

His best-known work however, was the invention of the two-electrode rectifying valve in 1904. This enabled effective radio sets to be made for the first time. The valve displaced Sir Oliver Lodge's primitive form of radio signal detection, and started the revolution in radio-communication techniques and broadcasting, greatly helped by the subsequent insertion of a third electrode by the American, Lee de Forest. To his great chagrin, Sir Ambrose did not think of inserting this third electrode himself, and patent lawsuits followed. He was elected Fellow of the Royal Society in 1892, at the age of 43, but other honours, although showered on him, did not come until very late in life: for instance, he was knighted in 1929,

and received the Faraday Medal of the Institution of Electrical Engineers in 1928.

A man of strong religious conviction, Sir John preached on the Resurrection, disputed the scientific basis for evolution theory and in 1932 became founding President of the Evolution Protest Movement. In 1935 he published a major book on the subject – *The origin of Mankind: Viewed from the standpoint of Revelation and Research.* He and Lady Fleming were regular worshippers at Sidmouth Parish Church.

When he died in 1945, aged 95, he was buried in the Churchyard of Salcombe Regis Church, Lady Fleming presenting to Sidmouth Parish Church a finely carved Litany Desk in her husband's memory.

Julia Creeke

31 HOPE COTTAGE

A Regency house, used over time as a residence and offices, public and private. The nationally acclaimed author, fisherman and WW1 civil servant, Stephen Reynolds, worked here from 1916 to 1919. It has been home to the Sidmouth Museum since 1970.

Hope Cottage, at the top of Church Street is next to the Parish Church. It is a listed, end of terrace, Regency building on three floors with a cellar and a small garden, which is now a parking area adjacent to Coburg Road.

Its history dates back to 1812 when Sir John Kennaway bought land from the joint owners, Samuel Cawley and James Amyatt. In 1815 a Bristol architect, William Nicholls, built the present Hope Cottage, 'bounded on the North by a row of houses called Amyatt Row and on the South by the Public Highway'. An extension was added to the northern aspect in the mid-19th century.

Sir John leased it initially as a private dwelling but from as early as 1836 it was a solicitors' office – Drake, Stevens and Lester. An unmarried sister of Mr Lester lived upstairs and remained a tenant until her move to Fortfield Terrace in 1865. For the remainder of the 19th century it was invariably legal premises but with varied other functions including local magistrates' sessions and Customs and Excise.

In 1844, John Radford purchased the house from Sir John for £380 and went into partnership with Alfred Lester. An 1857 Directory indicates that Mr Lester was solicitor agent to the Lord of the Manor and Mr Radford, Clerk to the Magistrates.

Mr Williams replaced Mr Lester and in 1863 the recently founded London and South Western Bank used Hope Cottage as its Sidmouth base for thirteen years, as one of its twelve branches, with the two solicitors as their agents. The metal security bars on many of the windows may date from this time.

Mr Williams died in 1873 and was replaced by James Orchard; his wife and children occupied the upstairs accommodation and in 1880 a son was born in the house.

Sidmouth Museum since 1970 (SVA)

About 1880, the solicitor Mr Orchard and family at the bay windows (Sidmouth Museum)

A photograph from about this time shows Mr Orchard and his wife and daughter standing at the open first floor bow windows fronting Coburg Road, and a housemaid and small child standing at the Church Street main entrance. John Radford became a well-respected and wealthy local citizen, working in Hope Cottage but living at Sidmount. In 1896 he gifted the Ham to Sidmouth Urban District Council, stipulating that it be used by the general public for 'recreation'. On his death in 1899 the ownership of Hope Cottage passed to his eldest daughter, Constance Mackintosh Radford.

Early in the 20th century, in addition to their legal duties, Mr Orchard was now Town Clerk and his new partner, Phillip Michelmore, deputy Clerk.

In 1916, at the height of the Great War, Hope Cottage again became vacant. Mr Orchard had died two years earlier and, in November, Mr Michelmore spoke to his friend, Stephen Reynolds, and offered him the tenancy. Reynolds was now a well-known Sidmouth figure. Ten years earlier, he had been an impoverished young writer from a middle class home and had walked to Sidmouth from his home town, Devizes. The fisherman, Bob Woolley, kindly allowed him to live with his family in their rented house in Bedford Square behind the Bedford Hotel. Stephen became an 'honorary' member of the family, adopted in all but name. He learned to fish and even to speak with the Devon dialect. He wrote *A Poor Man's House* based on his ongoing life with the Woolleys and it became a critical success. He was now the articulate spokesman for the local fisherman and his highly influential articles in the national press were noticed by the civil servants in London. He was the major contributor to the so-called Devon and Cornish Committee (1913) to improve national inshore fisheries. In 1915 he was appointed Fisheries Inspector on South West Naval Command, an onerous and crucial role with a coast line of 750 miles. His office was still in the cramped and noisy Woolley house. Phillip Michelmore knew that the situation was difficult and had been exacerbated by recent flooding of Bedford Square. Stephen and the Woolley family readily accepted the opportunity to lease Hope Cottage which was still owned by Miss Radford. Stephen wrote enthusiastically to his aunt:

> I am to have the first floor – three rooms, unfurnished, and a bathroom, while the Woolleys will have the ground floor (kitchen, etc, and dining room) and the three bedrooms on the top floor. Then if my work takes me away for any time, they will be able to lock up my study, and let the dining-room with my two bedrooms. What specially appeals to Mam 'Ooley is a back door, to avoid muddy boots etc, right through the house; to Bob, the bathroom, I think, and to me, the chance of quietness.

They moved in mid-November and the first floor was used for 'fisheries business'. It is likely that Reynolds's office was the Museum's present Dr Bob Symes Room. Stephen was now receiving paid help from a fisherman turned clerk, Harry Paynter, and also from an academic, Harold Wright, who lived in Sidmouth with his family. Reynolds was an intermediary between the West Country fishermen and the Admiralty in Plymouth – an invidious role. Many fishermen were in the Royal Naval Reserve (RNR) and had been recruited at the outset of war, including 11 members of the extended Woolley family but, in 1916, the Royal Navy was determined to conscript the remaining fit ones, which would have destroyed the industry. Reynolds fought tirelessly and, generally, successfully on their behalf. In December 1917, he moved his sleeping accommodation to the Retreat (now the 1922 Club), perhaps for extra quiet, but continued to work in Hope Cottage. He was offered, but turned down, an OBE, a new award for non-combatants in the home front.

In the December 1918 General Election, shortly after the Armistice, Reynolds mischievously hung from the house a Red Flag as well as a Union Jack. No Labour candidate was standing locally and memories of the murder of the Russian royal family were still fresh in people's memories. Reynolds reports a conversation between Bob Woolley and an angry passer-by:

> 'Do you know what that red flag outside your house means, Mr Woolley?'
> 'I haven't rightly taken much notice o'it: I been too busy wi' the herrings.'
> 'It means the first step to REVOLUTION!'
> 'Oh,' said Bob, 'that's it, is it? And a bloody good job too!'

In February 1919, Stephen Reynolds died of influenza; he was only 37 years-old. A remarkable and lengthy tribute was paid to his work in the official 1920 HMSO report *Fisheries in the Great War*, and he is now recognized as one of the major figures in the Devon home front.

The Woolley family continued to live in Hope Cottage until 1927 but, in the meantime and two years earlier, the owner Miss Radford, had generously gifted the building to Sidmouth Urban District Council with the requirement that it should be used as '…a free public library and reading room, or, if desired, for a museum or for any philanthropic, educational or scientific purpose.' A local newspaper suggested that the diaries of Peter Orlando Hutchinson and John Tindall could be displayed.

The Council accepted the gift and was using Hope Cottage for meetings in 1928; the Museum Print Room on the first floor was the Council Chamber. However, the Council prevaricated to

such an extent that it was not until July 1936 that it became the Sidmouth branch of the Free Library. Fortunately, Miss Radford lived to see the event but died later the same year. There is a plaque dedicated to her on the side of the building.

Stephen Reynolds in WW1 when a civil servant (Sidmouth Museum)

In its early history, a room was set aside as a picture gallery which included Sidmouth historic prints. The library occupied the ground floor and the Council continued to sublet the two upper floors. Local residents remember the library well including the strict rule of silence. It became a branch of Devon County Library in 1946.

In 1970, the lease for Hope Cottage was granted to the Trustees of the Sid Vale Association to which the Museum belongs. The Museum, previously located at Woolcombe House (see separate chapter), was officially opened in May 1971. The Town Council remain owners of the building.

Constance Radford's wishes continue to be fulfilled.

Nigel Hyman

---

32 HUNTERS MOON *formerly Salcombe House*

A fine Georgian house, built in the late 1700s. Once home to Sir William Cockburn, Dean of York, and his colourful family. It was then owned by members of the Cornish family, prominent in Salcombe Regis, and great local benefactors.

The 1775 Land Tax returns show Mrs Brutton as the holder of a plot of land adjacent to the Byes, for which over the previous seven years she had paid £337 to buy the copyhold. A few years later it notes that there is a house and barns and a

holding of 20 acres (8 ha) of land. All the way along the Byes were strips of agricultural land running up the slopes of Salcombe Hill, none particularly large because they had to be farmed with nothing more than human labour – a horse and cart, simple plough and a scythe: most were rented, but some owned outright. Salcombe House was built on just such a holding. It is believed that Mrs Brutton built the house and her husband is noted as the Reverend Mr Brutton who was presumably related to a Mr Brutton of Cullompton who had previously rented a cottage on the site. However, there must have been funds to build this quite substantial plain Georgian house. Later additions include the fine centred Ionic porch (now glazed in) with an elegant parapet, and a small belvedere or clock tower with a weather-vane.

When Mrs Brutton died, her daughter sold the house to the Reverend William Jenkins, Vicar of Sidmouth, who by 1800 is listed as the occupier. It was not unusual for vicars, in order to increase their income, to move out of the rectory if it was large and imposing, and let it to others, whilst they moved into a smaller and less expensive property. This is exactly what the Reverend Jenkins did, letting the Vicarage as a lodging house. By 1802, the Reverend Jenkins was also in possession of the adjacent land holding, but subsequently let it to a J Hook. Salcombe House was on the east bank of the Sid in the Parish of Salcombe Regis and since Waterloo Bridge was not built until 1820, access to the town was either through the ford, or for pedestrians over the Mill Ford footbridge. This inconvenience made the east bank much less fashionable.

By 1822, Salcombe House was owned by one of Sidmouth's most colourful characters, the Reverend William Cockburn, who that same year was made Dean of York – he was to remain so for the rest of his life (he died in 1858). He or his sons were to occupy the house for the next 25 years. The Dean was well-known in Sidmouth because he could frequently be seen striding about with an umbrella slung over his back – probably the first umbrella to be seen in Sidmouth. This was a new fashion in England, although they had been known in India for years.

The first mention of him in Sidmouth comes some years earlier in March 1813, when the 16 year-old Thomazine Leigh, daughter of the Leighs of Slade House, Salcombe Regis, dances with him at a ball and comments in her diary 'Mr Cockburn danced as usual with me – sweet man'. One may suspect that the Dean had an eye for a pretty, vivacious young girl.

The Dean was well connected, his mother was Augusta Anne Ayscough, who married Sir James Cockburn, 8th Baronet. Lady Cockburn was painted by Sir Joshua Reynolds with her three sons. The baby in her arms is the young William Cockburn and the picture is now in the Wallace Collection. His two brothers were both to become distinguished – James (born 1771) became a General and was Governor of Bermuda, and George (born 1772) an Admiral. He was in command of HMS *Bellerophon* when Napoleon was taken to St Helena, and subsequently became Admiral of the Fleet and First Sea Lord.

William Cockburn was born in 1773 and educated at Charterhouse School and St John's College Cambridge, gaining his MA in 1798, before entering the Church in 1800. Although he spent part of the time at his parish, he was a regular visitor to Sidmouth spending part of each year here with his wife and family.

His wife, Elizabeth, née Peel, was the sister of Sir Robert Peel, who became Prime Minister and remains famous for his founding of the London Police Force, who were known as 'the Peelers'. Dean Cockburn married her in 1805 and three sons were born to them, James, Robert and George. The Dean was a great lover of hunting and it wasn't long before he bought Higher Chelson, towards the northern end of Salcombe Regis Parish, where he stabled his horses and kennelled his hounds. The land consisted of 430 acres (174 ha) but, because it was so poor, had been left as sheep run. The Dean however broke up a considerable acreage and put it under the plough to grow oats to feed his horses, although the crops were invariably poor in quantity and quality.

Sadly Lady Cockburn died and left him to bring up three sons who grew to be handsome men, and were to become as passionate about hunting as their father. 'We'll find horses' they used to say to the Whips and 'you find the necks'! On one occasion Jack Tidd, one of the Whips, jumped his horse down and landed in an apple tree, the horse fell through, but the rider got caught by the branches. To get him down quickly, Robert Cockburn resorted to the whip; but the fox was gone. Unfortunately, the hunting was often poor because there were so many badger earths, but occasionally they got a good run. On non-hunting days they ran beagles and fought cocks at Core Hill on Sundays. At one time, the inn sign at the 'Hare and Hounds' on Honiton Common bore their portraits painted by their own hands – alas, the original is long gone.

Before the land was enclosed there was a race course on the Down, as the grassy flat land on top of Salcombe Hill was called. The Cockburn boys were regular participants in the racing and the partying afterwards. However, nothing would deter them from the Hunt, not even the funeral of respected Mr Guppy. They were on the way there, dressed in their frock coats and black gloves, when they espied a fox and gave chase, keeping the funeral waiting for four hours.

The Dean remained a widower for some years and went to live at Cotford House for a short time, and then at his farm at Chelson, leaving Salcombe House to his sons. Robert, his middle son, was paying court to a lady, Margaret Pearce, the daughter of Colonel Pearce, with a view to marriage. The Dean took his son severely to task arguing with him about the unsuitability of the match – 'She is too young for you Bob – it would not do at all!' However, the next thing was that six months later in 1830, the 57 year-old widowed Dean, married her himself. She was a handsome woman and made the Dean an excellent wife for the remainder of his life but it caused a terrible family rift and Robert left Sidmouth for a time.

The Dean having acquired the living of Kelston near Bristol in 1832, subsequently spent part of his year there, part at York and the remainder during the hunting season in Sidmouth. The Dean who had a very pugnacious side to him was in constant dispute with the scientific community because of his frequent published writings, where he tried to reconcile the natural world with the scriptures. As a 'biblical literalist', geology and particularly geochronology were particularly against the Dean's ethics.

York Minster suffered two fires during his time as Dean, the first was extinguished after much effort on the part of the city's inhabitants. It was started by Jonathan Martin, a staunch Methodist and brother of John Martin, the artist, famous for his sweeping biblical landscapes, such as the *Plains of Heaven*.

The Dean then appointed a night watchman to guard the Minster every night and set about organising the repairs, which he did not do particularly well.

The second fire in 1840 was nearly a disaster and could easily have burnt the Minster down. The fire was finally extinguished after heroic efforts and immediately, when the scale of the damage became apparent, a subscription was started to raise funds for the Minster's repair. By 1841, things came to a head over the Dean's unwise financial management of the repairs, when a Prebendary accused him of simony, because unfortunately when the bills came in, the money wasn't there to pay them. The Dean was taken to court on the charge. Litigation followed, involving the Archbishop of York and other senior churchmen, and they resolved to depose the Dean. He appealed against the verdict to the Queen's Bench, who ruled in favour of Cockburn, when it was found he had not embezzled the money, merely spent it on other things relating to the Minster. He was acquitted, much to the satisfaction of his congregation amongst whom he was popular. The judges were particularly disparaging about the Prosecuting Attorney who happened to be Regis Professor of Civil Law at Oxford, saying that he was ignorant of the applicable laws.

The Cockburn family out hunting on Salcombe Hill (private collection)

Sadly, the Dean was to outlive all three of his sons, who all died within a five-year period, two in the same year. James died in 1845 aged only 38, Robert in 1850 aged 42 and George in 1850 aged 37. James and Robert died at their father's Kelston Rectory, but George died at Core Hill House, Sidford where he had been living since his marriage.

After the deaths of his sons, the Dean tried to sell Salcombe House, but the auction proceedings were interrupted by the arrival of Charles John Cornish, whose elder brother had inherited the family home of Salcombe Hill House. Charles Cornish announced that the Dean was indebted to him and that Salcombe House was the security and that he had the papers to prove it. The auction was hastily terminated and Charles John Cornish became the possessor of Salcombe House.

The Dean had already left Sidmouth and sold Chelson. He died just eight years later at Kelston, aged 88. He had inherited from his brother, George, the Cockburn Baronetcy in 1853, and became the Reverend Sir William Cockburn of Langton. Salcombe House was now another house in Sidmouth to be occupied by a member of the Cornish family.

Charles John (1802-1879), was the second son of George and Sarah Cornish, of Salcombe Hill House (not to be confused with Salcombe House). This house is situated on the lower slopes of Salcombe Hill on what is now Hillside Road, then a delightful rural location overlooking the Sid Valley, and was built by George Cornish and his wife Sarah (née Kestell) about 1805 as a family home. Sarah, an only child, brought with her on marriage many of the old Salcombe Regis Copyholds which had devolved upon her orphaned Clapp mother.

George had spent time in India as ADC to the Governor General, but returned to England in 1799 to resume family life with his young wife and baby. The family was eventually to number six surviving children – four boys and two girls. Like his eldest brother, George James Cornish, Charles John went to Corpus Christi College, Oxford, but his interests were very different. He joined the cavalry of the Honourable East India Company on the Bengal Establishment and in 1827 was appointed Deputy Judge Advocate General to the Field Forces, with the rank of Captain.

On hearing of his father's death, he returned from India in 1830. The ship sailed in August, arriving off Start Point on 14 December. Leaving the ship, he got into an open boat and, after 30 hours sailing, landed on Sidmouth Beach the following night, walked up to Salcombe Hill House and was welcomed at the door by his mother, who recognised the sound of his footsteps.

He married his second cousin, Elizabeth Rhodes, and resigned his commission. He requested to qualify for a magistrate and his mother gave him the old house of 'Thorn' and its lands in Salcombe Regis. It was a few years later that he acquired Salcombe House by the River Sid and its farmland. When his mother died, he inherited South Combe Farm, Salcombe Regis, all of which he farmed with much enjoyment as a true countryman. In his day, there was plenty of field sport in Salcombe Regis, including the hunting of roe deer and shooting of black game on the open commons above the cliffs, and partridge on the lower fields.

He carried on the duties of a magistrate for more than 40 years, with a sense of kindness and discipline which settled

Salcombe House in the late 19th century (Sidmouth Museum)

many disputes without them ever reaching court. He kept up the old rural customs at his house, such as the Christmas burning of the 'ashen faggot' or Crying the Nick (or Neck) to celebrate the end of the harvest. He recorded local history and in particular that of the ancient estate of 'Thorn' on North Hill.

The Salcombe Regis Thorn Tree was deeply rooted in the ancient memories of the local villagers and their belief that the welfare of the Parish depended on the maintenance of this tree. Thus, when the tree was blown down, the people were greatly disturbed, but all was well as Mr Cornish had a new one planted 'with music and a general holiday for his tenants'. His grandson, Vaughan Cornish, had a granite monument erected beside the Thorn Tree with an inscription stating its ancient origin.

Although there were six children of the marriage, only one of them was to live at Salcombe House in their adult life, and that was William Floyer Cornish who occupied the house for a few years from 1881. About the turn of the century, the house was let to Charles and Georgina Blathwayt. Charles Blathwayt had held a senior post in the Indian Civil Service. There were several children of the marriage born in India. His youngest son, Henry Wynter Blathwayt, was born in Maharashtra, India, but educated in England. He joined the Royal Field Artillery and, after service in India, his brigade was sent to the WW1 Western Front. By this time, he held the rank of Major and, while commanding an RFA Battery at Bourlon Wood, he was killed in action in 1917 aged 30, leaving a wife and four children. He was buried in the British Cemetery at Orival Wood, Cambrai. His father had died shortly before his death and his mother gave up the house shortly after the War ended. His family's service in the Armed Forces was to continue in WW2 when his eldest brother, Christopher, became a much decorated member of the Special Operations Executive. Upon the departure from Salcombe House of the Blathwayts, Charles John Cornish's grandson, James George Cornish (1860-1938) resigned his incumbency and returned to live in his grandfather's old home, who had died in 1879.

James George Cornish, was yet another member of the Cornish family to go into the church, but it was here at Salcombe House that he spent the last nineteen years of his life. He now devoted himself to life as a country gentleman. He bought back several of his great-grandfather, George Cornish's, farms that were being sold, which included Northcombe, and resisted any attempt to develop the lands in his care. He used his experience and the availability of local stone from the long disused quarry at Dunscombe in setting in train the building of St Francis Church, Woolbrook. He also provided a new and reliable fresh water supply to his tenants at Churchtown, Salcombe Regis.

His greatest gift to the village of Salcombe Regis, and indirectly to Sidmouth, was the gift of land in the Salcombe Valley to be preserved to prevent it being developed and it remains so to this day – in the care of The National Trust since 1986. His brother, Vaughan who also had inherited some of his grandfather's lands joined with Reverend James Cornish in doing the same, thus preserving much of Salcombe Hill and the Salcombe Valley for public enjoyment. A large stone just beside the gate on the coast path on top of Salcombe Hill records the gift, together with lines from a poem by John Keeble, a great friend of George and Sarah Cornish's children who were brought up at Salcombe Hill House. James's only daughter, Miriam Mavis Page (née Cornish) was also a benefactor, giving Soldiers Hill Field to Sidmouth UDC to preserve the land from development.

Just before his death in 1938, the Reverend James George completed writing a book, *Reminiscences of a Country Life,* published after his death, detailing his life as a country parson and his life at Salcombe House. It was the cusp of WW2 and,

from 1939 to 1940, Salcombe House was used as a home for evacuated mothers and babies. It is likely that during the War, the house was requisitioned for use by the RAF who had taken over almost all Sidmouth's hotels and larger houses.

In 1947, Salcombe House was back in private occupation. A Miss Dorothy Wilmot is listed as a piano teacher and must have been a member of the Christian Science Church because, in 1950, there was a regular Sunday service in the house. It seems likely that she had her mother, Mrs B

James George Cornish when a Church of England vicar (Frontispiece of Reminiscences of a Country Life)

Wilmot, living with her and the house was being run as a guest house because, in 1953, a newspaper entry records 'Salcombe House is still being run as a guest house by Madame B Wilmot'. The next year there was a report of a sale of furniture and effects from the house. So presumably the guest house had closed by then.

In 1957, a further newspaper entry records 'Bishop's Court Hotel formerly Salcombe House', but that venture seems not to have lasted long because the following year the Fisher family bought the hotel and members of the family still own it to this day. It was renamed 'Hunters Moon' by the new owner's wife after the country house in Ivor Novello's musical *Perchance to Dream*. She was one of the original members of the Sidmouth Musical Comedy Society which was run by another member of a well-known Sidmouth family, Gerald Knight, who, for many years, ran a retail business in the town.

From the outside, the house appears little altered from the days when members of the Cornish family lived there and most of the fine trees they planted still grace the grounds, which enjoy vistas over the lawns of the Byes.

Julia Creeke

A late Victorian house, visited on a family holiday in 1908 by the author and artist Beatrix Potter (b.1866 – d.1943).

As the 19th century drew to a close, Sidmouth had for the first time a resident Lord of the Manor, Colonel John Balfour. The Colonel took great interest in the affairs of the Manor, which for centuries had languished under absentee Lords. Colonel Balfour inherited the Manor on his 25th birthday and during his minority his Trustees had attempted to restore it to a sound financial footing, but overstretched their available resources, and so certain areas of land deemed suitable for development were sold off. The break up of the Cotmaton Estate on the death of Commander John Carslake had added further areas of land suitable for development and from the 1890s, large detached villas were built, many of them designed by the local artchitect RW Sampson who was employed by the Manor. A number of these were available for renting.

'Hilton' in Seafield Road was just such a property and, in April 1908, Mr Rupert Potter rented it for a family holiday, arriving with his wife and daughter, Beatrix. Their association with Sidmouth had begun in 1898 when they had rented

Beatrix Potter at 'Hilltop', her Lake District home

'Cottymead' in Cheese Lane, and in the intervening years at least six holidays had been spent in Sidmouth, the last late in December 1908 at 'Meadhurst'. Both houses are now demolished.

The Potters had developed a pattern in their holidays: two weeks in the spring would be spent in the West Country whilst spring-cleaning went on at their London home, 2 Bolton Gardens. Then, in the summer, a large house was rented in Scotland or the Lake District for an extended stay, before returning to London in the early autumn.

These holidays allowed Beatrix Potter the chance to escape London, giving the rare opportunity to paint and sketch from nature, the creatures, flora and landscapes that interested her. Her life in London was always restricted; the result of over-protective parents and, after her last governess, Annie Carter, left to marry, she spent many hours alone in the old nursery suite amusing herself. She and her brother had always been interested in wildlife and probably because she was alone so much, she began to keep wild creatures as pets, and to sketch and paint them; some of these creatures even travelled with Beatrix on holiday.

Beatrix Potter was 32 when she first visited Sidmouth and had already started writing to children illustrated and minature letters. Many of her famous animal characters first appeared in the stories contained in these letters to children and were frequently based on her own pets or other animals she encountered. Peter and Benjamin Bunny were her own pet rabbits, Peter and Benjamin Bouncer, Jeremy Fisher her pet green frog, Hunca Munca one of her pet mice, and Squirrel Nutkin, one of two red squirrels she had bought from a dealer. Mrs Tiggy Winkle, the hedgehog, was a particular favourite with Beatrix. Tiggy died only weeks after the publication of the little book which was to make her name famous as a by-word for household cleanliness.

The children who received these letters loved and treasured them, keeping them safely for years, so that when Beatrix began to write the books, most were still with their recipients and could be borrowed back; the black and white illustrations worked up into finished watercolours, new ones added and the stories edited for clarity of storyline.

During the early years she was writing the letters to children, her consuming interest was in British fungi, which she was studying, going frequently to the Natural History Museum whilst working on a long series of watercolours to illustrate her work, which she had high hopes of publishing. Whilst staying at 'Cottymead' she painted, on 16 April at Sidbury Castle, a watercolour of Bracket Fungus: that watercolour still survives.

On the following day, 17 April, she wrote an illustrated letter to Noel Moore, the son of her last governess, Annie Moore, and the recipient of the famous Peter Rabbit letter. The letter from Sidmouth was all about a dog called Stumpy who had inherited his old clergyman master's cottage and l0/- (50p) a week, and who lived with his later master's housekeeper, Miss Hayward. Stumpy was apparently a dog of grave and solemn manner who would give Beatrix a large white paw. Miss Hayward kept the house, and Percy the cat lived with Stumpy on his l0/-, in a thatched cottage where Beatrix's brother was also sleeping. Presumably there was not enough room at Cottymead, which Beatrix tells Noel Moore was 'on the edge of town all surrounded by fields and lanes'.

Peter Rabbit had been published in 1902, followed by Beatrix's own favourite The Tailor of Gloucester, and Squirrel Nutkin in 1903; Benjamin Bunny followed in 1904. As the success of the little books grew, successive titles followed ever more quickly over the next 11 years, sometimes three a year.

After rejection by a number of publishers, Peter Rabbit was eventually published privately by Beatrix and copies sent to friends, relations and their children. Its success was immediate and more copies were requested. Frederick Warne, a family-run firm, finally agreed to undertake publication. Norman Warne, the youngest of the three Warne brothers, was put in charge of handling the books and Beatrix became a regular visitor to the Warne family home.

Clifton Beach, in a painting entitled 'Sidmouth' by Beatrix Potter (V&A)

Friendship between Beatrix Potter and Norman Warne grew and he eventually proposed marriage. Beatrix's parents were scathing and condescending about the match and for some time Beatrix had delayed telling them. She and Norman Warne eventually became engaged, but he almost immediately fell ill and six weeks later died of leukaemia, leaving Beatrix heartbroken, and forcing her to return to the claustrophobic life her parents imposed.

The death of Norman Warne, and the success of the early books, was the catalyst which drove her to produce increasing numbers of books to help her overcome her grief and achieve greater financial independence. She now had a reasonable income of her own and was about to purchase 'Hill Top', for she had become captivated by the Lake District. Notwithstanding that purchase, she was still expected to accompany her parents on holiday regularly.

At 'Hilton', in 1908, the weather had apparently been 'horrid' and she longed to get home, also Norman Warne's mother had died and Beatrix's letters written from Sidmouth were to his sister, Millie, with whom Beatrix had become great friends. There was one last recorded visit to Sidmouth at the end of that year, the family staying at 'Meadhurst', but thereafter she spent as much time as her family permitted at Hill Top, Sawrey.

From her late teens, for about 13 years, Beatrix had kept a diary written in a code which she had devised herself. In it she recorded the family's travels and daily events and doings.

Hylton today (SVA)

Sadly, the entries had ceased by the time of the Sidmouth visits and there are only some letters and drawings to tell of her visits to Sidmouth. There are two lovely watercolours, one of rocks and cliffs at Clifton Beach entitled *Sidmouth* and another *The country above Sidmouth*. There are drawings of the town and one of Knowle Cottage together with many pencil and watercolour sketches of the surrounding scenery. An original drawing of a stile is in Sidmouth Museum's collection.

Whilst at Falmouth in 1890, Beatrix Potter had started to write the first of her 'little tales' — ten year's later in 1901 she finished it at Sidmouth, and called it *The Tale of Little Pig Robinson*. In the story, Sidmouth was to become 'Stymouth' and Sidford 'Styford'. Two of the illustrations, one coloured and the other black and white, have as backgrounds the valley of Salcombe Regis. Although it was written before the publication of *Peter Rabbit*, it was, except for the American editions, the last of the little story books to be published.

There exists in a private collection, a first edition of *Jemima Puddleduck* inscribed in Beatrix's own handwriting and sent from Meadhurst, to the little daughter of one of the maids who had worked for the family prior to her marriage. By then it was l930, Beatrix Potter was 64, married to William Heelis, a Lake District solicitor, and had become immersed in the farming life of the Lake District and the breeding of the famous Herdwick sheep. Her eyesight was not so good, she no longer painted and had lost all interest in writing, which had made her famous as one of the greatest children's authors of all time.

Julia Creeke

End paper of a first edition of Jemima Puddleduck inscribed by Beatrix Potter and sent to one of her young admirers in Sidmouth

34 KENNAWAY HOUSE *formerly Church House (originally Fort House)*

A fine Georgian house, one of Sidmouth's landmarks, built in 1805 and subsequently bought by the Kennaway family of Escot. In 1906 it was acquired as a church house for community use and over time fell into disrepair, before being restored by a charitable trust in the 21st century.

Fort House (now Kennaway House) was built at the edge of the Fort Field by a Captain Thomas Phillipps for his wife, Harriet, née Amyatt. Initially, local intelligence had it that it had been intended as a place where receptions and parties might be held for the elite of Sidmouth society, instead of having to content themselves with the Assembly Rooms, where the company was 'not always of the best sort'.

However, on completion, Captain Thomas and Harriet moved in and made it their home, naming it 'Fort House' as, in the centre of the view to the south-west, was the Fort at the southern edge of the Fort Field (see separate chapter).

Sir John Kennaway (1758-1836), the 1st Baronet, and his brother Richard were the sons of an Exeter wool merchant of Scottish descent and, aged about 14 and 16, the two brothers went off to India and joined the service of the East India Company. In due course Richard amassed a considerable fortune in the employment of the Bengal Board for Trade. Through his diplomatic skills, John became ADC to the Marquis Cornwallis, at whose suggestion he was nominated for a peerage for his diplomatic services in bringing about a treaty

Fort House seen from Fort Field, 1816. From a painting by Henry Haseler (Sidmouth Museum)

with Tippoo, Sultan of Mysore, whose conniving with the French caused the British many problems, culminating in the Mysore Wars. In 1791, Captain John Kennaway accepted a baronetcy and became 1st Baronet of Hyderabad.

Twenty-one years in India had taken its toll on the brothers' health, but with fortunes made, they returned to England and jointly bought Escot from Sir Walter Young. In 1797 Sir John Kennaway married Charlotte Amyatt, daughter of James Amyatt of Freemantle, Hampshire, and sister of Harriet Phillipps. The two men almost certainly knew each other in India where James Amyatt was a former nabob and East India Company stockholder. He died in 1813 leaving all the land he owned in Sidmouth to another daughter, Mary. On the death of Captain Phillipps, the Kennaways came to occupy Fort House. In 1808, Escot had burnt to the ground in three hours. Sir John, Charlotte and their children, who were eventually to number twelve, had migrated to another house on the estate at Fairmile. For the first two years, Sir John brought his wife and family to Sidmouth for the summer season. Finding he did not much care for their temporary home at Fairmile, he soon became the owner of Fort House. It was to be many years before Escot was rebuilt, and he and the family enjoyed life at Sidmouth, so it was not long before Sir John and his growing

family were in almost permanent residence at Fort House and several of his younger children were born there.

Sir John was a very Christian man and a strong evangelical, and, as 'Escot' burnt, he was unconcerned saying, 'May God's holy will be done and may this worldly loss be conducive to our spiritual gain'. During the years spent in Sidmouth, he planned the rebuilding of Escot, finally choosing as his architect the then little known Henry Roberts. The new house was completed in 1836, the year Sir John died, but he had been almost blind for the last eight years of his life. With his death, the family returned to live permanently at Escot. The Kennaways continued to own Fort House, and it was let.

As Sidmouth's population grew, concern was expressed at the inadequacy of Sidmouth's churches, for the old Parish Church was not a large building. Backed by the 6th Earl of Buckinghamshire, himself a clerk in holy orders, and other 'well disposed persons', Sir John, 1st Baronet, gave land for All Saints' Church and, helped by others, £2,600 was subscribed for the church building which was completed in 1837. Sir John regarding his contribution as a 'thanksgiving' for the rebuilding of Escot. In 1848, the 2nd Baronet gave further land for All Saints' School and again, a few years later, for the Vicarage for All Saints Church.

Theodore Mogridge, the writer of one of Sidmouth's guide books published in 1836, records that the Reverend James Blencoe was renting Fort House, and in the succeeding three Censuses (1841, 1851 and 1861) he is recorded as occupying the house with his staff of five.

The 3rd Baronet, Sir John Henry Kennaway, was a fine scholar. He was an imposing figure and a great character, and is said, with his long beard, to resemble the figure quoted in Edward Lear's verse written some years previously:

There was an Old Man with a beard,
Who said, 'It is just as I feared! –
Two Owls and a Hen,
Four Larks and a Wren,
Have all built their nests in my beard'

He was, like his predecessors, a staunch churchman and involved with all kinds of religious and philanthropic work, and used to come over to Sidmouth and lead hymn singing on the beach with the local fishermen. In 1870, he entered the House of Commons and sat as Member for the Honiton Division (which included Sidmouth) until his retirement in 1910. For the last two years, he was Father of the House of Commons, thus representing Sidmouth at Westminster for a total of 40 years.

Sir John had succeeded his father, the 2nd Baronet, in 1873 and, at a public auction held in December 1876, he parted with some more of what remained of the family's land holding in Sidmouth. Fort House was sold in 1879, and Mr William Hine Haycock of 'Belmont' was the purchaser. Sir John now put up for sale the land adjoining it to the west that now forms the Putting Green, but it was not sold. Lot 6, however, which was part of Blackmore Field generated spirited bidding. It was eventually knocked down to the Trustees of the Manor for the then huge sum of £2,680. Fort House was back on the market in 1888 as, not long after Mr Hine Haycock (the owner) returned to live in London, he decided to dispose of his considerable holding of property in Sidmouth. It remained unsold until his death and was eventually sold by his Trustees in 1905 to Mr Richard Hatton-Wood who was also the owner of 'Belmont'. There had been a higher previous offer from developers who wished to demolish it, but the Trustees felt that Mr Hatton-Wood's proposed use for it was more in keeping with the late Mr Hine Haycock's philanthropic views.

Opening of Church House, 1906, with the 3rd Baronet Sir John Kennaway in front (Sidmouth Parish Church PCC)

Kennaway House after restoration (SVA)

Sir John was present at the ceremony held in the spring of 1906 when the house, after repair and alteration, was dedicated by the Bishop of Crediton for use as a church house for the benefit and use of the community. It had been bought in 1905 by the Trustees of the late Mrs RH Hatton-Wood of Belmont on the instructions of her husband. Sir John Kennaway made a speech at the ceremony which was attended by Mr Hatton-Wood and many local worthies in which he said that:

> The house had always been a great feature of Sidmouth, and if it had been pulled down to make way for rows of modern houses it would have been a great loss to the town. They were proud of Sidmouth, for they did not think it was like other places (great applause) and when they had a feature in their midst like that, they were very glad to preserve it, and they heartily thanked Mr Hatton-Wood for all he had done.

Thereafter, until 2007, the house was known as 'Church House'.

At the outbreak of WWI, it was requisitioned for war use for the Territorial Cyclists, who unfortunately caused a floor to become 'gravely concave', and the general state of the building gradually declined.

The curtilage of Church House was considerable, but over the years parts were sold off to produce funds for its upkeep. A large part of the garden of 'Nortongarth' (at one time occupied by Sidmouth Urban District Council) was disposed of to the Council in 1926 and became part of the Putting Green. Barton House and part of its garden were sold in 1932; the garden being added into the Putting Green. Barton Cottage was disposed of in 1936. Aurora was put up for sale in 1960 and realised £3,433 (see separate chapter). After all these sales, only an area of land in front of Church House was left.

As the 20th century progressed, the Church no longer needed such a large building, although the Parish Office remained located there together with a flat for the Curate. A library founded in 1900 occupied most of the ground floor, but failed financially in 1970. However, the Office of the Registrar of Births, Marriages and Deaths remained in the building until the end of the century. In WW2 there was an ARP centre in the building. Over the years it was a venue for local authority education courses, bazaars, social gatherings and exhibitions, all of which helped finance the building's upkeep.

By 1999, the Trustees of Church House were facing a huge bill for large-scale repairs and the building's future hung in the balance. The future looked perilous with imminent closure, and the likelihood of sale, demolition and redevelopment.

A local outcry produced a search for a rescue plan and with the Trustees boosted by additional members, a plan for the house's future use as a Community Centre fit for the 21st century was drawn up. A part of the roof collapsed just after a Restoration Fund had been launched. Between 2001 and 2005 architects were appointed, detailed plans drawn and costed, applications made to the Heritage Lottery Fund and further fund-raising undertaken. Finally, work began to restore the old building and make it fit for its new role. In 2007, the *Sidmouth Herald* asked its readership to decide on the building's future name – should it be: 'Fort House', 'Church House' or a new name 'Kennaway House'? Kennaway House it was. After more than 200 years, the old house remains an attractive feature of Sidmouth and provides a venue for a wide range of events, exhibitions and social gatherings.

Julia Creeke

35 KINGSWOOD HOTEL *formerly The Marine Baths*

Opened as baths and treatment rooms in 1895, for a variety of ailments, and used during WW1 for the treatment of convalescing officers. It was closed in 1935 and incorporated into the adjacent Kingswood Hotel.

In Regency times, there had been baths in Sidmouth and, in October 1819, a report stated that His Royal Highness the Duke of Kent had been conducted by Mr John Wallis of the Royal Marine Library to the Old and New Seawater Baths. The Old Baths had been established opposite the London Hotel and had been in operation for some years. Their proprietor, Mr Higham, greatly improved them, having added a shower bath to his establishment. The New Baths were situated in Prospect Place in one of the pair of houses adjoining what is now the Mocha Café. In the 1830s there were bathing facilities at Stocker and Longman's premises in York Terrace and,

between 1851 and 1866, 5 York Terrace also had a spell of use as Butter's Baths, offering hot and cold sea-water baths.

In the late 19th century, a guide book claimed 'the presence of good baths in a health resort constitutes a great attraction' and this was very much the sentiment in Sidmouth where it was felt the lack of such facilities detracted from the town's reputation. In 1893 a prospectus appeared giving particulars of the newly formed Sidmouth Baths Company and inviting the public to subscribe for shares; the Manor Estates being the instigator and largest shareholder.

A major redevelopment of part of the seafront was proposed, to include the demolition of all the Regency lodging houses of Portland Terrace, which had stood at a different alignment to that of the buildings which replaced them. The buildings at the eastern end aligned with the present Dukes, previously the Marlborough Hotel, whilst those at the Marine

Place end (the western end) followed the line of the present Hotel Riviera. There was a separate triangular area of garden at the eastern end, and all the houses of Portland Terrace had front gardens of varying sizes. Under the new development, all these gardens were largely dispensed with as the new buildings were to follow the line of the Esplanade road. It thus became possible for the Baths Company to acquire a site for the new baths at the western end of the re-development, and to combine this with a new mens' Social Club.

In 1894, construction of the new baths and treatment rooms commenced to the designs of RW Sampson, the Manor's architect, and they were opened in the spring of 1895. Various types of bath and treatment were provided. In some, sea-water was warmed, diluted and charged with carbonic acid in an attempt to replicate the waters at Nauheim, a popular German spa. Cures for a wide range of complaints were advertised by the Company, some undeniably spurious because of the poor medical knowledge of the times, but the baths proved popular initially, and a visitor's book contained many plaudits from satisfied customers.

During the First World War, as part of Sidmouth's war effort, convalescent officers were treated to relieve adhesions and contractures following serious wounds. The treatments at the Baths, and the results achieved, were so successful that they were used as a future model for the rehabilitation of those who had suffered serious injury. By the War's end, the Baths were getting dilapidated and were shut through a shortage of money to modernise them.

The Brine Baths (Sidmouth Museum)

1924 saw the re-opening by Mrs Balfour, wife of Colonel Balfour, Lord of the Manor of Sidmouth, with a number of well-known doctors present. Further funds had been put into the company for updating and refurbishment, but only in a few of the earliest years of operation was a dividend paid to shareholders. Almost throughout their existence, the baths only broke even, or more often ran at a loss, and finally the Manor decided it could not sustain this loss further and they were closed for good in 1935.

The Social Club, which shared the baths building, was a popular institution in pre-WWI days and when Edward VII died, the Proclamation of the Accession was read from the first-floor balcony to a large crowd assembled on the Promenade. Before the establishment of radio, when the Sovereign died, the Proclamation of the Accession had to be read in public in towns all over the country.

With the closure of the baths, the building never found a satisfactory use and was finally assimilated into the adjoining Kingswood Hotel, although one of the downstairs rooms remains as a reminder of its former use.

Julia Creeke

Therapeutic baths (Sidmouth Museum)

The house was commissioned in 1808 by Lord le Despenser, and then spectacularly transformed and expensively furnished by the eccentric Thomas L Fish after he took ownership in 1821. The grounds were no less astonishing, with architectural and water features, exotic plants and rare animals and birds. Mr Fish opened both the cottage and the grounds for public enjoyment, enhancing Sidmouth's reputation nationally.

Had Knowle Cottage survived more or less unaltered in its original form, it would now be probably the greatest cottage orné in the country. Sadly its fate was to be otherwise, and by the end of the 19th century it was unrecognisable from its original appearance. When he created it, Thomas Stapleton, Lord le Despenser (1766-1831) declared that he was 'building a thatched cottage upon a grand scale of 40 rooms'.

Why Lord le Despenser decided to build in Sidmouth remains conjecture, but when building commenced in about 1808, Sidmouth was being frequented by members of the nobility and persons of fashion. Lord le Despenser was well known in Regency society, a vain, capricious and difficult man, who it was said used to visit the site of his new cottage whilst it was being constructed and, if he found the slightest thing not to his liking, he would order the workmen to undo their work and start again. This not only aggravated the workforce, but slowed construction. Whilst visiting Sidmouth to oversee the work, his wife, Elizabeth (daughter

Lord le Despenser, who built Knowle but never lived there. Painted in Rome by Anton Maron (private collection)

of Samuel Eliot of Antigua), and their family were lodged at 1 Fortfield Terrace whilst he rented 5 Clifton Place. It was said by the locals 'that he stayed up all night and laid in bed all day'.

Lord le Despenser was Thomas Stapleton, 6th Baron le Despenser of the Leeward Islands. His grandfather was born in Nevis and Despenser had a small sugar operation there at Mont Pellier. His income was largely derived from sugar. He had inherited Mereworth Castle in Kent, built in the 1720s, one of the five great English houses copying the classical villa designed by Palladio, the Villa Rotonda. This line of Despenser Barons should not be confused with the much older line associated with Sir William Dashwood, of West Wycombe Park and of Hell Fire Club fame.

It appears that by the time Knowle Cottage was finished and furnished, Lord le Despenser had lost interest in the project for some reason. It had in the end to be completed by one of the top London firms of architectural joiners and carpenters, Lee & Cox, under the supervision of Sir John Soane's Office, where John Lee had been articled. However, he did not like architecture and transferred to joinery. For work done between 1809 and 1811 they were paid £6,414, an enormous sum then. As well as carpentry, the bills also list stone grotto flinting, pebble paving, thatching and work on a dairy, coach houses, and greenhouse. Soane's Bill Book also lists work by local contractors including an organ in the Music Room, a stable, well-digging, laying a road, making a rustic wall and gate, rustic trellis and finishing the verandah. Between May and November, Soane's Office Day Book records 'entering bills' and 'making accounts'. Mr Spiller subsequently made surveys on Soane's behalf which amounted to £60.13.0d (£60.65) as work on the Cottage must by then have been complete.

The Curator of the Soane Archive writes: 'There is only one document in Soane's private correspondence which summarises all the bills for Lord Le Despenser and corrects some prices. It makes it clear that Soane had not visited Knowle Cottage as he writes to Lord le Despenser: 'It is also to be observed that reference being made to the prime cost of these articles of which a judgment can be formed without seeing the work, that several of them appear to be overcharged'. The total of the entire contract including the day work, amounted to the then staggering sum of £8,744, equivalent to around £1 million today.

Peter Orlando Hutchinson (POH), the great commentator on Sidmouth life, knew a local man, Mr Piper, who had worked on Knowle. Piper said that the front was rough flints collected from inaccessible and dangerous places on Peak Hill and not from the more usual gravel pits. When POH asked him why this had been done, he replied: 'I's suppose that them flints as was easy to get was too cheap for a lord'.

Lord le Despenser then placed the property for sale in an advert in *The Times* of 9 April 1812, the sale being held at noon on 28 May 1812. The result of the sale is very unclear, although the Reverend Edmund Butcher states that the Marquess of Bute was occupying the house. It is beyond doubt, however, that the Knowle Cottage estate was sold in 1821 by a William Fauquier to a Mr Thomas Leversidge Fish.

Mr Fish was to own Knowle for 40 years and would reside there during 'the season' – normally July to September. He made considerable alterations to the house and grounds, transforming Knowle into something spectacular. Then he made it famous. With few precedents, if any, he threw his house and gardens open for public inspection, once a week in

Knowle Cottage – the garden as it appeared circa 1823. From a painting by Isaac Fidlor (private collection)
Photo: Martyn Gregory Gallery

the season, free of charge. The effect was phenomenal – visitors were attracted in very large numbers, both from the immediate locality and from around the whole country.

Contemporary accounts describe something close to mania on these open days, known as 'Fish's Mondays'. For example, John Harvey's *A Guide to Knowle Cottage* published in 1837 said:

> If a stranger perfectly unacquainted with Sidmouth...placed himself at the entrance to that delightful town, he would be absolutely astonished at the constant and rapid influx of persons in every kind of vehicle, who are straining forward with ardour which no obstacle can impede and no impediments overcome. Every variety of vehicle, every species of carriage, from the lordly barouche to the 'respectable gig'...are dashing along, conveying hundreds of cheerful faces all bent on one object – pleasure, and all pursuing it at one pace, a steady gallop.

Of Thomas Leversidge Fish we know relatively little. He was born in 1784 at Walworth, now in the London Borough of Southwark, to Thomas and Sarah Fish. By 1798 his mother and only sibling were dead, and in 1818 his father died also. When he himself died in 1861, the obituaries said three main things about him: that he was immensely wealthy, dubbed 'the

Mr Thomas Fish and an unknown lady in the garden (private collection)

Golden Fish' (he inherited a sum equivalent to around £100 million in modern terms, including an estate of 400 pubs); that he was a lifelong bachelor; and that he was eccentric.

A lasting eccentricity, he was to live throughout his life in the street where he was born, Penton Row. This was an 'unaristocratic locality', the obituaries observed, implying correctly that someone of Thomas Fish's substance would normally retain their town house in a prestigious location such as Belgravia or Kensington.

His frugal lifestyle also attracted comment – 'he was scarcely ever to be seen abroad and partook most sparingly of the simplest kind of diet', although he did ensure that his servants ate well. He maintained a carriage and coachman but never used them, choosing to hire transport instead. Nevertheless: 'two of his horses (a pair nearly milk white) might be seen daily attached to a very antique curricle, driven by an equally antique coachman, around the streets of Walworth for exercise'.

His greatest eccentricity however was Knowle, his 'celebrated show house', as the newspapers called it. We don't know what drove him to create such an extraordinary place, although it is possible that some of the inspiration came from the Vauxhall Pleasure Gardens, which were less than a mile from his home at Penton Row. From childhood, he would have heard the music and seen the illuminations there at night, and he probably would have visited. What he did at Knowle differed in a number of key respects, but it still had something fundamental in common with Vauxhall Gardens – it was a spectacle, contrived to divert, impress, amaze and astonish.

On the open days, the general public were given more or less free run of Knowle Cottage, including the main rooms on the ground floor, where the Grand Suite of reception rooms and the Morning Room were located, and the first floor, where there was a suite of bedrooms and a Breakfast Room. All were decorated lavishly and adorned with artworks, ceramics, objects d'art and precious stones. There were quirky items also, such as taxidermy specimens, birds in cages, gold and silver fishes in large bowls, and mechanical birds.

The Grand Suite of rooms was opulent and dramatic. It was over a hundred feet (30m) long, with the upper parts of the windows being coloured or painted glass. John Harvey's 1837 Guide said that the chief attraction of the suite was:

> ...the splendid collection of bijouterie and most splendid Dresden china which graces the centre and sides of the whole length of rooms. There are seventy tables, large and

small, placed along the centre and sides. They are all covered in with the choicest specimens of the art of the jeweller, and with the ingenious and elaborate specimens of fancy clocks, as Genevese and Parisian can alone manufacture.

There cannot be less than a thousand articles in these rooms, all the most costly patterns, and choicest workmanship. … They comprise the richest specimens of china vases, groups of china, bronze, French clocks, which are disposed around the rooms with great judgement and taste.

Among the paintings in the middle room of the Grand Suite were three watercolours by Thomas Fish himself, all said to be of good artistic quality – *Tintern Abbey*, *A Moonlight Scene* and *Sunset After Rain*.

Immediately outside, surrounding the house on the main and eastern fronts, was a verandah:

…three hundred and fifteen feet [96m] in length and nearly twelve [3.7m] in width, and …entirely supported by oak pollards, which are completely surrounded by ivy, roses, myrtles and flowering creepers …and around each …circular flower stands …three thousand five hundred plants in total.

Throughout the verandah there were large china vases, and compartments with marble fountains, statues or other items on display. From vantage points there were 'truly magical peeps of the ocean'.

The grounds were no less amazing. They totalled over 30 acres (12 ha), including land leased from John Carslake of Cotmaton and William Lyde. The gardens were extensive, with upper and lower lawns, parkland, a conservatory, domed aviary, a grotto and Gothic summerhouse.

There were a vast number of unusual plants and shrubs from all over the world, several fountains (one fountain is said to have had a 40 ft (12m) jet) and pools, in one of which there were frequently a pair of black swans swimming, an amazing collection of foreign birds and brightly coloured macaws on stands. In the outer park were all kinds of animals, more often found in a zoo, but at the time still a wonder. These included two Indian buffalos, zebras, Cape Sheep, alpacas, a gazelle, kangaroos (several bred at Knowle), wallabies, emus, antelopes and a camel.

In a print of 1826, an agave is shown in bloom, with its 20ft (6m) flower stem. These take 20 years to bloom and it was not

Verandah, circa 1834. Painting by CF Williams (private collection)

until 2017 when one flowered again in Sidmouth, in the front garden of a house in Salcombe Road, to the wonder of all, since it had survived every winter for 20 years, yet its home is usually in the Mediterranean.

Occasionally there was a mishap, as when two wallabies escaped into the town, causing much amusement, especially as they proved very tricky to re-capture.

It is obvious why Knowle Cottage and gardens attracted such a huge influx of visitors, from every section of society, sometimes six or seven hundred a day. However, there was never a free-for-all, as the crowds were closely controlled – only 30 persons were admitted to the house every 15 minutes, they were kept moving, and attendants were in place throughout the house and grounds to keep watch and answer questions. Babies, dogs and baskets were not allowed. Moreover, the public could not take a visit for granted, as the *Sidmouth Journal* observed later in the century:

the drawback was that with the slightest sprinkling of rain the gates were closed and then, no matter from how far visitors had come or how socially important, 'no admittance' was the inexorable decision.

View from the drawing room, circa 1834.
Painting by Isaac Fidlor (private collection)

The same article in the *Sidmouth Journal* also gave an insight into Mr Fish's whereabouts during the open days:

> ...it is said that on no occasion was the owner to be seen, but that he amused himself by watching, from an invisible spying place, the demeanour of the crowd, and was annoyed or gratified as he saw indifference or pleasure manifested.

Although Mr Fish was eccentric, and lived quietly and modestly, he was not a recluse, and he was a very generous host. This is evidenced from *Woolmer's Exeter and Plymouth Gazette* of 13 October 1838, which reported that he had hosted an evening dinner at Knowle for nearly 200 of the nobility and gentry from around Sidmouth, prior to his departure to London that year. The Grand Suite was lit by candelabras, and the grounds lit by lamps:

> which were ingeniously arrayed to represent interesting devices, such as imperial crowns, stars, anchors, etc, all terminating in an illuminated fountain, which through the long vista leading from the Drawing Room had the appearance of a magnificent cascade... The refreshments, which were the most sumptuous, consisted of every delicacy of the season, and the peculiar excellence of the wines was justly appreciated.

The evening culminated in a 'merry dance', which commenced soon after 10pm and continued to a 'late hour'.

Unfortunately there were thefts from the house. Goldfish were taken in 1848, with the felons being caught and sentenced to four months hard labour. Plate and silverware were stolen in 1853, prompting Mr Fish to suspend visits, much to the dismay of visitors and locals alike. However, some time later he relented and visits were allowed again.

Thomas Fish died in 1861, leaving all his property to a friend, Thomas Frederick Marson, a solicitor of Rickmansworth Park, Hertfordshire, who, like Mr Fish, had been born in the Newington parish. Reportedly, Mr Marson had married a lady whom Mr Fish, when young, would have liked for his own wife. Nevertheless, he retained the friendship of Mr Marson, although he himself never married. The closeness of the friendship was demonstrated by two of Marson's children, born in the 1820s, being given the middle name of Fish.

Mr Fish had created a family tomb in Newington Parish Church, obtaining the necessary consents to unite his parents, sister and two grandparents there. However, in 1859, Mr Marson had had built a relatively modest tomb in Kensal Green Cemetery (now in the Royal Borough of Kensington and Chelsea), and it was there that Thomas Fish was buried in 1861. The only other burial in the tomb at the time was Mr Marson's grandson, who had died as a child.

There is little tangible to mark the 40 years spent in Sidmouth by Mr Fish. The shell grotto still survives, located in the garden of a bungalow, built on what was once part of Knowle's land. It has been carefully restored by its custodians, but is not open to view by the public. There are also two items in the parish church – a bell Thomas Fish gifted in 1844, and a stained glass window dedicated to him in the north aisle, donated by Thomas Marson.

There were two other memorials dedicated to him, sponsored by local tradesmen, in thanks for allowing public access to the cottage and grounds 'to the great benefit of the town'. One was a lamp standard outside Knowle and the other was a flagstaff on Salcombe Hill hangar. Sadly, neither survive.

Thomas Fish nevertheless left a significant intangible legacy – whereas Emanuel Baruh Lousada was seminal in bringing Sidmouth to the attention of the aristocracy and senior gentry, Thomas Fish did so across a wider spectrum of society. He raised Sidmouth's profile nationally and enhanced its reputation, to the continuing benefit of the town and its wellbeing.

Thomas Marson, having acquired Knowle, immediately disposed of all the animals and birds, and opened up the park, cutting down many fine trees to create new views. Then, in an advert of 1861 in *The Times,* a sale of the contents and Estate was notified. Some of the contents sold, but the Estate did not. The house proved hard to sell and it seems likely that it was still unsold on the death of Thomas Marson in 1867 at the country estate he had bought in Hampshire, Highfield Park. He was buried in the tomb at Kensal Green. Later, there were two further Marson burials in the tomb, another grandson and a daughter-in-law, the mother of the two grandsons. According to the *Sidmouth Journal*, the next owner, Richard Napoleon Thornton, made the purchase from the executors of Thomas Marson.

Richard Thornton (senior) was a City banker, whose father was a founder of Lloyds Bank. Richard (senior) had also founded a ships' commodity broking business, which during the Napoleonic Wars had contracts with the Navy Board for the supply of hemp and masts. This became critical when the Baltic was blockaded to British shipping. Thornton sent his brother to live with the expatriate community in St Petersburg and through contacts succeeded in getting supplies of hemp out of Russia (the main source), and also masts from the Baltic states, when the Americans stopped supplies following independence. It was said that Thornton knew of the victory at Waterloo before the British government, and Thornton signed a major contract with the Navy as Waterloo was being won. This was the foundation

of his fortune. He had his two nephews in the business with him as he had no children, except one illegitimate son, Richard Napoleon Lee, who bore his mother's (Alice Lee) surname. The 'Napoleon' was added by his father who said he had much to be thankful to Napoleon for, although he hated him.

Richard Lee went to Oxford and studied for the Bar and was admitted at the Middle Temple in 1860. When his father died in 1865 he inherited £400,000 of his father's enormous fortune on condition that he changed his name to 'Thornton'. When Thornton (senior) died, he left the largest commercial fortune yet made by a single person – £3,000,000. So Richard (now) Thornton gave up the Bar for the life of a country gentleman. Thornton senior's two nephews inherited the remainder of the £3,000,000 fortune divided between them. One came to Exeter and built Streatham Hall, now part of the University Campus and gave the County Cricket Ground to the City. The whole family were keen cricketers and Richard Lee, when at Oxford, played for the University side.

This inheritance enabled Richard Thornton to buy Knowle. He at once started making alterations whilst he and his new wife, Ellen Jones, lived at Peak House for two years. To celebrate his marriage, a large party dined at the London Hotel and afterwards the grounds of Knowle were open to the public and amusements provided. Over the next ten years he continued to make further alterations. Gone was the last of the house's great thatched roof to be replaced with scalloped

Jet d'Eau and grotto, circa 1826. Painting by George Rowe (private collection)

Garden with rare birds, circa 1834. Painting by CF Williams (private collection)

tiles and bands of plain ones; he also extended it. He built new tropical plant houses, and a pineapple house, vineries and laid out an Italian garden and a new kitchen garden. He bought more land, improved the boundary wall and took away straggling hedges, replacing them with stonework. He altered the entrance to the grounds and built the two lodges. He also built the head gardener's cottage, later sketched by Beatrix Potter (a copy of this drawing is in Sidmouth Museum), which is located near the corner of Broadway and Knowle Drive, and still exists today, externally almost unaltered.

The house was furnished by the top cabinet-maker of the period and he had beautiful stained glass windows made by an Exeter craftsman. One item of Knowle's furniture resides with the V&A collections in London. The house and grounds became once again a show place, but Mr and Mrs Thornton were generous hosts and benefactors to Sidmouth and were very popular. Many celebrations took place there, including their son's coming of age, and the festivities when the railway finally arrived in 1874. He did much to support the game of cricket in Sidmouth and improve the Fortfield Cricket Pitch. (See also chapter on Fort Field.) He also gifted the last two bells to the Parish Church to make a peal of eight bells. There were other less obvious benefactions to local people that went largely unnoticed.

It was not surprising therefore that when his health began to fail there was much concern locally. Sadly he died at the age of only 43 in May 1876, greatly mourned and lamented. The size

New entrance of Knowle Cottage, circa 1878

of his funeral bore witness to the feelings of the local population. The testament to this was the following report:

This was the funeral of a private gentleman, without a single tenant, but whose additions to the town's attractions and kindness and liberality to its inhabitants, had awakened a sense of loss in hundreds of tradesmen and others, who were not in the slightest degree personally or pecuniarily affected.

His funeral procession was considerable and mourners filled the enlarged Parish Church to overflowing. Richard Napoleon Thornton was then laid to rest in the Churchyard, leaving his son, the Reverend Richard Thornton Thornton, to inherit his estate. It wasn't long before he married and the couple decided that Sidmouth was not to be their home. He attempted to sell the house and estate, but to no avail. It seems that perhaps all his father's building work had made the house and gardens too big, but the estate was not of a large enough acreage to attract the kind of buyers who wanted a country seat.

In the end, the Reverend Thornton lived on at Knowle until 1882, acting as Curate to the Reverend HG Clements, Vicar of Sidmouth, and playing cricket for the local team with his two brothers, so that he became known as the 'cricketing parson'. He scored several centuries for Sidmouth. He was a man with a breezy affable personality and great charm, who, like his father, was very well liked by all. Eventually, at the third attempt, a buyer was found for the house and grounds. Knowle was never again to be a private house – it was turned into a hotel. The estate was carved up piecemeal, part being sold as the site for the building of a convent and various houses.

The head gardener lodged a rather sad advert saying that after 16 years of service he was now looking for other employment and detailing all his skills. However, it is likely that in the end he was retained by the newly-formed Sidmouth Knowle Hotel & Baths Company to manage and tend their very substantial gardens as they intended to turn Knowle into a top class hotel for Sidmouth, which was urgently required now that the railway had reached the town.

Knowle was to remain a hotel for 76 years, but its fortunes were to fluctuate. The Company raised the necessary funds through debentures and it was soon known that the backers were the Trustees of the Manor Estate. On the death in Paris in 1863 of Edward Hughes Ball Hughes, the owner of Sidmouth Manor, it was put up for sale, and sold to Mr GE Balfour of

Manchester in 1866, who then purchased 'Powys' for his Sidmouth home. Not long afterwards, his wife died of blood poisoning following a tooth extraction and in 1869 Mr Balfour died in London, leaving three orphaned children. Trustees were appointed to oversee their upbringing and it was intended that the eldest, John Edmond Heugh Balfour would inherit the Manor Estate on reaching his 25th birthday. The Manor then totalled 690 acres (280 ha) with an income of £2,267. The Trustees over time set about increasing this by buying additional assets, hence the purchase of Knowle and their move into hotels. Their aim was the provision of a reasonable income from the Manor and to fund the building of a Manor House for the Lord of the Manor. The new Manor House was built on General Slessor's old estate, opposite Knowle, which they had bought for the purpose.

Some work was done on Knowle to fit it for its new use as a hotel of 25 bedrooms, and it opened on 7 August 1882; its first visitors arriving on 10 August. The hotel, however, made initial losses and, to remedy this, ten plots of building land were sold in 1887.

In 1890 there was a royal visitor to the hotel – the Empress Eugenie, widow of Emperor Napoleon III. She lived in England for many years at Sundridge Park, Bromley, Kent and travelled under the pseudonym Comtesse de Pierrefonds. Peter Orlando Hutchinson records that she stayed for a few weeks and attended Chapel at the newly-constructed Convent close by at the top of Broadway. She drove out, walked about, visited the Royal Glen and was apparently charmed by the situation of Knowle. She left by train on 23 April 1890, having been presented with a bouquet of roses by Dr Pullin's daughter, 'and before the train started, Mrs Lindemann of Sidholme, the richest lady in Sidmouth, presented the Empress with a handsome bunch of Napoleon Violets'.

However, the losses at Knowle persisted and finally the Court of Chancery directed that its major debenture holder, who turned out to be Kenneth Balfour, younger brother of JEH Balfour, now Lord of the Manor, bring an action to force the sale. This he did and was able to buy the hotel and 24 acres (9.7 ha) as a going concern for £10,000.

Kenneth Balfour was now a hotel owner and it reopened at Easter 1892 with the following report in the *Morning Post*:

THE KNOWLE HOTEL Sidmouth Devon.
This first class home like hotel, unique and most charming in situation and character will be reopened next Easter

holidays, refurnished most luxuriously by Messrs Maples and redecorated and under new direction, but the same capable management. Extensive structural improvements, excellent cuisine and wines, sound sanitary arrangements, 20 acres [8.1 ha] of grounds, fruit and flowers, fine climate, hunting, fishing, golf, cricket, tennis etc: terms moderate, either *a la carte* or *en pension*, own omnibus and porter meet all trains.

The hotel flourished and soon there were plans being drawn up for a major extension, but the extension wasn't so much an extension as a complete rebuild of the old house, making it ever afterwards unrecognisable. It was now a large three-storey building, the upper floors of which enjoyed a magnificent view of the sea and valley. Just ten months later it reopened, but its new clientele were no longer aristocrats and gentry but the affluent self-made business, professional and artistic people who arrived by train for a holiday. To look after them, the hotel employed 30 staff. Unfortunately, the criminal fraternity had become attracted to this new source of wealth frequenting Sidmouth, and there were a number of thefts from guests staying a Knowle.

The effects of the Great War on Knowle were limited. It remained open, but its German Manager, Adolf Hoch, was placed under arrest as an 'alien', and so the hotel lost its license to sell liquor, and its Managing Director, Mr Slade, had to take over its running.

The hotel continued to be well patronised and in the 1920s there were a lot of guests from the arts fraternity. It still

Knowle when it was a hotel (Sidmouth Museum)

attracted people of note like Rajah Brook of Sarawak who came with his family, while he indulged in some fishing. In 1931, the owners decided that they could well do without much of the estate, particularly the part that had been used for Knowle Nursery. The local architect RW Sampson planned the division of the land into various building plots and, in addition, a number of the existing houses and buildings were sold off.

At first the impact of WW2 was not great, but then the hotel was turned into a convalescent home for boys who were evacuated from the London area for their safety.

In late spring 1942 came a major change in the fortunes of Knowle, when the entire property was requisitioned by the Government for use as the Medical Training Depot of the RAF. Almost all the hotels in the town were requisitioned and it became in effect an RAF station – RAF Sidmouth – for the training of medical staff and orderlies. At Knowle, there were lecture rooms and administrative offices on the ground floor and living accommodation for the Aircrew Officers' Training School above. One night, Knowle got sprayed by cannon fire by a German aircraft, but thankfully there were no casualties.

One of the former WAAF Officers told the story of the use of a bath at Knowle for the illicit distillation of liquor to be used in a punch at a big party. Unfortunately, the distillation went awry and instead of merriment following the consumption of the punch, everyone got very depressed. In spite of the War, Christmas festivities were celebrated in the traditional way with decorations, holly and a meal of turkey and Christmas

The hotel lounge

pudding. In 1944, RAF Sidmouth was closed and the whole operation was moved to RAF Halton, leaving many of the hotels empty for the remainder of the War. They were gradually de-requisitioned from 1945 onwards, although Knowle was one of the last to be released in spring 1947.

The hotel finally reopened on 1 May and, on Saturday 3 May, the Knowle Hotel Company held a weekend house party for 70 guests to mark the reopening. However, on 8 October, they announced that Southern Railways were to become the new owners and this would allow them to promote the hotel to attract visitors to Sidmouth. The hotel's business grew over the next few years with some quite distinguished guests staying, such as General Sir William Slim, Commander of the 14th Army in South East Asia, who stayed in 1948. In spite of the success of the hotel, in 1951, British Rail, who had taken over the hotel, announced they were selling it by auction; but bidding only reached £35,000 and it was withdrawn. A month later, a sale to a small local Sidmouth consortium was concluded.

One of the leading members of this consortium was Mr Drake, owner of Drake's Farm (located adjacent to the Byes alongside Sidmouth Road) and other areas of potential development land. However, he was a working farmer and, to the amazement of guests, this man would come striding into the hotel, often wearing his muddy wellingtons, and dressed in his brown working overall, the waist tied with binder twine. He looked like a farm labourer and his appearance gave no hint that he was actually one of the owners.

The Ministry of Housing and Local Government, in an effort to boost tourism, surveyed many historic hotels producing a list of 80 which, according to the *Sidmouth Observer*, could not be demolished or their use changed, without reference to the local planning authority. Knowle was on this list and there was also a supplementary one which included many others which were also considered of merit and worth preserving. The list had been drawn up on behalf of the Brewers' Society and it was intended to put plaques on them.

Through the 1960s, Knowle Hotel continued to trade, but the directors now looked at disposing of further building plots, particularly those facing on to Broadway and another on Knowle Drive. Many of the Councillors on Sidmouth UDC were not particularly happy when presented with the application to build, and at least one site had to go to appeal before permission was granted. By 1964, the whole of Knowle Grounds was covered by a Tree Preservation Order.

The next phase of the history of Knowle came as a total surprise to Sidmouth residents when the Council announced in 1967 that it had been negotiating to buy the Knowle Hotel. Part of the building would be used as offices for Sidmouth UDC and the remainder would be converted into flats. This would ensure the future survival of the beautiful grounds with their fine trees which could then be kept open for the enjoyment of all Sidmouth's inhabitants. This was the start of a long period of uncertainty over the future of Knowle which finally culminated in the Government, in spite of financial austerity, agreeing in February 1968 to provide the funding by way of a loan. This allowed the UDC to purchase Knowle and a month later the Council sold their old offices at 'Nortongarth' for conversion to flats.

Through all this, the hotel had continued to trade, but its doors closed for the last time on 28 September 1968.

The Director of the Folk Festival now took a keen interest in Knowle and floated the idea of constructing a grass arena there, as the Festival was rapidly out-growing its other venues. The meadow which was the proposed site was, at the time, covered in brambles, fallen trees and other rubbish and, although the Council was not against the idea, there was no money.

There was, however, enough money to hold a big reception for 300 to celebrate the move to Knowle and the opening of the new offices at which the redoubtable Councillor Ted Pinney presided in his role of Chairman of the Council. The pure size of Knowle soon brought its own problems and the Council spent much time in debate on various matters including the Folk Festival's request for an arena and car parking. It wasn't the arena that caused the problem, but the parking in the grounds which was flatly refused.

In 1970, the question of the Folk Festival's use of the Knowle raged on, but eventually agreement was reached for an all-grass arena with no car parking.

The defeat of the Wilson government brought the Tories to power and their favoured option for local government was a two-tier system which led in 1974 to local government reorganisation and the demise of Sidmouth UDC. Knowle was to become the main offices of the new authority, East Devon District Council (EDDC). The cost of converting Knowle for this purpose was estimated at £250,000, notwithstanding the tenants of the flats all had to be re-housed first. However, in 1973, a year before the UDC was disbanded, the Finance

A large Monterey pine in the grounds (SVA)

Committee agreed that all the grounds around Knowle should be dedicated as a public open space: only the land around the main building and that set aside for a car park for the new authority was not to be included in the order. The Council's Clerk said this would make it very difficult for the land to be taken over for development once it was a dedicated public space.

The building, once such a beautiful and unique house, had been so altered over the years, often insensitively, that there was nothing left of its original form and it became architecturally so debased that there was nothing left worth saving. EDDC decided to move to modern offices in Honiton and sold the site to a developer, who obtained planning consent, on appeal, to build a complex of retirement homes.

Sidmouth has enjoyed unfettered access to the beautiful grounds for more than 45 years and its residents have been determined that no matter what happens to the building they want the grounds to remain an open space to which they have a permanent right of access.

Sidmouth Museum has agreed to take a fireplace which includes rare, handmade Ravesteyn tiles. Further tiles from another room and of similar provenance but a different design will also be displayed. One of the two fine marble fireplaces with the RNT (Richard Napoleon Thornton) monogram will also find a new home in the Museum.

Julia Creeke

38 LIFEBOAT HOUSE (site of)

An arched doorway is all that remains of the original Lifeboat House, built in 1870 to house Sidmouth's first lifeboat, the *Rimington*. Today, the lifeboats are housed in the building opposite.

Sidmouth's fishermen had always acted as the town's unofficial Lifeboat men, going to the aid of any vessel in distress, if the weather permitted boats to be launched from the beach. As coastal trade increased in the 19th century and Sidmouth became increasingly popular as a seaside resort, with people pleasure boating and sailing, a properly maintained and manned lifeboat was proposed as being very desirable for the town, and the recently formed Royal National Lifeboat Institution (RNLI) became involved.

A Lifeboat House was built on a piece of rough land at the eastern end of the Promenade and separated from York Terrace by Potbury's Coal Yard, whose gateposts were made from two redundant cannons from the old Fort. The land had been used in the 18th century for the building of schooners for the Newfoundland trade.

Apparently there was one steam vessel built there, as recorded by Thomazine Carslake in her diary for 27 September 1859: 'Into the town to see the first steam vessel ever built in Sidmouth launched – but she was only got to the wall!' Such was the excitement that the launch day had been declared a holiday in the town and an Ottery Band had arrived. (Why not the Sidmouth Band?) Hundreds of spectators turned out and there were boat races preceding the main event. The ship was named *Alice* – a steam vessel of 120 tons built by Captain WS Andrews and named after his second daughter. Her size caused problems hauling her out of the building yard, and by the time she arrived at the Esplanade, it was already getting dark. By the next day it was blowing a gale. Finally on 3 October she was 'got into the sea with a tremendous plunge head foremost and shot into the sea' and taken in tow by the *Sir Francis Drake,* another of Captain Andrew's ships, and towed away to Lowestoft to be fitted out.

Captain Andrews lived at 'Salcombe Mount', Salcombe Regis, and owned a shipping business, bringing coals into Sidmouth and taking timber, mostly elm, out for use in ship-building. He was accused of encouraging farmers to denude the local hillsides of elm which he stored in his timber-yard located on the Ham close to the Alma Bridge. There were two Andrews brothers involved in various business ventures, but the businesses as a whole seem to have run into trouble and their Lowestoft shipyard was sold in 1859: by 1861 both brothers were in prison for debt.

The last two vessels to be built on the Sidmouth site were both yachts. In 1861, the *Star of the Exe* was hauled across the road like her predecessors and then allowed to slip down the shingle into the sea, before being towed round to Exmouth for rigging and fitting out. The last yacht was one of the most interesting – called *Rip Van Winkle,* she took to the water at 6pm on 4 June 1862. She was built by Robert Charles Leslie, an able writer and fine marine painter born in 1826. (See chapter on 10 Fortfield Terrace).

In Sidmouth he made friends with Harry Conant, a fisherman, and together they built by hand a little gaff yawl called *Foam*. With the help of this fine seaman, Leslie embarked upon building the *Rip Van Winkle*, for the keel and planking of which Conant had espied a fine old elm in Farmer Grip's orchard hedge and this, with the aid of a wheelwright, was felled and taken to a meadow in Sid Road opposite Sid House, where it was sawn and left to mature.

The yacht was built by local craftsmen with Leslie's help and supervision: all the materials being locally produced down to the blacksmith-made nails, and Harry Conant made all the sails to a plan drawn up by Leslie to the then rare Bermudan rig.

In March 1869, the *Sidmouth Directory* reported that Mrs Rimington of Streatham had offered to donate a lifeboat for Sidmouth, but many in the town were not convinced of the need for such a boat and besides there was no place to accommodate it permanently on Sidmouth's exposed shore. Eventually, Mr GE Balfour, who had recently purchased the Manor, offered to donate a site on one corner of Ham Lane for the Boathouse and tenders for the construction were invited. However, the construction costs contained in the first tenders were somehow 'leaked', 'whereby others were enabled to go below them'.

During the month of August, notice was received from the RNLI that they were anxious to place the boat on station before the autumn gales. Nevertheless, by the beginning of September there had been little progress on the boathouse but, in spite of this, it was still intended to send the boat.

The lifeboat, surprisingly, did not arrive by sea but by train. She was delivered by rail to Honiton Station on 22 September and the next day a deputation from Sidmouth went over to fetch her. They took with them eight fine horses loaned to the Lifeboat Committee and Mr Chamberlain, proprietor of the Royal York Hotel, who was to act as 'master of the horse'. In Honiton, people turned out in great numbers to see the strange sight of the lifeboat on its transporter. At Sidbury, the Church bells rang a peal and the street was lined with people. At Sidford there was a large crowd of spectators, including some members of the crew who came out to meet the boat, which was finally parked in a field at Temple Street belonging to Mr James Pepperell.

On the 25th, the streets of Sidmouth were decked with flags, bunting and arches over the road and crowds arrived from all over the district to see the procession to the Boathouse.

The procession was headed by the 2nd Devon Volunteers under the command of Colonel Lousada, with the Lifeboat on her transporter pulled by the same eight fine horses and flanked by the Coastguards somewhere near the middle. The Town Band, who had given their services free, brought up the rear. The progress of the procession was unfortunately greatly hindered by the triumphal arches which spanned the road,

whose builders had failed to comprehend the height of the lifeboat on its transporter with its masts stepped and her crew with oars held upright. The result was that they kept getting tangled up in them and several fell down, and the crew, all of them Sidmouth fishermen, used some rather 'salty' language to describe events.

Eventually, the procession reached the Lifeboat Station, where a grandstand had been built for the ladies, and the heights above the Alma Bridge were thronged. The Reverend Clements, Vicar of Sidmouth and Chairman of the Lifeboat Committee, blessed the boat, and Mrs Thornton, wife of Richard Thornton of Knowle, with a gaily decorated bottle named the boat *Rimington*; then, with the securing ropes cut, the boat on its transporter was pushed into the sea, which was quite choppy. Unfortunately, no one had remembered to let go the fastenings on the transporter and the Coastguards had to wade into the surf and cut the boat free, to loud cheers from the crowd. The boat then gave a display after which she was pronounced thoroughly seaworthy by her crew. A large team of horses was required to recover it and haul it up the beach again.

By December, the boathouse was still incomplete; the lifeboat having stood out in the rain for nine weeks, the *Sidmouth Directory* acidly noting: 'It took nearly 3 months for a stranger to build what any one of a dozen Sidmouth masons could have erected in half the time'.

The lifeboat crew contained members of most of the Sidmouth fishing families and when called out, the boat crew wore cork life-jackets and were distinguished by their red woollen hats. There were two launches of the *Rimington* in 1873, but apart from practice launches it was four years before the boat's services were required to rescue six from the schooner *Wave* of Guernsey. The total number of lives saved during the boat's years of service was 32.

The *Rimington* was involved in an extraordinary Royal occasion when, on 23 May 1881, Prince Alfred, Duke of Edinburgh (second son of Queen Victoria), accompanied by the Duchess, arrived off Sidmouth in HMS *Lively* to inspect the Preventive Station. The Prince held the rank of Vice Admiral and had spent most of his life at sea in the Royal Navy. *The Lifeboat Journal* recounts the proceedings as follows:

The Rimington processing through the town (Sidmouth Museum)

Proceeding in a steam pinnace from HMS *Lively* towards the shore, the steam launch was struck by a sea which nearly capsized her. The Lifeboat which had been got out in readiness for inspection was at once launched and proceeded alongside where their Royal Highnesses and their party were taken into the Lifeboat. Mr Floyd, the Lifeboat Secretary, who had gone out in the *Rimington,* sat on the gunwale to make more room and promptly fell overboard – two of the crew, Conant and Bartlett, going in after him, fished him up and were all hauled, safe but soaking, back on board and eventually the Royal party were landed to the applause of a large crowd. It was decided that it was too risky for the Royal party to return to HMS *Lively* and so Mrs Davidson of Richmond Lodge, Elysian Fields, lent her carriage for them to travel to Exmouth and Mr Chamberlain of the York Hotel supplied four horses. The Royal party travelled via Peak Hill, it being a lovely bright day, but their troubles were not over when the postilions in coming into Exmouth ran the carriage pole into an omnibus.

In 1885, the *Rimington* was replaced by a larger and more modern lifeboat, the *William and Francis*, but it was seldom called out and made only one significant rescue in 1911, going to the aid of the Schooner *Maria* of Geestemunde and saving six of her crew.

Occasionally, for some major celebration, such as Queen Victoria's Jubilee in 1887, the Lifeboat would be taken from the Boathouse on its wheeled carriage pulled by a team of eight

horses to join a procession through the town centre.

The Lifeboat facility at Sidmouth was withdrawn by the RNLI in 1912 partly though lack of use and partly because a faster steam-powered lifeboat had been stationed at Exmouth. The Boathouse became part of Dean's Garage, which was demolished in 1986 to make way for a block of flats. The door surround from the old Boathouse was incorporated as part of the side entrance to the

Pediment of the old Lifeboat House (SVA)

flats and still bears the initials RNLBI carved on the pediment, although the stone is now very eroded. Sidmouth's present lifeboat is located on the other side of Ham Lane and is supported by voluntary contributions.

Julia Creeke

---

39 LITTLECOURT – *formerly Violet Bank Cottage*

Built in the late 18th century as a summer retreat by the 5th Duke of St Albans, the grandson of Charles II and Nell Gwyn. Later the residence of his son, the distinguished naval commander Admiral Lord Amelius Beauclerk.

In 1700 there still existed in many parts of Sidmouth remnants of the mediaeval strip system of cultivation; some of these had already been enclosed by walls and banks, and now formed gardens and orchards. Just such a series of strips of orchard existed between the upper part of Seafield Road, then known as Sandyway, and Station Road, then called Fortfield Road.

The southernmost orchard known as 'Hemphaye' contained a cottage which, in 1713, Sir Edmund Prideaux (4th Bt.) and the absentee Lord of Sidmouth Manor (he lived at Netherton near Farway) sold freehold, with a 2000 year lease on the Orchard.

The word 'haye' or 'hayne' is of mediaeval origin and in Devonshire means a meadow cut for hay. Below Hemphaye Orchard was a large triangle of land known as Courthaye and Little Courthaye. At the end of the 18th century, Hemphaye Cottage and Orchard and the adjoining Little Courthaye were sold to the 5th Duke of St Albans forming a site of approximately one acre (0.4 ha), and on this land Violet Bank

Cottage was built. More 'house' than 'cottage', its exterior was plain in comparison with the cottages orné which were to follow only a few years later in Sidmouth.

The Dukes of St Albans were descended from Charles II and his mistress, Nell Gwyn. The 5th Duke inherited in 1768 and his third son, Lord Amelius Beauclerk, born in 1771, was thus a great great grandson of Nell Gwyn and the King. In 1782, at the age of 11, he entered the Navy in which service he had a long and distinguished career, gaining his first command, the *Juno*, at the age of only 24. He served throughout the Napoleonic Wars in various ships. In 1802, the 5th Duke of St Albans died and Captain Lord Amelius Beauclerk, who was serving with the Channel Fleet, came to his father's funeral. He was in attendance on King George III, who had been ordered to take the sea airs, and was staying at Weymouth.

In 1796, Captain Lord Amelius, whilst commanding the frigate *Dryad*, captured, off the coast of Ireland, the French frigate *La Proserpine* after a fierce 45 minute fight. Twelve years later whilst blockading Toulon, that same frigate was recaptured by the French. On board was Lieutenant John Carslake whose home, Cotmaton, faced Lord Amelius's Violet Bank across Seafield Road. John Carslake was taken prisoner by the French and was not to see his home again for nearly six years.

Lord Amelius went on to become an Admiral of the Red in 1830, Commander-in-Chief at Plymouth and Principal Naval Aide-de-Camp to William IV. He continued to hold the appointment under Queen Victoria until his death in 1846, at which time he had been a close associate of the Royal Family during four reigns. A letter written to Lord Hertford (founder of the Wallace Collection) describes the festivities of a New Year's Eve at Brighton Pavilion in 1833, when the King danced a country dance with Admiral Amelius as partner: 'the sight of the King and the old Admiral going down the middle hand in hand was the most royally extravagant farce that ever was seen'.

The original house then called 'Violet Bank'. From Butcher's Guide to Sidmouth, 1820 (private collection)

In 1820, a Miss Bryett, who kept an academy for young ladies, was renting Violet Bank and, in 1823, the property was sold to John Carslake, who added the second storey and canopied balconies on the first floor – it was renamed 'High Bank' and became part of the Cotmaton Estate.

Throughout the remainder of the 19th century, the house was let to a succession of genteel families for periods of up to three years, including members of the Lousada family of Peak House. From 1871 to 1874, the Reverend and Mrs Baring Gould rented the house. He was Vicar of All Saints and a relative of the Reverend Sabine Baring Gould of Lewtrenchard Manor (near Lydford), author of the hymn *Onward Christian Soldiers*. Some years after the death of John Carslake, High Bank was put up for sale at £1,600 but failed to find a buyer and was once more rented out for £120 p.a. It was for sale again in 1891 when the property included the adjoining Hemphay Cottage, a coach house and stable. It was bought by Mr and Mrs Walker whose daughter married Mr Gore who had purchased Cotmaton House from the Carslake Estate.

The Johnson family took the house in 1906, changing its name to 'Littlecourt', a reference to the original name of the land on which the house was built. Mrs Johnson who continued to live there until 1930 was well-known for her work with the local troop of Boy Scouts. At her funeral, there was a wreath of white flowers from the indoor and outdoor staff at Littlecourt. For some years, it became a popular hotel until reverting to a private house: its landscaped garden has featured on BBC's *Open Gardens*.

Julia Creeke

Littlecourt in 2019 (SVA)

40 1 FORE STREET *formerly* THE LONDON HOTEL

This was built in the late 1700s, and was the starting point for the London coach. On the first floor were the Assembly Rooms, Sidmouth's evening social hub in the Regency period, and an important entertainment venue later.

For seven summers in the late 18th century, the Reverend John Sweete, Rector of Buckfastleigh, went on a series of peregrinations in the County of Devon, illustrating and recording in his sketch books and diary the places he visited. In 1795, he passed through Sidmouth where he stayed at the London Inn, recording that the rooms were neat and clean, and that the town's Assembly Rooms, which were situated there, were well attended.

In 1797, another traveller, one John Skinner, described the London Inn as follows:

> A good Inn called the London Inn kept by civil people where there is a Table d'Hote at a moderate expense. They have beside a spacious assembly and card room where they meet six evenings in the week during the season, which are generally well attended, the subscription being half a guinea and two shillings [62p] on coming into the room on a ball night.

The London gained its name as the starting point of the local coach which connected with the London Mail Coach – the stables were located further up the town. The London for many years played a central part in the town's social life for, apart from the Assembly Rooms, there was also a Card Room. Throughout Regency times there was a ball during the Season every Wednesday and it was said that the floor had an excellent spring, but 'the want of a Master of Ceremonies to effect introductions for those without previous acquaintance with any of those assembled was often remarked on by visitors'.

Towards the end of 1811, it had been agreed to commission an engineer to study the feasibility of constructing a harbour in the Ham. On 3 February 1812, at the London Inn, a meeting was convened, at which Sir Joseph Scott took the chair, and at which it was decided to accept Mr Crocker's estimate for £15,352 and to submit the plans for inspection at the Marine Library. Thomas Jenkins, who had inherited the Manor from his great uncle, now took issue with the plan and in the *Exeter Flying Post* of 10 September 1812 announced his intention of petitioning Parliament for an Act to make a harbour at or near Chit Rocks. There was division within the town as to which plan was the more favourable, but with the Napoleonic Wars again raging across Europe, both plans were shelved.

The great gale of November 1824 left the town centre flooded beyond the junction of Fore and Old Fore Streets where it was easily possible to row a boat between the two streets. In the vicinity of The London the water was more than 3 ft (0.9m) deep.

In the summer of 1831, when the Grand Duchess Hélène of Russia occupied 8 Fortfield Terrace (see separate chapter), she brought with her a Russian Band. They gave a series of well-patronised concerts at the Assembly Rooms to a fashionable audience; the ladies seated on long forms, the gentlemen standing in groups at the edge of the Room. All Sidmouth was fascinated by this Russian House Band whose members wore long tunics with waist sashes and pantaloons tucked into high boots. The Landlord of the London about this time was Mr Hetherington, who for many years had been butler to the late Emmanuel Baruh Lousada of Peak House.

The London Hotel before conversion into shops (Sidmouth Museum)

During the Duchess's visit there was a Ball and the *London Morning Post* of 11 July 1831 carried the following report of the festivities:

The Ball at Hetherington's London Hotel on Wednesday last was most fashionably attended; upwards of 140 distinguished individuals honoured it with their presence, among whom was Prince Gargarin and several of the Russian Noblemen and Gentlemen in the suite of the Grand Duchess. The Room was beautifully and tastefully chalked, with the English and Russian Arms, and superbly decorated with a magnificent profusion of luxuriant flowers and the Ball went off with so much éclat that it is proposed that another shall take place at the above Hotel in the course of ten days, when the Grand Duchess and her Ladies of Honour will attend. [For illustration of the band playing, see chapter on 8 Fortfield Terrace.]

A lecture in the Assembly Rooms, painted by PO Hutchinson 1857 (Devon Heritage Centre)

There is no record of whether this second Ball ever took place.

Another of the literary figures who knew Sidmouth, although he did not live there, was William Makepeace Thackeray the novelist. His mother and stepfather lived near Ottery St Mary at Larkbeare and he used Sidmouth and the London Hotel as one of the settings in a novel, *The History of Pendennis,* renaming it Baymouth, and the London became the Baymouth Hotel, which he described in some detail. Interestingly, there exists a pen and ink drawing done at the time of the Grand Duchess's visit depicting her Russian House Band playing in the Assembly Room. This drawing bears out Thackeray's description with the gentry sitting on long forms at the front and the tradesmen and their ladies standing at the back. The 'them and us' social demarcation was very much in being in the late 1820s when Thackeray knew the hotel.

On 13 August 1840 an advert appeared in the *Exeter Flying Post* announcing:

London Hotel, Sidmouth, a Grand Evening Concert, Saturday, 22nd August at 8 o'clock precisely. Mr Lavenu has the honour to inform the nobility and gentry that he has succeeded in engaging Mr Liszt, who on this occasion will perform his Grand Gallop Chromatique, Marche Hongroise and morceau choices from his celebrated recitals and a grand duet with Mr Mori.

Also on the programme was Mademoiselle de Varney of La Scala, Milan and Miss Louisa Bassano and Mr J Parry, all singers. 'Mr Lavenu will preside at the piano. Family tickets to admit 4, 21/- [£1.05] single tickets 6/- [30p] to be had of Mr Cawsey and Mr Harvey'. Liszt had agreed to tour the South of England in August and September 1840 and the tour opened in Chichester on 19 August.

Liszt stayed in Exmouth from where, on 24 August 1840, he wrote to Madame d'Agoult, who at the time was the recipient of his attentions. It seems that up until then the tour had not been particularly successful and Liszt complained: 'Our concerts are very mediocre! Lavenu is losing rather a lot of money up to now. The costs are enormous, but I regret that he does not do better business, for we have only been to small places up to now with the exception of Southampton and he is banking on Exeter, Plymouth and Bath to make it up'.

It seems that Liszt had not been well and complained of running a high fever for three days, but was feeling somewhat better and had found: 'A sensible doctor who promises to stop the fever without resorting to violent means. He is the sort of man you can trust and I am convinced that I will be better soon.' Of Sidmouth, Liszt said: 'The countryside that we have been through is most delightful, Sidmouth seems particularly beautiful and everywhere there are wonderful parks'. For a central European, the sight of Sidmouth's high red cliffs and green valley in mid-summer made sufficient impression on Liszt to warrant a special comment to his 'dear' Marie d'Agoult to whom he had already written two previous letters from London and Chichester.

Even with the establishment of other hotels in the town, the

London continued to be prominent in the town's social life. That commentator on local life, Peter Orlando Hutchinson, records in his diary a Christmas Ball at the London Inn on 19 December 1862: 'Went to the Christmas Ball at 9.30 this evening, gentlemen's tickets 7/6 [37 p]. Tea, refreshments and supper difficult to get at and uncomfortable to take!' He complained that the size of the ladies' dresses with their crinoline petticoats extended with steel hoops had attained ridiculous dimensions and that it was impossible to walk close to them without stepping on skirts or flounces.

Towards the latter part of the evening it was amusing to see strips of blue, red or white muslin or shreds of silk, which had been trod or torn off by these collisions lying on the floor or driven about by the whirlwind of these fleet dancers.

The London's decline set in gradually as the century wore on, and the Assembly Rooms, which had seen fashionable gatherings, were frequently reduced to trying to improve the education of the town's lower classes by arranging 'penny readings', the cost of entry being one penny. It was, though, still the venue for many sociable cricket dinners over the years but, by the end of World War One, although a comfortable hotel, it was mainly patronised by commercial travellers. Its owners were Bert Goodwin and his wife. Bert had been on the Edwardian stage and was renowned for his renderings of comic songs. He was also a keen cricketer, but had only one stroke – 'a great whirl of the bat which was entirely

Looking up Fore Street with the London Hotel on the left with a large hanging sign. A mid 19th century photo (Sidmouth Museum)

inconsistent in its ability to connect with the ball. If connection was achieved the results were startling'.

As the years went on the London declined still further until its reputation and appearance discouraged all but a small minority, and eventually it was sold in the early 1980s for conversion to shops. Sadly, what remained of the Georgian Assembly rooms was ripped out. Few now even realise that this building was once the heart of Sidmouth's social life.

Julia Creeke

---

41 LUSWAYS

Former home of John Yonge Anderson Morshead (b.1846 – d.1913), who in 1910 completed the most comprehensive historical account of the parish of Salcombe Regis.

Lusways was a large mid-Victorian house on the slopes of Salcombe Hill with a fine large garden and enjoying views across the valley to the west. When it was built, it was surrounded by open farmland. On an existing late 18th century map of the lower slopes of Salcombe Hill, a long strip of land running up Salcombe Hill on the north side of the road is shown. It is clearly marked as 'Lands of William Clapp and the Poor of Sidmouth'. It must have continued as agricultural land for probably another century, because the first building to be developed on it was 'Lusways' (Salcombe Hill Road). This house was occupied for many years by John Yonge Anderson-Morshead (1846-1913) and his wife Helen after he retired from Kensington, following a career as a barrister.

His father, the Reverend John Philip Anderson-Morshead (1809-1881) had been Vicar of Salcombe Regis Parish Church, and was a most popular vicar, spending twenty-seven years as the Vicar of Salcombe Regis Parish. In those days the Vicarage was what is now called 'Soldiers' Hill House', opposite the Church. There were six sons of the marriage and sadly their mother, Letitia, who was the daughter of the Reverend John Yonge, Vicar of Puslinch in Devon, died when she was only 48.

When their father died, his sons gave the money to construct Trow Pump and its housing in his memory. This was an important and much-needed improvement in local amenities. Until then the residents of Trow hamlet had to carry all their water from a spring low on Orleigh's Hill, a quarter to half a mile up the steep, rough track of Shoot Lane, before reaching their cottages. This task was often given to the older children who would carry it home in buckets held away from their bodies by wooden hoops. The new well initially ran dry and had to be deepened to the exceptional depth of 98 feet (30m), but still ran dry and failed in 1907, and finally, using steam power, was deepened to 126 feet (38m). It took 15 minutes of turning the pump wheel just to raise the water to the spout, a task usually given to the children. Water was finally piped to a tap in the adjacent lane in 1915.

John and Letitia's eldest son was John Phillip Yonge who was brought up in the Vicarage together with his siblings, all of whom went to Winchester and were exceptionally talented in

different ways, and all were fine cricketers. Edmund was a man of amazing ability as well as of fine physique – a great Alpine climber, as well as a classical scholar. John, after university, became a barrister and it would be hard to say what he did not know – poetry, the classics, law, geology, and the history of Salcombe Regis in minute detail from the conquest of it by the Saxons to the end of the reign of Queen Victoria. He eventually wrote it out in full in a great Manuscript History. Sidmouth is lucky to have

John Yonge Anderson-Morshead

had Peter Orlando Hutchinson to chart Sidmouth's history in five great volumes. What is not generally known is that Salcombe Regis has something very similar and equally comprehensive.

John Yonge Anderson-Morshead spent many years trawling through and copying all the ancient deeds, all of them in Latin, relating to Salcombe Regis, held in the Archives of Exeter Cathedral, as the Dean and Chapter had been gifted the Manor in 1149 AD by the then Bishop. These included rolls from the ancient Manor Courts held at Thorn Farm by the Cathedral's Steward; alas, no English translations are provided because John could read and translate mediaeval Latin – just one of his many talents. He also copied and collected together every piece of information that he could discover relevant to the Parish over the centuries, from whatever source, including memories of the inhabitants. Eventually these were bound together into a heavy volume, *Collections on the History of Salcombe Regis*. In the front of the volume there is a note that this volume was presented to the Vicar and Churchwardens of Salcombe Regis and their successors in 1910. Three further copies were made, one kept by the compiler, one presented to Bishop R Kestel-Cornish as Lord of the Manor, and the last to the Exeter Library of the Royal Albert Memorial Museum. The original and one of the copies now reside in the Devon County archives.

The volumes provide an unparalleled source of information about the Parish, but their sheer size makes them unwieldy and they are rather impersonal, recording as they do a multitude of facts on every conceivable subject relating to the Parish and its history; only in the later section of the volume do the people themselves begin to speak.

John Yonge Anderson-Morshead was an influential figure in the Parish, becoming Chairman of the Parish Council and controller of the Parish Volunteers, but he died in 1913. Lusways was known for its fine garden with many early flowering shrubs. A red rhododendron in the garden still blooms regularly in early spring alongside Salcombe Hill Road and is of considerable age.

All four of John and Helen Anderson-Morshead's sons served in the Great War. Captain Raymond, Captain Pentyre and Sub Lieutenant Duke Anderson-Morshead served with distinction, but it was their second son, Rupert, who made the ultimate sacrifice. He was appointed to command the 2nd Battalion the Devonshire Regiment in March 1918, and in May they were deployed to hold a quieter section of the Front near the River Aisne. On 26 May, they were moved forward to Les Bois des Buttes but, just as positions were being consolidated, the Line came under a massive enemy artillery assault. The German Infantry followed, supported by tanks and aircraft, and broke the Devonshire's Line. The Devons fought manfully until reduced to holding just one trench north of a canal and Rupert Anderson-Morshead was last seen rallying a handful of his men and directing fire as the enemy closed. He was never seen again and was one of 28 officers and 552 men from the 2nd Devons lost that day. The unit, in recognition of their incredible courage, was collectively awarded the Croix de Guerre avec Palme. Rupert Anderson-Morshead had been awarded the DSO earlier in 1918. He is commemorated by a tablet in Salcombe Regis Church as are seven others from the Parish.

John Yonge Anderson-Morshead is now best remembered for his manuscript history of the Parish. In WW2, Lusways became a nursing home and a number of Sidmouth mothers had their babies delivered there. It was subsequently turned into flats, the fate of many large Sidmouth properties in the 1950s when people could no longer get staff to help run them or gardeners to care for the gardens, nor had they the money, because of heavy taxation, to pay their wages.

Julia Creeke

42 MARYCOURT

One of the finest houses designed by notable local architect RW Sampson (b.1866 – d.1950), built in 1913 in Queen Anne style.

Marycourt is one of a number of houses that RW Sampson built for his own occupation, and is said to have been named after his eldest daughter, Winifred Mary Sampson.

Robert Sampson was born on 7 March 1866 in Shoreditch, London. He trained as an architect at the Royal Academy and Architectural Association Schools during the 1880s and joined the London architectural practice of Robert Cunninghame Murray. The Sidmouth Manor had engaged RC Murray to provide architectural services to the Manor Estate, and in 1891 Robert Sampson came to Sidmouth as the firm's representative. Sampson settled in Sidmouth and, following expiry of the initial contract with the Manor, decided to establish his own architectural practice in the town. He remained in Sidmouth for the rest of his life. His output was prolific, and many of the buildings we now see in the town were designed by him.

For some years after his arrival in the town, Sampson was fully engaged in work for the Manor Estates. The Lord of the Manor, John Edmond Heugh Balfour, ably assisted by his solicitor and agent, William Hastings, had

*The architect RW Sampson
(Sampson Society)*

embarked on an ambitious programme to raise the profile of the town and upgrade the town's facilities. The Manor offices and adjoining concert hall (now the Manor Pavilion complex) were built in the year of Sampson's arrival. It was here that Sampson had his drawing office. The building was shared with William Hastings until 1928 when they both moved to Fortfield Chambers, a building designed by Sampson on the opposite side of Station Road. Among a number of commercial ventures, the Manor Estates upgraded the town's gas and water supplies. Brine baths were built on the Esplanade to enhance the facilities available for tourists. New hotel accommodation was financed, including building the Victoria Hotel (see separate chapter) which was opened on 4 March 1904. Sampson was involved in all of these projects, designing the Victoria Hotel, his largest building, whilst still in his thirties.

The Manor promoted the creation of high quality modern housing, and in doing so sought to exploit the Estate's own land-holding. The Bickwell Valley Road was constructed in 1900 and opened up an entirely new extension to the town. It was here that Sampson designed large Edwardian villas set in extensive grounds, all built in a loose form of Arts and Crafts style.

However, Sampson believed that good housing design should not be the exclusive province of the wealthy. His work encompassed the full range of house types, evidence of which can be seen throughout the town. He designed all of Sidmouth's early Council houses, including the schemes at Sid Park Road and Arcot Park. At the official opening of Arcot Park in 1927, Neville Chamberlain, then Minister of Health, declared that it was the best Council development he had ever seen.

The initial success of Bickwell Valley convinced the Manor Estates to extend the scheme into adjoining land. In September 1906, the Manor acquired an additional block of land between Bickwell Valley Road and Convent Road and more houses were built, including Marycourt.

The design of Marycourt contrasts sharply with the informal style of the Arts and Crafts houses built earlier in Bickwell Valley. It is essentially a formal composition in a Queen Anne style. The house has two forward projecting wings to each side which enclose a formal entrance courtyard leading to the centrally-placed front door.

The house is constructed with a soft orange brick, probably from the Manor Estates own brickworks. There is extensive use of brickwork detailing, including expressed quoins at each corner of the building. The roof is covered with plain clay tiles, a roofing material often used by Sampson. Much of the first

floor is enclosed in a mansard roof arrangement, again using plain tiles. The mansard roof is supported by a decorative cornice. The gable ends of each of the projecting wings are extended above the roofline in a parapet fashion and appear to mimic a Dutch gable style. To complete the formal approach, the roof is surmounted by a belvedere topped with a weather-vane incorporating 'RWS', Sampson's initials.

The northernmost projecting wing originally included all the servants' accommodation, discretely accessed from an inner hall and complete with its own staircase. The main hallway runs across the house from the front door to the formal staircase at the southern end. In common with many of his houses, Sampson inserted large windows in Marycourt at the half-landing level, enabling light to flood into the hall and landing areas. The principal living areas and bedrooms all lie to the south and west of the house in order to gain maximum sunlight and outward views over the extensive garden areas. All these rooms are provided with deep timber-framed windows with leaded lights.

Although Marycourt is regarded by some as Sampson's finest house, his occupation of it was relatively brief. By 1918 he was living in a house on the Bickwell Valley road, and moved regularly over the following years. In the late 1930s he built the last of the houses for his own family to occupy. This final house was a large thatched cottage on Sidbury Hill, which he named Shatterway.

Whilst living in Sidmouth, Sampson devoted much of his time to musical activities. He was a prominent member of the Amateur Operatic Society, taking leading roles in Gilbert and

Sullivan productions, in addition to painting scenery and acting as stage manager. He also organized fund-raising concerts for local organizations such as the Cricket Club. Throughout his life he was a keen amateur artist.

Robert Sampson died at Shatterway on 20 April 1950, aged 84, and is buried in Salcombe Regis Churchyard, having designed his own gravestone. Following his death the *Sidmouth Herald* reported that 'Mr. Sampson's connection with Colonel JEH Balfour was responsible for practically the whole of the architectural layout of modern Sidmouth, including the Victoria Hotel and many outstanding buildings'.

Martin Mallinson

43 MAY COTTAGE

Sidmouth's first hospital from 1885 to 1891.

There is a print of May Cottage of 1826, showing a pretty neat thatched cottage, although it is likely that it was probably built over 100 years earlier and is thus one of Sidmouth's oldest surviving buildings.

For many years John and Ann Potbury lived in the Cottage. He died aged 51 in 1832, but Ann lived to the age of 90 and, since she was born in 1773, could remember the 'old' Sidmouth before it began to become a fashionable place. John Potbury ran a coal and timber business (now Bradfords). John Potbury's son, another John Potbury, went to sea as a young man, after which he followed in his father's business, but on his own account he also carried on a flourishing ironmongers. About 1876 he took over the upholstery and cabinet-making business of Mrs Ann Farrant, which was to be continued into the 20th century by John Potbury senior's two grandsons as Potbury and Sons, the well-known Sidmouth business still trading today.

In 1872 it was first suggested that there should be a cottage hospital for poor people. In 1875 a committee was formed but the scheme was abandoned for two reasons. First, there was lack of support from most of the local doctors. Their opposition to a hospital may have been because of concern of extra work, or the fear of 'outside' doctors consulting in Sidmouth. A second objection was that the new railway (1874) would allow patients to be transported easily to Exeter.

In 1884 the scheme was raised again, largely due to the efforts of the solicitors at Hope Cottage, Mr Orchard and Mr Radford, as well as the Reverend Trepplin's wife. A meeting was called, which was held at Barton Cottage. May Cottage was proposed, but, surprisingly, the genial vicar, the Reverend Clements, was initially opposed to it. Several owners of local businesses were on the committee, including Mr Field (the draper) and Mr Trump (the grocer). Mr Hine-Haycock, the well-liked owner of Belmont and benefactor to Sidmouth, chaired the initial meetings, but was shortly to leave the town to live in London. Finally, May Cottage was agreed in principle.

In early 1885, Annie Leigh Browne, the prominent local benefactor, generously guaranteed to pay the rent of May Cottage for 5 years. She was the grand-daughter of John

May Cottage, from an old print after the painting by George Rowe, 1826 (Sidmouth Museum)

Annie Leigh Browne aged 14 (courtesy of the Trustees of the Sidmouth Old Dissenter Meeting)

Annie Leigh Browne in later life (Sidmouth Museum)

Carslake of Cotmaton by his daughter Thomasine and Samuel Woolcot Browne. The Lord of the Manor, Colonel Balfour, who owned the property, also offered to assist with costs. In March, Miss Williams was appointed as nurse and the cottage was now completely repaired and fully furnished for its new role as a 'cottage' hospital. It was supplied with an operating table and surgical instruments. The hospital had four beds and the first patient was described as a young woman with rheumatic fever; clearly medical confidentiality did not extend to poorer people.

In the same vein, *Lethaby's Sidmouth Journal* in April 1885 wrote:

We have no wish to beat up for patients, but feel justified in saying that there is now provided for the poor of Sidmouth, and its immediate neighbourhood, at a merely nominal cost, such help towards recovery from sickness and disease, both as to residence, nursing and medical attention, as is often unattainable by persons of far superior positions in life. Subsidies of 10s 6d [52p] may recommend one patient annually, and in the same proportion for every 10s 6d subscribed.

A total of 21 patients were admitted in the first year. The service continued until the opening of the purpose-built Victoria Hospital nearby in 1891.

May Cottage did not last long as the Town's hospital, because in 1889 an anonymous donor offered the sum of £500 towards the cost of building a proper hospital for Sidmouth. The Manor Trustees then donated a site, which led to further donations being received, which allowed a purpose-designed building to be erected at a cost of £1,200. There were ten beds and, with the agreement of Queen Victoria, it was named the Victoria Cottage Hospital.

Over the years, there have been a number of extensions to the Victoria Cottage Hospital, the last but one, costing several million pounds, being paid for by the Comforts Fund from accumulated donated monies. It was opened by Princess Anne. Until very recent times the Hospital's name still included the word 'Cottage' linking it to May Cottage.

After its brief use as a hospital, May Cottage was bought by Miss Annie Leigh Brown to preserve it, and let as a private residence. It later became a guesthouse. For many years it was famous for a wonderful passion flower which covered the front of the cottage but, sadly, it never recovered properly from the winter of 1963, and another very cold winter finally killed the struggling plant. Alas, it has never been replaced.

Julia Creeke

The house as it is today (SVA)

From the late 18th century, an open-fronted thatched shelter known as the 'Shed' occupied this site. It was replaced in 1809 by a two-story building, also with a 'shed', and was home temporarily to Wallis's Marine Library.

The 'Shed', as the building which first occupied this site was called, was possibly the first building actually fronting the Esplanade and dated from the time when Sidmouth's charms first began to attract visitors in the early 1780s. It may possibly have been associated with the house next door (now Beach House) which was also of early date.

In appearance it resembled the present wooden shelter on the west end of the Esplanade. It was larger, with a glazed western end and thatched roof, open to the sea along the front and fitted out with wooden benches. It became a popular place of resort for the minor gentry and those of fashion where, in fine weather, they could congregate to discuss the latest news and topics, and enjoy the view. It was particularly frequented when the latest editions of the papers and journals had just arrived from London; usually they were about three days behind date, and were on sale at the Marine Library next door. This Library had been founded by Mr John Wallis, son of a London bookseller, in 1803.

A view across the beach toward the Shed with its glass windows. The thatched top to the wall of St Peter's Chapel is visible on the left. Facsimile copy by PO Hutchinson in 1879 of original by TW Upton, 1802 (Devon Heritage Centre)

Such had become the popularity of the Shed as a place of resort that John Wallis succeeded in acquiring it for redevelopment as part of his extended Marine Library. Being a successful businessman, he did not do away with the concept of the Shed, for he doubtless realised that this was one of the attractions which helped bring the public to his Library.

Wallis demolished the old Shed and replaced it with a neat two-storey Georgian brick building. John Wallis's extended Marine Library opened to the public on 20 June 1809. About two-thirds of the ground floor facing the sea was given over to the replacement 'Shed' and a contemporary writer said that:

'...it was neatly painted and ornamented with stone pillars which supported the large and handsome billiard room in which was an excellent table'.

The new Shed was benched round on three sides with the front open to the sea and still continued to be known as the Shed.

John Wallis's original Marine Library in a print of 1810

The remaining third of the building to the east was a small shop premises for the new Library. The Reverend Butcher writing in 1810 says:

Articles of fancy as well as information and utility may be met with. It is supplied every day with the London and provincial newspapers and several of the most popular periodicals are found on its tables. A variety of toys and trinkets and articles of greater utility occupy the shelves. Books, dissected maps and a circulating library complete the establishment. The front part of the shop is appropriated to the readers of newspapers and magazines, but in the summer a convenient back room is also prepared.

Just as now, things were busier in the summer. The billiard room had four sash windows facing the sea and a decorative tablet was placed between the two central ones.

John Wallis did not run his library from this site at Prospect Place for long because, in 1813, he moved further westwards along the Esplanade to new premises at what is now the Bedford Hotel. For years thereafter at the new premises the Library continued to be known colloquially as 'The Shed'. (Read more about the Library in the chapter on the Bedford Hotel.)

Once the Library was gone there were changes. 'The Shed' did not last long. The first floor billiard room remained for a time in use by the baths situated next door at 1 Prospect Place. When the baths closed the property became two lodging houses. The old Library building on the corner of the Promenade became a residence, 3 Prospect Place. For over 80 years now it has been occupied by a business which is one of Sidmouth's features, the Mocha Café.

Julia Creeke

The library (on the right) now converted to a residence. Detail from Sidmouth's Long Print 1815 (Sidmouth Museum)

45 NORMAN LOCKYER OBSERVATORY

Founded by Sir Norman Lockyer (b.1836 – d.1920), previously Professor of Astronomical Physics in London and founding editor of Nature. Now owned by a charitable company, it is a centre for amateur astronomy, meteorology and radio-astronomy, and a champion for science education.

How the Observatory came to Sidmouth

The Norman Lockyer Observatory sits on top of Salcombe Hill about one kilometre east of Sidmouth. At 167m altitude, it looks over the Sid Valley and, from many places in Sidmouth, its silver domes can be seen amongst the trees on the skyline. It has a long and distinguished life having been founded by Sir Norman Lockyer as The Hill Observatory in 1913. Since 1920, it has been known as the Norman Lockyer Observatory, or NLO. In addition to its historical importance, it is home to the Norman

Lockyer Observatory Society and is a centre for amateur astronomy, meteorology, radio-astronomy and the promotion of science education. This Society has a current membership of about 300, all amateurs from a variety of backgrounds, and, apart from providing facilities for members to pursue their interests, the Society maintains the site, develops the facilities and opens them to the public. It is a foremost example of how Sidmouth is a town of arts and science.

The site has four main assets: the telescopes, the planetarium, an orrery, and the Lockyer Technology Centre. These will be described later and will be better understood if a description is given as to how the observatory came to Sidmouth. The answer is simple: Sir Norman Lockyer, his marriage to a Sidmouth lady, and his long and active retirement.

Norman Lockyer was a Victorian polymath with Victorian values of a good brain, endless curiosity, driving ambition and a forceful personality. He was born in Rugby in 1836, the year before Queen Victoria came to the throne, and died peacefully in his garden on Salcombe Hill in 1920 aged 84. His educational preference was for languages, becoming fluent in French, German and Greek; he never studied at university yet was awarded a Doctor of Science (DSc) degree from both Cambridge and Oxford. In his twenties, he borrowed a telescope from a friend he met on a train and this was the catalyst for his, largely amateur, interest in astronomy, a science in which he excelled, becoming the first Professor of Astronomical Physics in the country. He identified a new element in the Sun, naming it helium – 27 years before it was discovered on Earth. He did much to promote the study of science in schools and the advancement of science amongst scientists: in this he had perhaps his greatest achievement – founding and editing, for 50 years, *Nature*, still the world's greatest scientific journal.

Norman Lockyer's father was a surgeon-apothecary but both his parents died before he was 19 years of age. After a short time as a student teacher, he passed examinations to enter the Civil Service, becoming a clerk in the War Office in London. At the age of about 24, he married Winifred James who was also a linguist, and they set up house in Wimbledon. Alas, she died 19 years later, leaving Norman to look after their young family of five boys and two girls. Twenty-four years later, aged 67, he married a 50 year-old widow, Thomasine Mary Brodhurst. Thomasine Mary (usually known as Mary) and her older sister Annie, used to come to Sidmouth as children to stay with their grandparents, Captain John and Tomasine Pearse Carslake. (See Cotmaton Hall for more information on the Carslake family. Please note that Thomasine can be spelt in many ways.)

Fascimile of the first edition, 4 November 1869 (Sidmouth Museum)

Mary had inherited land on the west side of Salcombe Hill. In 1909, six years into their marriage and when Norman was aged 73, they built a house on this land and it became known as 'The Lockyer House'. A priority was that the house would include a dome in which Norman installed his beloved 6¼ inch telescope. They retired to Sidmouth in 1911 but, even at the age of 76, Norman was determined to continue his astronomical studies and built an observatory on the top of Salcombe Hill. At that time it was devoid of trees, allowing a good view of the horizon, and with good ground cover which would minimise distortion of telescopic images caused by rising warm air. Establishing this observatory would cost money but luckily Norman was well connected. Prince Arthur, Duke of Connaught, was President of the Appeal Committee, and the sum was soon found. It became known as The Hill Observatory and, at this stage, contained two 10 inch (25.4 cm) refractors. Norman's 6¼ inch (15.9 cm) refractor telescope remained at his house. By 1913, the observatory was operational, with a house (the Long House) containing a library and laboratory, and providing back-up for the work carried out in the domes. After seven active years in his new observatory, Norman died in 1920.

In the early 1930s, a further telescope was added, known as the Mond Equatorial or Astrograph. Sir Robert Mond, a supporter of the Observatory, provided funds for the equipment and to build the new dome.

Sir Norman's son, James, took over as Director, changing its name to The Norman Lockyer Observatory, which has been its title to this day. It remained active until James's death in 1936. But astronomy was changing: larger and larger telescopes were being built on the top of high mountains, at considerable cost, and Sidmouth's observatory could not attract funds to keep it going. In 1945, the University College of the South West of England (which subsequently became Exeter University in 1955) took over the running of the observatory. Although the College's Department of Physics used the site, there was no Chair of Astronomy, and research at the observatory ceased and, importantly, maintenance of equipment stopped in 1961.

Fortunately, this valuable asset was saved by the newly formed Sidmouth and District Astronomical Society who, in 1975, sought permission to use the engine room as a meeting room, and the two 10 inch telescopes. At the same time, the Sidmouth Amateur Radio Society asked if they could use the building to house their equipment. Both these requests were granted but, after only eight years, a further threat to the future of astronomical sciences in Sidmouth and the prime site on top of Salcombe Hill, appeared.

By 1983 Exeter University had no further use for the site, coinciding with increasing demand for housing (and in the West Country, caravan parks) in attractive locations such as Salcombe Hill. The University decided therefore to sell the site. A similar scenario was unfolding on the opposite slope of Peak Hill. The citizens of Sidmouth were appalled as it could not be guaranteed that the District Council would not approve building on these sites. After protracted negotiations, East Devon District Council (EDDC) purchased the nine acre (3.6 ha) observatory site, the National Trust purchased adjacent farm and woodland, and the people of Sidmouth (through the Sid Vale Association/National Trust Landscape Fund) purchased 200 acres (81 ha) of land at the top of Salcombe Hill. Part of the deal was the sale by the University of Norman Lockyer's 'Long House' as a private dwelling, and the Porter's Lodge. The present layout was established.

Restoring the observatory, which at that time contained two refractor telescopes, was a major task as neglect, theft and vandalism had taken their toll. The valuable 10 inch refractor (the McClean telescope) was sent to Newcastle upon Tyne for renovation – this was not easy as the lens had been stolen, but fortunately Sinden Optics of Newcastle possessed the original records so that an exact copy could be made. One of the vacated domes (the Mond dome) was converted into a small planetarium with an additional building attached to it providing meeting rooms and a radio research room. Considerable credit must go to the Council who funded this project and especially to the amateur enthusiasts in Sidmouth district who planned the facilities and carried out much of the work. Continuity was provided by Donald Barber, who had worked with James Lockyer and contributed substantially to the restoration. The Sidmouth Amateur Radio Society and the Sidmouth and District Astronomical Society were permitted to use the premises, under an annual licence, with the requirement that the observatory be open to the public on nine occasions during the year. The NLO was formally re-opened by Patrick Moore in 1989. Membership of the Societies grew and visits, especially by schoolchildren, became very popular and it soon became clear that further building was needed. The EDDC backed these proposals, paying for the building, while members of the NLO fitted it out. In 1995, Patrick Moore revisited the NLO to open a brand new 60 seat planetarium and meeting hall. Norman Lockyer's faithful old 6¼ inch telescope was installed in the now vacated Mond dome; its 135 year-old lens being found to be in excellent condition.

Sir Norman Lockyer beside his telescope (NLO)

The NLO presently enjoys great popularity amongst the large number of amateur enthusiasts and the increasing number of the general public who visit on Open Evenings to view the sky and, on Open Days, to attend lectures, exhibitions and demonstrations, including the planetarium. The NLO contributes significantly to the success of Sidmouth's annual Science Festival.

Norman Lockyer – the scientist

In this account of the establishment of the observatory on Salcombe Hill, the essential and central role of Norman Lockyer is very obvious. But why did he achieve such fame? Borrowing a telescope from a friend he met on a train is an unlikely beginning. But it was so – Norman was hooked by the excitement of astronomical discoveries which were happening thick and fast in Victorian Britain. He bought his own 3½ inch (8.9 cm) telescope and began, as many do, by observing the moon. His accuracy and enthusiasm became known and he joined a Moon mapping project led by the President of the Royal Astronomical Society. In 1862, aged 26, he constructed an 8 foot (2.44 m) long telescope, housing a 6¼ inch (8.9 cm) lens, which had to be carried into his garden to view the sky, to record *inter alia* Titan's transit of Saturn.

The Observatory now (courtesy of John Maclean, member of NLO)

The 1860s was a time when science was emerging from being a hobby for gentlemen and Norman saw a need for a journal which would publish new science. Together with Alexander Macmillan, he launched *The Reader* in 1863, with himself as editor. Norman was asked to 'look after the science' and reported on the proceedings of the Royal Society and the British Association, so that he became personally acquainted with scientists such as Darwin and Huxley.

A move to Hampstead in 1865 allowed Norman to build his own observatory and he began studying the Sun. A spectroscope attached to his telescope allowed him to examine the solar spectrum; a valuable method for identifying elements present in the Sun (and elsewhere) as each element causes distinct lines in the spectrum. Working independently but exactly at the same time, Norman and a French scientist, Jules Janssen, showed that the Sun was composed largely of hydrogen: for this they were jointly awarded a gold medal by the French Academy of Sciences. He also confirmed the presence of sodium, calcium, barium and other elements, but there was a set of lines in the yellow part of the spectrum which did not correspond with any known element. In 1870, he named this new element helium after the Greek Sun God, *Helios*. Twenty-seven years later, helium was discovered on Earth in the mineral Cleveite: we now know that helium is the second most abundant element in the universe after hydrogen. His examinations of the region surrounding the Sun led him to label the envelope of glowing gas, the Chromosphere.

The Reader had a short life of four years and was replaced by a new journal *Nature*, first published in November 1869 with Norman Lockyer as founder editor: he was then aged 33 years. He remained Editor of *Nature* for the next 50 years, a remarkable achievement. His scientific research continued to be centred on the Sun and, beginning in the 1870s, he travelled far to observe solar eclipses and sun-spots. Astronomers must have a phlegmatic personality as on one of these trips to Sicily, which involved the use of two gunboats to transport his astronomical equipment, at the moment of eclipse the sky was cloudy. He was luckier on an expedition to India in 1871.

At the same time as his amateur research progressed, Norman became increasingly involved in improving science education in this country. He was appointed Secretary to a Royal Commission led by the Duke of Devonshire to look into this matter. The Report appeared five years later and called for a massive increase in state spending on science, resulting in the creation of a new government department; its successor still exists today. Just one example of his contribution was that he pressed for scholarships to be granted to Empire and Commonwealth students to come to our universities – Ernest Rutherford was one of the first, subsequently providing an understanding of the source of solar energy as one part of his outstanding contribution to science.

One positive result for Norman was that his Solar Physics Laboratory would be state-funded and located in South Kensington; later, in 1887, he was appointed Professor of

Astronomical Physics at the Royal College of Science (now part of Imperial College, London). In the mid-1870s, he was seconded to the new Department of Science and Arts to organise an exhibition of scientific instruments, also in South Kensington. This was opened by Queen Victoria in 1876. The exhibition became an annual event and was the forerunner of the Science Museum, South Kensington, we know today.

His achievements were well recognised: apart from the medals he received, he was elected Fellow of the Royal Astronomical Society in 1862, Fellow of the Royal Society (FRS) in 1869, and knighted in 1897.

Lady Mary Lockyer was a scientist with considerable interest in education, *inter alia* helping to establish the first women's hall of residence in London University. In 1882 she attended the Solar Physics Observatory and therefore was a student of Lockyer. She married Bernard Brodhurst in 1885. After Bernard's death, Mary married Norman Lockyer in 1903. Mary was then 51 and Norman 67 years. She was elected Fellow of the Royal Astronomical Society. She died in 1943 aged 91 years; both Sir Norman and Lady Lockyer are buried in Salcombe Regis churchyard.

Thus, Sir Norman Lockyer's legacy to astronomy, scientific education, and to Sidmouth is considerable. Norman and his son, James, would be proud that his hilltop observatory has developed to become a very successful centre for amateur, but nevertheless significant, research and provides education and entertainment for a wide spectrum of people.

The Observatory now

Presently, the site contains the Lockyer Technology Centre, three major telescopes (one historic and two modern), an orrery, and a planetarium, as well as the Donald Barber lecture theatre, meeting rooms and other facilities for members of the NLO. The Technology Centre is an important centre for meteor detection as well as other scientific studies. The three telescopes are the Lockyer 6¼ inch, used by Norman for his major discoveries, the Kensington refractor and the McClean refractor: all are equipped for several uses. The Victoria dome was built in about 2000 and houses the 12 inch (30.5 cm) reflector, while the Connaught dome was built in 2012 to house the 20 inch (50.8 cm) reflector. The 19th century orrery is a mechanical model of the Sun, Earth, Moon, planets and major asteroids: it has been restored to full health by members of NLO. The planetarium has had two projectors. The first came from the USA via St Luke's College, installed in 1995 and used for 10 years. The second and present Spitz projector came from the Royal Greenwich Observatory: NLO members transported the projector and reassembled it in its present position. The Norman Lockyer Observatory Society is a company with charitable status. In 1995, it obtained a 20 year lease of site and buildings from EDDC. This has now been renewed.

Andrew Rugg-Gunn

46 THE OLD JAIL – *(site of)*

Sidmouth's first jail was built in about 1862, alongside two cottages for the town's policemen. It remained on the site until the 1890s.

For centuries before the founding of Police Forces, the only law enforcement was through local Constables and Night Watchmen. They were appointed by the local Justices of the Peace and were dispatched, under their authority and direction, to deal on the Justices' behalf with local disturbances or to arrest felons apprehended by others and take them into custody when that was necessary. This worked reasonably well in small towns and villages, but in larger towns and cities there were regular patrols. For that purpose every town and city had its local jail. Law and order had been carried on in England in this way since an Act of 1637. It was further regulated in an Act of Parliament of 1707 and continued so until the 19th century.

Minor misdemeanours were usually punished by the Justices ordering time spent in the stocks, and Sidmouth's stocks stood beyond the south-west corner of the Parish Churchyard between the steps and the road. The pillory was used for some of the more serious misdemeanours, and was sited on Mill Lane (now All Saints' Road) at Mill Cross, close to the Old Meeting and the top of the path that led across Blackmore Fields from the Parish Church. In the stocks, the feet were clamped in holes cut between two boards, but in the pillory, both head and wrists were clamped whilst the victim stood. In both cases the victim might be pelted with rotten fruit and eggs or other unmentionables, but the use of the pillory was outlawed by Act of Parliament in 1837. The stocks fell out of use in Sidmouth in the mid 1830s.

In London, as the city grew, the system proved unsatisfactory and in 1829 Sir Robert Peel's government passed an Act which allowed the formation of the Metropolitan Police, but only for Greater London. In 1839, policing was extended by the County and Rural Policing Act to allow other Police Forces to be set up voluntarily; Wiltshire being the first county force. It was not until 1856, when the County and Borough Police Act was passed, that policing

Rear wall – all that remained of the two cells before the present reconstruction. (SVA)

became compulsory for the whole of the United Kingdom.

The first record of Sidmouth having a policeman was in 1851 when Peter Grant, described as Police Officer, was living in Amyatts Row. This was well before the formation of the Devon Constabulary in 1857, when it was ordered that police stations, strongrooms and cells be provided at various locations. It was ordered that at Sidmouth the following provision should be made: two cells, and cottages for two constables. There seems to have been some delay because it was not until 1862 that there were official plans and specifications for a Police Station. The architect was an Ottery St Mary man, J Digby, and the mason was a Sidmouth man by the name of J Turner.

This first Police Station was built on a plot of land on the west side of Mill Street opposite the site of the town's mill and close to the Ford. Here, in the north-west corner, a pair of two storey cottages were built to house the newly appointed Police Constables and their families and, in the opposite corner, was the building housing the two cells. It is possible that this plot of land belonged to Sidmouth Feoffees and was leased, because in due course they had possession of the pair of cottages and the site, and remained so until the land was sold and redeveloped in 2015. How long the police station remained on this site is not recorded, but in late Victorian times the 'station' was moved to Newtown and shared between two adjacent properties. Both had lock-ups in their gardens. John Copplestone, with his wife and four children, lived in number 17, now called Copplestones, and Charles Pratt, with his wife and five children, lived in number 19. The cooking of their respective wives was so good that prisoners enjoyed their time in custody. Sadly, the lock-ups no longer exist.

Not long after the Devon Constabulary was formed, we have one of the early reports in our local Press of an affray in the middle of Sidmouth. It was such that today it would have resulted in equal outrage by Sidmouth's normally law abiding majority. The press report is recorded thus:

December 5th 1867.

We much regret that Sidmouth is to be numbered with those towns in which the 5th of November continues to be marked by rough conduct and a wanton destruction of property.

If the outbreak had arisen from distress or oppression though it would not excuse the folly, but might be urged in mitigation. But no such cause existed and there is scarcely a town where greater kindness is shown to the poor or greater liberality manifested.

And how was it repaid by many on Guy Fawkes day? Why by terrifying the peaceable inhabitants, extorting money from defenceless householders, and maliciously destroying the property of tradesmen.

It was not until nearly 9 o'clock that any uproar was made. About that time a number of men and boys, masked and with flaming balls in their hands paraded the streets, first tarring and burning Mr Pidsley's shutters, breaking the windows and throwing the lighted guy into the house.

At Mr Webber's the violence was much greater and the damage more considerable, indeed but for the firm hand and resolute assistance of some of the gentry it was feared that the whole house would have been pillaged and burnt down.

The following Thursday a number of tradesmen assembled at Mr Smith's residence where they consulted a Magistrate. The Magistrate cordially promised all assistance within their power. He expressly stated that the letting off of fireworks or the carrying of lighted balls through the streets was illegal and the offenders are likely to be taken into custody. He remarked that it would have been better if constables had been called out, but that if constables had been enrolled some would have attributed the disturbance to that cause as a provocation.

Most of the work for the Constables in Sidmouth involved petty crime by over-exuberant youths and drunkenness by their elders, especially on a Saturday evening, when it was the custom to make a round of the local pubs and drinking places. To remove any causing nuisance by being so drunk come closing time that they were abusive and 'legless', they were unceremoniously hoisted on to a hand cart and taken to the little Jail in Mill Street, close to the Ford, where they were dumped into the lock-up for the night until they sobered up. They were then released on Sunday morning. If they had been particularly troublesome they might be charged to appear before the local Magistrates.

The police station finally moved to specially built premises in Temple Street in 1911, but there was much consternation locally that it had been built in front of an old house, instead of on the site of the redundant gas works which were an eyesore. In the 1980s, the little lock-up in Mill Street was still complete with its sloping slate roof, barred window overlooking a small enclosure and a wooden door, painted green. At the rear, two small barred windows overlooked the adjacent alleyway. The Sidmouth Feoffees, who oversaw many of Sidmouth's old charity bequests, owned the surrounding land where there were the pair of two storey cottages which had become substandard housing and were empty, their tenants having been re-housed elsewhere. The Feoffees wished to demolish them and sell the land for re-development to generate the highest return from their asset. To clear the site they demolished the cottages and, at the same time, the little lock-up was demolished, leaving just the rear wall as a reminder of what once stood there. It was hoped, when the original Blue Plaque scheme was underway in the late 1980s, that it would be possible to affix a plaque to record the building's previous use and prevent its demolition. But the request from the SVA was rejected and the owners suggested it would be better to do so when the redevelopment was complete. Alas, too late to save it.

Julia Creeke

47 THE OLD MEETING

First built as a Nonconformist chapel in about 1705, sharing a thatched roof with the White Hart Inn. It was rebuilt in 1886, and then further extended in 1939 to include a meeting room.

By the reign of James I the first stirrings of another religious reform were evident as people became disenchanted with the Church of England. Twenty years later they began to leave England for the Americas where they could practice their religion unhindered. Under Cromwell, Puritanism was imposed upon the Church of England, but the restoration of Charles II in 1660 and the Act of Uniformity saw the re-imposition of the former liturgy. Many resented this and left their parish churches as a protest, so the Nonconformist movement grew rapidly, but persecution soon followed. Charles II gave a temporary Indulgence, but it was quickly withdrawn. Finally, in 1687 King James II issued his Declaration of Indulgence giving the Nonconformists leave to meet and worship. The Toleration Act of 1689 gave orthodox Nonconformists statutory freedom, enabling them to build the first meeting houses.

After the temporary Indulgence, it is known that by 1672 Nonconformists were worshipping in Sidmouth at the house of a widow, Jane French, and at Bucklye, Sidbury, the home of Richard Carslake. Descendants of this Nonconformist family remained for 250 years supporters of Sidmouth's Old Meeting.

Samuel Stodden, a staunch Nonconformist, living in Sidbury (1672) and Sidmouth (1693), was a member of the Exeter Assembly and described himself as 'Medico-Theologus' – a medical theologian. The Exeter Assembly minutes record that Samuel Stodden had been Minister at what was then known as the 'New Meeting House' in the present location at Sidmouth where Mr William Palk was ordained as Minister on 17 October 1705. But the next year, the Exeter minutes record a dispute involving Sidmouth's congregation. This was over the 'newly erected Meeting Place' which those in Sidbury felt should have been built at Sidford to serve both communities.

After Samuel Stoddon senior's death in 1706, the dispute rumbled on with claim and counter claim involving Stoddon's son and a Mr Serle, who claimed that the Meeting House and dwelling house (presumably for the Minister) at Sidmouth had been left to them under Samuel Stoddon (senior's) Will and had cost £214.11.8 (£214.58). At a further Exeter Assembly in 1708, the two men were urged to transfer the property to trustees at Sidmouth. No more is heard of the matter, but in 1715 the 'learned and excellent Dr Bennett Stevenson' was settled at Sidmouth and had 250 'hearers' – a sizeable congregation.

During the 18th century, the congregation seems to have flourished. It was drawn not so much from the landed families, who tended to remain in the established church, but from those engaged in commerce, people such as Captain Follett. A member of a family of Nonconformist tenant farmers, he had made money in the Newfoundland fisheries, where the family operated vessels out of Topsham. Other family members, similarly engaged, owned Trepassey Plantation on the west coast of Newfoundland. One of the last members of this family to live in Sidmouth was Abraham Follett, a pillar of the Chapel and, like his forbears, a farmer and shopkeeper.

As the American War of Independence gained momentum, a number of influential colonialists, who were Royalists, left America for Britain: most were Nonconformists; amongst them were Judge Curwen and the Reverend Isaac Smith. Judge Curwen, a Judge of the Admiralty Court of Massachusetts, lodged with a member of the Follett family, so they may already have been acquainted with each other through maritime interests in the New England States. The Reverend Isaac Smith, who was the Judge's friend, graduated from Harvard in 1767, and had been a tutor there until his sudden departure in 1775 for England, where he had a brother. Judge Curwen writes of his friend: 'He was an esteemed preacher and liberal minded man' and like many of the second and third generation American refugees, did not fit easily into English life with its social conventions and were homesick for America. Judge Curwen left in 1784 and, after the peace, so too did the Reverend Isaac Smith, to finish his degree. He later became Librarian at Harvard College from 1789-91, and then Preceptor of Dummer Academy, near Newburyport, Mass.

In the Reverend Butcher's 1820 Guide to Sidmouth, he states: 'The Old Dissenting Chapel is situated at the north entrance of the town, at the corner of Mill Lane. It is a small, white, thatched building, measuring forty-five feet [14m] long and twenty-three [7m] broad. Its exterior appearance is very humble.'

There is also a description of the Old Meeting in 1835 in *A History of the Presbyterian and Baptist Churches in the West of England*:

> …the end of it is in line with the street, yet the traveller sees no sign of a place of worship. It is connected with a dwelling house on one side by a low wall, in which is a door from the street opening into a small yard. From this yard the Meeting House is entered and the interior neatly fitted up.

This would have been the Meeting House to which the Reverend Edmund Butcher was appointed Minister in 1798. He left London through ill health and initially lived at Burscombe, Sidbury. He was not what is called a popular preacher, yet was well-liked and remained throughout the Regency period. He retired in 1820, at which time he was living at 9 Fortfield Terrace which he had just purchased from the Reverend William Cockburn. He had been gifted land by his friend, Emmanuel Baruh Lousada on which he built 'Helens' in Cotmaton Road where he lived for some years with his family. Gradually his religious views altered and he embraced Unitarianism. On his retirement, a presentation of plate was made by the congregation recording their 'gratitude for his invaluable pastoral services during 20 years'. His health deteriorated while he was living at 9 Fortfield Terrace. He became well-known as the author of Sidmouth's first guide books. Originally apprenticed to a linen draper in London, a friendship with the Reverend Hugh Worthington led him to train for the Nonconformist ministry at Daventry Academy and, after some time at Sowerby, Yorkshire, he returned to live in London at Leather Lane, Holborn, before circumstance brought him to Sidmouth. (See also the chapter on 9 Fortfield Terrace.)

At the Old Meeting, he was succeeded as Minister by Mr ML Yates, who had been a shipper and dealer in limestone. In 1807 with William Good he established the Exmouth and General Bank. Following close on the death of his wife in 1811, came failure of the Bank and his business assets had to be sold to defray debts. Fortunately he owned some property which included 'Fairlynch' at Budleigh Salterton and in due course he decided to train for the Ministry. He remained as Minister until 1825, when he moved to Cullompton to take up his Ministry, dying there in 1847. Nonconformity had now grown so much in popularity in Sidmouth that a second Chapel had been built at the west side of the Marsh, the present day Ham.

Lady Lockyer, younger sister of Miss Annie Leigh Browne, recalled the Old Meeting in the 1860s, before it was altered.

She and her sister used to stay with their grandparents, Commander and Mrs John Carslake, and accompany their grandmother, Tomazine, in her bath-chair to morning service. There was also an afternoon service at 3 o'clock, but no evening service, for lighting in the chapel was by candle only and a large Dutch chandelier was then in use. Later, oil lamps were installed. The music for the hymns was provided by two men, one with a cello and the other with a violin, usually much out of tune. There were high pews, each with a little door forming almost a small room and furnished with red cushions. High straw footstools were provided which the children liked to stand on so they could look out over the top of the pew. In 1880 these high pews were lowered.

A report in a newspaper *The Inquirer* of 1886 tells more of the circumstances then pertaining:

> Adjoining the Old Meeting and indeed covered by the same thatched roof, was a house built as a parsonage, but which was converted into an inn [the White Hart] at a time when it was not regarded as a scandal to seek support for religion from the higher rent which is obtained from traders of intoxicants. The public house became a nuisance to the neighbourhood.

List of benefactors (SVA)

The rent obtained of £28 had been enough to pay the Minister's stipend. About two years previously, the landlady had died from a fall, but nothing could be done to abate this nuisance because the lease had not expired, but the Local Board came to the rescue, by offering to buy the house, so Mill Lane could be widened and the junction with High Street improved. Mill Lane was now re-named 'All Saints Road'. The land not required, they sold back to the Chapel's Trustees.

The Trustees, with the money so obtained, together with funds initially raised for the purpose of converting the Inn to shops, began work to rebuild the Old Meeting. The Chapel was given a new roof, a new front wall, gothic windows, a new porch and carved barge boards on the front gable: the walls all white painted, but the interior still retained much of its former character including the high pulpit and gallery. On her death in 1936, Miss Annie Leigh Browne, left a sum of money for the building of a new schoolroom adjoining the Chapel which later became a hall. Currently the Chapel has only a small congregation, but is still in use.

Julia Creeke

48 THE OLD SHIP

This tavern was a rendezvous for smugglers and a place for storing contraband wine and brandy. It closed as a public house in 2011.

The former Old Ship Inn is one of the oldest of Sidmouth's buildings, reputedly dating from the late 15th century, originally grouped with others around the Parish Church. Being higher ground, this area was less at risk from flooding, as to the east the land was marshy since the River Sid flowed to sea further west than now. By the 17th century, the building was probably being used as a tavern, for it seems to have become a haunt for those engaged in smuggling. At least one passage, now bricked up, led towards Church Path and another to what was later the grounds of Blackmore Hall.

By the last half of the 18th century, the British aristocracy and wealthy merchants had developed a taste for fine wine and brandy, and whenever war with France erupted, supplies were curtailed. The local fishermen, whose trade gave them an intimate knowledge of the coast and whose livelihood was always uncertain, could find an additional source of income if they could clandestinely land such goods, and any part of the coast remote from authority and with sheltered beaches was an ideal location for smuggling. In the earlier part of the 18th century, the major smuggling was conducted further east in Kent, Sussex and Hampshire, but as the authorities there became more effective at breaking up and arresting the gangs, so smuggling moved further west.

By the time of the Napoleonic Wars, the shortage of wine and brandy was so acute that fortunes could be made dealing in contraband. With wages depressed and prices rising due to the effects on the economy of war in both Europe and America, many in East Devon were prepared to become involved, in spite of the risks they ran if caught – often impressment into the Navy. Surprisingly, there is little evidence of Sidmouth's fishermen being directly involved; perhaps they already had an additional income source providing boat trips and ferrying visitors to other coastal locations which mitigated against involvement in smuggling. Also, the beach was exposed and open to public gaze. However, there is some evidence of involvement by the local population in the distribution of the ill-gotten gains landed in the area, particularly in Salcombe Regis. Beer was the 'mecca' of local smuggling with the Rattenbury family at the forefront. In the 1840s there was an affray on Sidmouth beach involving Rattenbury's son and his accomplices who had been apprehended for smuggling, although by this time they had sunk the kegs offshore.

Originally, the Preventive Service was land-based and consisted of the Riding Officers under the direction of the Customs Service, whilst the sea-going side operated the Revenue cutters under the Board of Excise. In 1822 the two services were combined together into the Coast Guard and with an influx of small ex-naval ships now surplus to requirements, and large numbers of men no longer required by the Navy, the new Coast Guard Service was relatively better manned and equipped and therefore better able to perform its role.

In the 19th century, smuggling gradually declined as the Coast Guard men grew more efficient, numerous and better equipped, and also as more and more wines and spirits were imported in the bottle instead of the cask. The four-gallon casks strung together could easily be flung overboard and recovered later should the Revenue cutter hove into sight – glass bottles could not be similarly treated.

In 1810, David Gould, the Solicitor acting for the Manor, tried to buy the Ship Inn from Captain Jenkins, who had inherited the Manor from his great uncle, Thomas Jenkins of Rome, but finding that as a result of the latter's poorly drawn up Italian Will, the title was suspect, David Gould took Captain Jenkins to court. On 1 August 1810, the court ruled that David Gould should pay Captain Jenkins the sum of £5,190 and that the dwelling, garden and stables be conveyed before 29 September. The protagonists, however, settled their differences amicably and the sale never took place, but it gives a good idea of the value of property at the time. Probably here there was greater value than normal because of what could be made from involvement with the smugglers.

The Ship was at the heart of the distribution network for smuggled goods in Sidmouth, most of the local worthies being the smugglers' customers. Indeed people like the Leighs at Slade House actually assisted the smugglers in hiding the contraband in their cellars before it was transported further inland. No doubt they had free supplies as recompense for their co-operation. Even the Magistrates, with one hand administered the justice if the smugglers were caught and with the other hand were the smugglers' customers. Almost every hostelry in Sidmouth was involved in some way even if it was only selling smuggled brandy.

In time, the Ship fell out of use as a tavern and sank to a notorious doss-house for vagrants, who cooked in one room on the ground floor and slept in a large dormitory upstairs. On one occasion, a man with a performing bear arrived seeking accommodation, but the inmates became so alarmed at the presence of a bear in their midst that a police constable had to be called and eventually the man was persuaded to seek accommodation elsewhere. For many years The Old Ship returned to its former use as a popular tavern, but with changing times it became less profitable and closed. Into the 21st century, it found a new use as a coffee house.

Julia Creeke

The Old Ship (SVA)

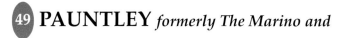

49 PAUNTLEY *formerly The Marino and*
MARINO LODGE *formerly Pauntley Cottage*

The Marino was a late Georgian house, set within beautiful gardens, with eminent owners over time. It has always been noted for the singular beauty of its cottage orné lodge on the opposite side of the road.

As you come down Cotmaton Road (originally called Mill Lane) from Peak Hill and before the crossroads with Bickwell Valley, on the left there stands a pretty little thatched cottage orné with a rustic verandah, a conical roof, and pointed arched windows, with a little thatched extension, which looks as if it might once have been a toll house. This is actually not so: it started life as 'the lodge to the Reverend Mr Hobson's', the owner of the big house on the other side of the road called 'The Marino', now called 'Pauntley'.

The Marino was a handsome late Georgian house of grey render under a slate roof with twin bays and a verandah over-looking 'a beautiful lawn and with a shrubbery, conservatory and walled garden'. A slightly later guide book of 1838 adds:

The Mansion, the well-designed and highly finished house of the Reverend Mr James Hobson. This gentleman has at great

Marino Lodge (SVA)

expense added much to the appearance of the house and the immediate neighbourhood. It stands at the summit of a sloping meadow enjoying a fine reach of ocean scenery and has a pretty rustic lodge situated opposite the entrance.

The Marino was admired not only for its garden, but for the beauty and uniqueness of its lodge, known now as 'Marino Lodge'. The guide book to Sidmouth published in 1817 and written by the Reverend Edmund Butcher says 'the Lodge belonging to the Mansion, which stands opposite the entrance into the grounds in Mill Lane, is an object of universal admiration'. It was admired then, and it still is, 200 years later. A guide of 1832 gives some idea of why it was considered so attractive: 'The ivy which creeps up its slender pillars and hangs in festoons from its roof gives it a simple elegance'.

Mr Hobson was to live in the The Marino for 50 years, dying in April 1860 at the age of 91. He is known to have been living at The Marino in 1810, although in 1816 he purchased the freehold of 2 Fortfield Terrace, along with the coach house and stables. Whether this was for his own use or to let is not recorded.

His first wife died in 1820, and he subsequently married a second time, his widow dying a few months after him. He does not feature much in the life of the town, although we know from a letter sent by Elizabeth Barrett (Browning) to her friend Mrs Martin that from time to time he called on them. It appears that he was never involved in the religious life of the town. He was interested in promoting education for the poor and was one of the ten guinea (a guinea being 21/- or £1.05p) subscribers to the Society for Promoting the Education of the Poor in Ireland, having been brought up in that country in Kilkenny.

In the late 19th century, Major Edward Hicks owned the house. He died of internal injuries after being thrown from his horse-drawn carriage outside the gates in February 1884. He was an ex-officer of the Bengal Infantry and was land agent to the Trustees of Lord of the Manor in Sidmouth.

In the late 1890s, John Tindall moved into The Marino with his family when he retired from Leighton Buzzard Bank, where

The garden front of Pauntley in the mid 19th century (Sidmouth Museum)

he was a partner. In due course he became a very influential person in the town. His daughter, Mary, died at The Marino in 1917, the only woman named on the WWI memorial plaque in Sidmouth Parish Church. She was a Red Cross military nurse, stationed in Exeter. The Tindall parents moved after the war to Cotmaton House. (More about John Tindall's time in Sidmouth can be found at the end of the chapter on Cotmaton Old Hall).

In 1923 a family by the name of Whittington, who were direct descendants of Dick Whittington, thrice Lord Mayor of London in mediaeval times, moved in. It was they who changed the name of the house to 'Pauntley', the name of the village where they had lived previously.

Pauntley later became the seaside home of the 3rd Viscount and Viscountess Hambleden. The Viscount's grandfather founded WH Smith & Sons, the stationers, although the family's connection with newspapers went right back to 1800. It was when the railways started to proliferate nationally that his ancestor obtained franchises for newspaper stalls on stations, boosting the family fortune, and ultimately allowed William Henry Smith to found the company WH Smith & Sons Ltd. He became an MP, Cabinet Minister and leader of the House of Commons. He died before a peerage was conferred and Queen Victoria granted this to his wife, Emily Danvers Smith, who became a Vicountess. It was the Second Viscount who inherited his father's Devon estate, became Chairman of WH Smith, and whose fortune built Mortonhampstead Manor (now Bovey Castle Hotel).

With the outbreak of WW2, Pauntley became the first big house in Sidmouth to be taken over and turned into a hostel to accommodate evacuated children from the East End of London. Pauntley had the distinction of being the first house in the country with a nursery centre for toddlers, thus allowing their mothers to go to work. The surrounding land was turned into allotments for the duration.

After the war, the Hambledens did not return to Pauntley, and Viscount Hambleden sold the house, which was converted to flats. He gave 'Pauntley Lodge', the little thatched cottage, to Sidmouth Urban District Council, with the condition that his chauffeur could live there as long as he wished. It soon became celebrated as the most charming and unique council house in the country.

In 1974, on the reorganisation of local government, it passed into the hands of East Devon District Council who finally sold it to the tenant, subject to strict conditions. With the building of a small new single-story house in the grounds of Pauntley, called 'Pauntley Lodge' the name of the much admired little thatched cottage reverted to a modern version of its original name 'The Lodge to The Marino', and it is now called simply 'Marino Lodge'. It remains one of Sidmouth's most singular and unique buildings and is Listed Grade 2.

Julia Creeke

In an early 19th century aquatint when called 'the lodge to the Marino' (Sidmouth Museum)

50 PEAK HOUSE

The original house was built in 1788 by Emmanuel Baruh Lousada, a London merchant of Jewish heritage. It became seminal to Sidmouth's rapid rise to become a desirable society resort, because Lousada was hospitable and influential. After a fire in 1903 the house was rebuilt by Sir Thomas Dewey, President of Prudential Insurance. Now converted into flats.

As late as the 1760s, Sidmouth remained a big village whose inhabitants made a living farming, fishing and shopkeeping, with some merchant families like the Follets and a few houses of minor gentry, like the Carslakes of Cotmaton. (More about the Carslakes of Cotmaton can be found in a separate chapter.) The mediaeval pattern of settlement was still evident with the farmhouses located intermittently along the streets, with the fields spread around the outskirts. The settlement was huddled behind the big shingle embankment which made up the back of the beach. All the houses close to the beach turned their backs to the sea. But things were about to start to change and, by the end of the 18th century, that change in Sidmouth was becoming rapid – it was on its way to becoming a fashionable small town.

One of the things which may have helped to kick-start this era of rapid change for Sidmouth was the building of one particular house – Peak House. The story began on 9 October 1788 when a gentleman of Jewish heritage by the name of

The original Peak House. From Butcher's 1820 guide to Sidmouth (Sidmouth Museum)

Emmanuel Baruh Lousada leased for one year at a rent of 5/- (25p) and then, next day, bought from Sir William Pole (who owned the Manor of Old Hayes, now Woodlands), Pick's Tenement, containing a house, garden and orchards and about twenty acres (8 ha) of land.

This was a remarkable purchase in view of Lousada's Jewish heritage. Few Jews in late 18th century England were buying land or a house because of uncertainty of their legal rights. However, those with wealth and confidence, as in Lousada's case, were usually successful. Property ownership went hand-in-hand with civil rights and full emancipation did not occur until 1890. Why Lousada decided to make this purchase in Sidmouth has remained a mystery. All that might be surmised is that Lousada thought that Sidmouth's surroundings were very attractive, far from London, relatively unknown and hoped his purchase might go un-noticed. He could have had little idea of what would happen to Sidmouth in the next thirty years and the way it would change the town forever.

Lousada's Sephardic ancestors hailed from Spain and Portugal where the family was of great rank. The Inquisition expelled the people of Jewish faith, while others fled, some to Jamaica and others to Livorno in Italy. Jamaica was still a Spanish possession and there they probably hoped to escape the horrors of the Inquisition. Those who went to Livorno rapidly became successful traders with the Levant, and before long some of them migrated to Amsterdam, at the time capital of the greatest trading nation in Europe. From there at least one member of the family came to London and, in the time of Cromwell, is recorded in a list of aliens living in the City of London. In the reign of Charles II, he was one of the three Wardens of the London Synagogue. Those of Jewish faith became Members of the Royal Exchange. They were not allowed to trade within the building but were granted an area under the portico which became known as the 'Jewish Walk'. In 1697, a new set of rules was instituted which limited the Jewish brokers to twelve in number. Among the licenses granted was one to Moses Baruh Lousada. Thereafter, the name disappears in London and the story crosses the Atlantic to the Caribbean.

In 1655, Jamaica was ceded by Spain to Great Britian and with that the Spanish residents became part of Britain's colonial empire. They had amassed large land holdings and continued to live on their estates in great style. It was from the now very wealthy Lousada family, resident in Jamaica, that Emmanuel Baruh Lousada was descended. His grandfather, also an Emmanuel Baruh Lousada, had moved on to live in Barbados, becoming a wealthy merchant exporting sugar and rum back to Britain on behalf of the plantation owners and importing goods to supply their needs. He died in Barbados in 1768.

Round about 1730 he sent one of his sons, Jacob Baruh Lousada, to London, probably to act as agent to receive and sell on the sugar and rum shipped by the West Indian merchants. He settled in London, marrying Abigail Lamego, daughter of Issac Lamego, another wealthy Jewish resident with an estate in Berkshire. It was to this couple in 1744 that Emmanuel Baruh Lousada (of Sidmouth) was born. Meanwhile, Jacob's brother, another Emmanuel Baruh Lousada, had plantations in Jamaica, which were inherited by his son, yet another holder of this same name. He was to marry the sister of the 'Sidmouth' Lousada – so his cousin was married to his sister. This was typical of these wealthy Sephardic families who lived within a close coterie of inter-family relationships.

Emmanuel Baruh Lousada married in 1778, Rebecca Ximines, the daughter of yet another wealthy Portuguese Jewish resident of Berkshire, and they settled in the Parish of St Martin's-in-the-Fields. Later the couple were to occupy a house at 4 The Adelphi. The Adelphi was designed by Robert Adam and at the time was one of London's smartest addresses, and has escaped demolition.

Emmanuel Baruh Lousada of Sidmouth was in partnership with David Barrow as 'Barrow & Lousada', whose business was principally with the West Indies. In the early 1780s, Lousada was part owner with David Barrow of a West Indiaman. He was also a subscriber to the London Dock Company and a board member of the Hon. East India Company. The fortune that was to build Peak House was therefore likely to have been based on sugar and rum. His wife Rebecca too was a member of another wealthy Sephardic family. These families formed a small but very influential group in the City of London and it was their fortunes that had helped sustain the Government financially when the War with America erupted in 1776.

Shortly after purchasing the 20 acres (8 ha) on Peak Hill, Emmanuel Baruh Lousada started construction of a house for his own occupation, looking across the valley with beautiful views of Salcombe Hill and the eastern cliffs. It was constructed of brick with a three-storey central block and a two-storey wing on either side. This house was the most influential property ever built in Sidmouth because it was almost certainly the catalyst to the development of the town. This was because Lousada was a man of influence and his wealthy friends and family members came to visit him. News of Sidmouth's delights was carried away in their memories to reach a wider audience. The fashion for the picturesque and the seaside was then fast developing and Sidmouth could offer both a romantic landscape and a beautiful coast. It was not long before Sidmouth's fame spread far and wide, bringing an ever increasing number of wealthy aristocrats and people of influence to sample its charms. Some of them were also to be captivated and built houses of their own.

Emmanuel Baruh Lousada, who now owned one of the finest houses in Sidmouth, continued to buy more land to add to his estate, so that towards the end of his life he had become one of the largest landholders in the town. He built several other houses, occupied by his relatives, and even Thomas Jenkins, the Lord of the Manor, had to buy land from Lousada in order to be able to construct Fortfield Terrace.

Lousada was extremely well-liked in the town and was a generous host. He was a member of various local committees and was honoured by John Wallis when he dedicated the famous Long Print of Sidmouth to 'Emmanuel Baruh Lousada'. Numbered amongst Lousada's friends was the Reverend Edmund Butcher, Minister at the Old Meeting, to whom Lousada gave a plot of land close to the upper gate of Peak House, so he might build a house for himself. It was an amazing friendship – a wealthy person of Jewish faith and a Nonconformist Minister. It seemed his ministry found favour with this influential gentleman who enjoyed the Reverend Butcher's society as well as his ministerial services so much, that he presented him with this valuable piece of ground near his own mansion.

Sadly, Lousada and his wife, Rebecca, had no children and when she died in 1820 he missed her greatly, the more so since his old friend, the Reverend Butcher, whose health was again failing, had left Sidmouth. Lousada however continued to involve himself in local life and, following the terrible storm of November 1824, he formed a Committee and set up a Subscription Fund at Barings Bank to aid those in the town who had lost everything, both homes and livelihood.

Peter Orlando Hutchinson recalled, in an 1876 Diary entry, a memory from his childhood: 'He was a very tired old man, and though I was a mere boy, he would invite me up to dinner without my father and mother'.

Peak House 1870 (Sidmouth Museum)

When his Arms were granted, they showed a bird with a sprig of sugar cane in its beak as a reference to his West Indian connections.

Unlike his wife, who was buried in the Sephardic Jewish Cemetery at Mile End, London, Lousada intended to be buried in the grounds of Peak House, and had himself selected the site where he wished to be interred. However, on his own death in 1832 at the age of 88, his family went entirely against his wishes and demanded that he too be buried at Mile End Cemetery. When he died, the Peak Estate encompassed all the land surrounding Peak House to the cliff edge as far up Peak Hill as Peak Cottage, and eastwards down to what was a rough track leading from the lane up Peak Hill, in later years part of Manor Road. This land included several houses, such as Belmont, Rosemount and Clifton Cottage. This latter had been built many years previously as a summer house where the Lousadas could take their guests for picnics. With increasing age, they had used it less and it was converted to a small cottage and let to Henry Haseler. He was a local artist and drawing master responsible for many watercolours of Sidmouth which were made into prints for selling to visitors to the town.

Emmanuel Baruh Lousada left a considerable fortune and, being childless, by his Will, Peak House and his land holdings passed to his brother, Isaac's, son, yet another Emmanuel Baruh Lousada. Although his uncle's fortune was made by trade with Britain's Caribbean colonies, there is no evidence that he had any direct connection with the plantations and therefore with slave ownership. The same could not be said of his nephew, who owned both plantations and slaves, as is evidenced by his applications to the Courts on two separate occasions for compensation for the loss of his slaves when slavery was abolished throughout the British Empire.

He had a sister Abigail Lousada (1772-1833), who remained unmarried and lived in London. She was a scholar and mathematician of unusual ability for a woman of her generation. She was the owner of a rare mathematical treatise, *Megarensis (Elements of Geometry)* by the Greek scholar Euclid, in the Paris edition, published in 1664. She also translated into English the mathematical works of Diophantes of Alexandria, which was a study into the history of Greek algebra. Although this was loaned to a fellow mathematician and intended for publication, this never came about, although she did publish some other mathematical papers under her own name.

As well as Peak House, he also had a London house. He had built Cliff Cottage in 1821 on the cliff-top site (now Connaught Gardens), which was part of his uncle's estate. He now let Cliff Cottage to the Kent family (more about them can be found in the chapter on Connaught Gardens). He made major alterations to Peak House, particularly the exterior. The red bricks were soft and the surface had begun to suffer from the effects of the salt laden winds. The second storey of the central block was removed, the exterior was faced and a large pillared porch in the then fashionable Greek Revival style was added to the garden front, making the appearance of the house unrecognisable from the Georgian house he had inherited.

Whereas his uncle had for forty years played a prominent part in the life of Sidmouth, this next Emmanuel Baruh Lousada was less heavily involved. He did however allow the field – which is now the Manor Road Car Park – to be used for archery practice by the Archery Club, and for many years thereafter it was known as the 'Archery Field'.

Like his uncle, he and his wife were also childless. By the time he died in 1853 he had amassed a very considerable fortune of £103,000. He left Peak House and much of this fortune to his nephew, John Lousada, who had left the Jewish faith and become a Christian. He was involved in the Parish Church and with various local committees. His sister, Mary, had married the son the Victorian sculptor, John Bacon, who lived at Sidcliff, and Bacon made two very charming pencil drawings of his daughter-in-law which still exist.

John Lousada, having inherited a considerable fortune, did not have the business acumen of his ancestors. In 1866, he let Peak House for two years to Richard Napoleon Thornton and his new bride, whilst substantial alterations were being made to Knowle Cottage which Thornton had just purchased.

Unfortunately, John Lousada made a number of poor investments, made worse by a financial recession, that greatly diminished his fortune and resulted in his having to sell Peak House. The auction took place on 18 September 1879. The buyer was the Trustees of the Manor Estates who intended to make large scale developments on the land, but fortunately these plans came to naught. There was general disquiet when the town learned that, instead, they had let it to some recently displaced French Jesuits. At the time it was said there were only four Roman Catholics in Sidmouth. These Jesuits used the house for training students for the priesthood, but were seldom seen and caused no trouble. When the foundation stone of the Convent Chapel was laid, they formed part of the procession. They were to remain for just three years before moving on to Hastings in 1883. The Manor Trustees then decided, in 1891, to rid themselves of the Peak House Estate whose grounds then totalled 24 acres (9.7 ha) with an additional 10½ acres (4.3 ha) of pasture plus some further acreages of land. The estate was sold to Miss Marion Kennedy of New Milton, Hampshire.

Miss Kennedy's tenure lasted just 12 years before she sold the Estate to Sir Thomas Charles Dewey Bart., by Conveyance dated 1 July 1903 for the sum of £8,500. Sir Thomas was to become President of the Prudential Assurance Company. He had only just completed the purchase of the house and grounds, and was considering plans for its improvement, when the house caught fire and was badly damaged. In an interview, Sir Thomas said that he 'felt the existing house would prove incommodious for his lifestyle but intended to build a new house on the site'. Demolition of the remains of the old house began shortly afterwards.

Many of the Georgian fittings like fireplaces and mahogany doors which had escaped the fire were removed for storage, and Sir Thomas then engaged the architect, Evelyn A Hellicar ARIBA. Hellicar was noted for his architectural scholarship, his church architecture (he was diocesan architect for Rochester Cathedral) and for the design of small country houses. The result was a dignified and pleasing house faced in Beer Stone, using many of the best fittings from the Georgian house. The new house, though, was built on a slightly different site from the old house, with a south-easterly view across the sea to Portland, views of Salcombe Hill and the eastern cliffs. It was not particularly large for an Edwardian country house and the garden front downstairs consisted only of a dining room, morning room, a through hall which opened onto a terrace, study and drawing room, with a long black and white marble-floored corridor at the back, connecting the rooms.

In later life, Sir Thomas used Peak House mainly in the summer months, as his main residence was at South Hill Wood, Bromley, Kent. Sir Thomas was very much a self-made man. He was born at Cheshunt, Hertfordshire, came to London as a young lad, and joined the Prudential as a junior clerk in 1857. At the

Sir Thomas Charles Dewey, by Bassano Ltd. 1920 (National Portrait Gallery)

time, the Prudential was a young company struggling for its very existence. The recently appointed Company Secretary, Mr Henry Harben (soon to become Sir Henry) noticed the lad's talent and, young as he was, made him his Chief Assistant. The path for Sir Thomas was set and it was to be ever upwards, and at just 34 he was installed as Industrial Branch Manager. He became General Manager in 1874, a position he still held when he completed 50 years of service to the company. He joined the Board of Directors as Deputy Chairman, becoming Chairman in 1910 and, in 1922, President, of a now large and flourishing business.

Sir Thomas was a born leader, firm of character and sure in decision-making, but he was also tolerant and generous, resorting far more often to praise than admonition. He was extremely popular with his staff and kept in constant touch with his superintendents and their assistants. He was a member of the Institute of Actuaries and had an incredible and quick grasp of figures. He was not particularly tall, with a handsome face, regular features, ruddy complexion and piercing blue eyes. He had a soft but well-modulated voice which carried well when he had to address large meetings, and walked with a quick springy step.

Sir Thomas generously offered the use of the house to be converted into a Red Cross Hospital in the Great War, as there

The rebuilt Peak House used in WW1 as a VAD Hospital (Sidmouth Museum)

was a desperate need for hospitals to accommodate the increasing number of casualties. He also agreed to continue to pay the taxes, rates and electricity. The hospital opened on 25 November 1916 with 53 beds divided between the three floors. When the first patients arrived at Sidmouth Station they were greeted by a considerable and curious crowd. The local paper reported the arrival of the injured, but concluded their report by saying: 'It is hoped that on future arrivals, that all except those having business at the station will have the good taste to stay away'.

Soon afterwards a large temporary building and two marquees were erected in the grounds and the total number of beds increased to 100. X-ray facilities and an operating theatre were installed. On 1 June 1917 the hospital achieved 'First Line' status, from which date convoys of patients were directly received from overseas.

The clinical staff included three medical officers and a consulting surgeon. There were also two matrons, ten sisters, eight staff nurses, a masseuse and an X-ray assistant. The main ward workforce consisted of 38 VAD (Volunteer Aid Detachment) nurses whose uniform was similar to the trained nurses with a red cross, but the sleeves were a light colour rather than dark blue. There were also volunteers running the laundry and kitchen services, as well as domestic cleaning. Sir Thomas continued to pay his gardening staff and allowed all produce to be used by the patients.

The medical costs were centrally funded, but other costs, including furniture, crockery, linen, periodicals, books and tobacco were provided by the Sidmouth community. Ambulant patients could visit the Ellis Little Cinema on Fore Street, free of charge, and were recognised by the required uniform for privates and NCOs which consisted of 'convalescent blues'; officers were permitted to wear their own uniform but with a blue armband.

The hospital was open for 26 months and during that time cared for 1,141 patients. It closed on 1 February 1919. At that time, Peak House was one of the largest VAD hospitals in Devon.

A Grand Fête was held at Peak House on August Bank Holiday 1922. This was to raise funds for the building of the War Memorial Club for returning veterans. Attractions included an aerial railway, a mile of pennies, a 'monster whist drive, maypole dancing, skittle alley, sports for children, dancing on the lawn 8pm till midnight, and a monster firework display.' Sidmouth certainly knew how to enjoy itself.

Sir Thomas Dewey was a man with an indefinable 'presence'. Devoted to the welfare of his business and its employees, he nevertheless found time for church work, municipal duties and charitable work. When he died in 1924 it was said that he was 'un-rivalled in his generosity, but used riches and success wisely and well'. He left a considerable fortune amounting to over £400,000.

In his Will, Sir Thomas Dewey left his property divided between his two children and a nephew. He left bequests including £2,000 to Sidmouth Parochial Church Council, £1,000 to the Building Fund of the Church Schools in Sidmouth, £1,000 to Sidmouth Cottage Hospital towards the building of a new wing, subject to an assurance being given to his Trustees, that no patient in the ordinary wards shall be called upon to pay any fees for medical attendance whilst in hospital. There were personal bequests too, with a life annuity of £100 to his housekeeper at Peak House, Mrs Louisa French, and two years wages to his outdoor staff with ten years service. He left his portrait by Herkomer, his bust by March, his silver gilt presentation desert service, a beautiful lace wedding veil and all the family silver to his son, Stanley. This was his only son – Sir Stanley Dewey – and he purchased their share of Peak House from his sister and nephew, becoming the sole owner on 29 April 1927. For the next 20 years, his family enjoyed life in Peak House but, with the outbreak of WW2, life for the Deweys changed. They played their part in the local war effort and there were lighter moments, such as the hay-making parties in the summer for children who lived nearby. However, shortly after the war, the Deweys sold the house to Mr Louis Lee.

This was not to be the end of the Dewey family's association with Sidmouth because, in 1957, his grandson purchased St Mary's, Hillside Road, a house originally designed by RW Sampson for two unmarried sisters. The Dewey family used the house mainly for holidays and remained for over 20 years before selling up.

Mr Lee made the west wing of Peak House into two flats, thereby reducing the size of the main house. He sold off the two lodges as separate dwellings and the Cliff Fields passed to Sidmouth UDC as public open space. Mr Lee lived quietly in the house for 30 years. He became well-known locally for the early new potatoes which he grew in the walled garden and which were sold in a local greengrocer's shop in the Market Place to a queue of willing purchasers.

By the mid 1970s, Mr Lee was finding the house too large and the contents of Peak House were auctioned off; Mr Lee moving to a small cottage in the Stable Courtyard, to the west of the house, where he lived for the remainder of his life. In his Will he left the walled garden to provide the site for a house for a retired member of the clergy. Peak House was sold on 19 October 1979 to Mr Anthony Barlow. The house was given Grade 2 listing in August 1980, preventing any significant alterations. By chance, a Mr and Mrs Philip Nicholas, who lived in a house on the Hatfield Estate, Hertfordshire, decided that they wanted to retire to a cottage by the sea. Since Mrs Jill Nicholas was disabled by osteoporosis, Philip, who had been a property developer and was of some means, set out to look for a suitable house located anywhere between Poole and Salcombe. He stopped in Sidmouth and by chance his driver took him to the wrong address and drove up to the front of Peak House where he met Anthony Barlow. Philip enquired if he had a property to sell and, after some consideration, Mr Barlow agreed to sell the ground floor. It was a happy coincidence.

Philip Nicholas carried out some minor alterations and he and Jill moved into the ground floor garden front flat. They came to love Sidmouth and the views of the coast and countryside enjoyed by their flat gave them constant pleasure, since Jill, who was in almost constant pain, seldom went out. It wasn't very long before Philip turned from a 'poacher and became a game keeper', since the SVA found his talents very useful, and he helped them try and stop a number of unsightly developments. He was instrumental in the negotiations with Exeter University which saved the Sir Norman Lockyer Observatory (NLO – see separate chapter) for Sidmouth.

Sadly he and Jill were not to enjoy Peak House for very many years and shortly after Philip's death, Jill suffered a stroke from which she made a reasonable recovery, but she decided the flat was too big and she moved further down Cotmaton Road to a cottage that Philip had purchased not long before his death. Jill became a wonderful benefactor. She gave £140,000 to Sidmouth Cottage Hospital to provide a new X-ray unit and endowed the Philip Nicholas Memorial Lectureship in Maritime History at Hull University in Philip's memory, thereby allowing the University to teach a degree in Maritime History in all but name.

Philip had a lifelong interest in maritime history and had a fine collection of both books and model ships, which lined the long marble-floored corridor in Peak House. His pride and joy was an ivory model of a French frigate made by the Dieppe ivory-carvers for the Duke of Orleans. Philip had bought it as a cardboard box full of pieces in an auction in London, and had it restored by the National Maritime Museum's restorer. Jill gave the entire model ship collection to the National Trust, who put them on show at Arlington Court, North Devon. The beautiful ivory model, that was in a glass case in the drawing room at Peak House, now has pride of place among the models at Arlington.

Peak House remains much as Sir Thomas Dewey built it, although the estate is now much reduced in size. Much of the land originally owned by Emmanuel Baruh Lousada has been built on and the Sidmouth Golf Course occupies a large area of the higher land on Peak Hill. After WW2, the Sidmouth UDC purchased the old Archery Field which is now the Manor Road Car Park, and East Devon District Council has a 101 year lease of Peak Meadow which is overlooked by the house. This prominently-sited house has played a seminal role in Sidmouth's history and development – in fact it could well be 'The House which started it all'.

Julia Creeke

51 ROYAL GLEN HOTEL *formerly Woolbrook Cottage*

A fine late 18th century Gothic villa with Regency interior. It was rented over Christmas 1819 by the Duke of Kent (4th son of King George III), the Duchess and their baby daughter Victoria (the future Queen Victoria). The Duke died of pneumonia a month after arrival.

In mediaeval times, there were three main areas of cultivated land locally: the Sea Fields, the Fort Fields and Western Fields. From a map of the Manor drawn at the time of its sale to Thomas Jenkins in 1787, it was clear that the mediaeval strip pattern was still extant and probably in use. Between these three groups of fields was a narrow wooded dell, sheltered and well watered by the Woolbrook, an ideal situation for a dwelling and, sometime between the late 17th and mid 18th centuries, a farmstead existed which in 1775 was still part of Manor Lands. Around this time it was acquired by a Mr King of Bath, who transformed this building into a picturesque Sidmouth Gothic Villa, with fashionable interiors – the delightful first floor drawing room is oval – and he named the house 'King's Cottage'.

In 1816 it was purchased by the mother of Major-General Baynes, who made some improvements and re-named it 'Woolbrook Cottage'.

On 24 May 1819, the Duchess of Kent gave birth to Princess Victoria. The Duchess was suffering from rheumatism and was

The house at the time of the Duke and Duchess of Kent's visit in 1819. From an aquatint of 1816 (Sidmouth Museum)

recommended tepid seawater baths by her physician, and the sea air of Devon was recommended to the Duke as of benefit to his wife and daughter. Besides, extensive renovations were planned for their apartments at Kensington Palace, which he proposed in future to make his permanent residence in order to save money. He was planning to sell his huge estate at Castle Hill Lodge, Ealing, to help repay his spiralling debts.

The Duke therefore employed an Exeter solicitor, Mr Turner, to look for houses in the fashionable areas of East Devon suitable for their accommodation. By October a short list had been made and, like any good husband, the Duke decided to inspect them personally. Ending his journey at Sidmouth, he decided 'to give it preference over all other towns in the area', and an agreement was reached with General Baynes to lease 'Woolbrook Cottage'.

The Royal Family with their seven month-old daughter, Victoria, arrived in torrential rain on Christmas Eve 1819 and settled into their winter home, their retinue being lodged at a house in The Fortfield belonging to Mr Rafarel (almost certainly 8 Fortfield Terrace which was called 'Rafarel House'). A soirée was held at which the local nobility and gentry paid their respects to their royal visitors. The local traders were patronised and Princess Victoria's first shoes were made by a Sidmouth shoemaker, John Taylor.

Charlotte Cornish, daughter of George and Sarah Cornish of Salcombe Hill House, wrote in her reminiscences about a visit to the Duke and Duchess. Charlotte's father, George, was Lord of the Manor of Salcombe Regis, and head of one of Sidmouth's leading families who were staunch members of the Established Church. He was a Deputy Lord Lieutenant of Devon, a JP and Major of the Rolle Troop of Yeomanry, so the command to take tea at Woolbrook Cottage on Sunday 6 January 1820 was perhaps not unexpected.

'We have been honoured with an Invitation or rather command to drink tea with the Duchess of Kent on Sunday next. I cannot imagine why she chose that day'. She then goes on to recount the meeting:

At eight o'clock we set off in chairs [presumably sedan chairs] for the Duke of Kent's Woolbrook Cottage. It is the

HRH the Duke of Kent.
Engraving from a painting
by William Beechey, 1818

first time in my life that I ever paid a visit of this kind on Sunday and I hope it will be long before I do so again. The Duke took us by the hand and presented us to the Duchess. We exchanged curtsies and sat down. The Duchess (a German by birth) speaks French. The Duke talks in French, German and English endeavouring to make conversation general. The Duchess nurses the infant herself. They appear very fond of each other.

There was an incident when the window in the infant Victoria's bedroom was broken by a young boy, supposedly shooting birds with a catapult, although some claimed it was a gun that was used. The Duke was very lenient in his reaction to what appeared to be an innocent accident urging that no action be taken against the boy, but asking that he make a promise of 'desisting from such culpable pursuits'.

The weather after Christmas was cold, with snow, and the Duke returned from an outing with his boots wet from the thawing snow, but, wishing to write some urgent letters (his letters from Sidmouth are full of instructions regarding the alterations at the Palace and additional work at his home at Amorbach, Germany) he did not immediately change them. By 9 January he had a feverish cold and a few days later developed pneumonia. His physicians were called but their ministrations probably did more harm than good and, on the morning of Sunday 23 January 1820, he died. Lord Rolle praised the Duchess's devotion, saying that for five days she had remained fully dressed.

The grief-stricken Duchess left Sidmouth with her daughter and attendants on 25 January in very inclement weather, travelling in eight carriages. Six days after the Duke of Kent's death, the ailing King George III died on 29 January and all arrangements for the Duke's funeral had to be immediately cancelled whilst the King's funeral took place. Eventually the new King, George IV, gave instructions for his brother's funeral.

Meantime, in Sidmouth, the Duke's body lay in state at Woolbrook Cottage on Monday 31 January and the two following days. A letter written, again by Charlotte Cornish, gives a vivid picture of the proceedings:

We all went. The room was quite dark except for candles which were larger than any 6 you ever saw and placed on very high candlesticks all round the room. The room was all covered in black and in the middle two coffins: one of which held the body, the other the heart. They were covered in crimson velvet and set with gilt nails all over, a brass plate

Duchess of Kent with Princess Victoria. By William Beechey 1821.
Royal Collection Trust/© Her Majesty Queen Elizabeth II 2019

on each with the Duke's names and titles. At the door were 2 men in black with black flags. Everybody in the place went to see it.

Mr Clench of the London Inn was commissioned to supply the hearse and coaches. The procession which left Woolbrook Cottage at about 9 am on 7 February 1820 was quite splendid. It was led off by the Salcombe Yeomanry riding two and two, followed by four men all in black with black cloaks and mounted, their horses all covered in black. Then came all 20 of the local tradesmen the Duke had employed, all mounted. The band of the 4th Dragoons was composed mostly of buglers and trumpeters. A man carrying a huge plume of black feathers preceded the mourning coach containing the coffin with the Duke's heart, accompanied by Major Parker with an escort of the 4th Light Dragoons. Following that, the hearse drawn by eight horses all caparisoned in black velvet with black plumes on their heads, their saddle cloths bearing the Duke's arms in gold and accompanied by an escort of the 4th Light Dragoons.

Contemporary photo of the Royal Glen Hotel (SVA)

There followed another two mourning coaches, bearing the chief mourners, each pulled by six horses and with an escort of Dragoons and the Duke's travelling chariot all blacked out, with two servants in black on the box, also with an escort on foot each side, and a large party of the 4th Light Dragoons. The procession ended with a further five carriages bearing others, including the Duke's Chaplain, the Rector of Sidmouth and the owner of the Marine Library, Mr Wallis. Finally 24 carriages of the local nobility and gentry followed. The procession left Woolbrook Cottage, went all along the Mall (the

Plaque recording royal associations (SVA)

Esplanade), and up through the town, the band playing the Dead March. It was witnessed by several thousand people (some said 10,000 – a huge crowd for those days) who had travelled from all over the district to see this amazing spectacle.

The procession travelled to Honiton, taking several hours to reach there, whence the local mourners said their farewells and the main cortège went on to Bridport. After three further overnight stops it reached Cumberland Lodge in Windsor Great Park on Friday: the burial taking place the following day.

After this short period of notoriety, Woolbrook Cottage became, once again, the quaint and pleasant residence of the Baynes family, who remained there until 1853. Major-General Edward Baynes, who took over the house from his mother, was a career soldier who first appears in the Army lists as a 1st Lieutenant in September 1771 and seems thereafter to have changed regiments almost as often as he changed shirts. The last regular British regiment in which he served as a Lieutenant-Colonel was the 5th Foot in 1805, after which he seems to have gone to Canada and joined the Nova Scotia Fencible Infantry as a Colonel. In 1812, as the threat of hostilities between the USA and Canada over the Niagara Frontier loomed, the Canadian High Command decided to augment the Canadian Fencible Regiments with another recruited from the Glengarry Infantry which had been disbanded in 1802, and of this new regiment Major-General Baynes took charge. It served throughout the war with the USA and was disbanded at Kingston, Ontario in 1816, after which Major-General Baynes retired from active service and returned to the UK where he settled down to enjoy life at

Woolbrook Cottage, after a short stay at Belmont House. He purchased part of the adjoining Western Fields from the Manor and added it to the grounds, and made some further small improvements to the property. On the death of Mrs Anne-Frances Baynes, Major-General Baynes's widow, the house was sold and the entire contents sold by auction in 1853.

Woolbrook Cottage was visited occasionally by several of Queen Victoria's children, curious to see where their grandfather had died, and where their mother had stayed as a child. Edward, Prince of Wales, came to the house on 1 October 1856, during an educational tour of the South-West. On hearing of the visit, a crowd of locals congregated outside, but the Prince left by a rear door, where a carriage was awaiting him. Through the generosity of Mr Edward Stanford of the Charing Cross Map Depot, who had retired to a house called 'Helens' on Cotmaton Road, a plaque was erected in 1907 recording the royal visits to Woolbrook Cottage.

The house's picturesque situation led to another name change in the late 19th century when it became Woolbrook Glen (finally to become the Royal Glen). The house even had a brief spell as an orphanage between 1878 and 1883 before becoming a guest house.

Its surroundings have altered and most of its original grounds are built over. On the east bank of the Woolbrook, a drive led up to the house, although the main drive followed the line of Glen Road from the north, beginning at Cotmaton Road. The whole length of the drive had public pedestrian access and was known as the 'Grand Walk'. The grounds were extensive, well-wooded and included much of the site of the present Victoria Hotel.

The main elevations of the Royal Glen have altered little since the time of the Kent's visit although there has been a modern extension eastwards at the rear. It is now a hotel and has received its final name the – Royal Glen – but much of its Regency charm remains in the interior. During WW2, it was used by the RAF, like almost all the other hotels in Sidmouth, as a unit of the Medical Training Establishment. Later, the original part of the building was designated a Grade I Listed building.

Julia Creeke

52 ROYAL YORK HOTEL

Sidmouth's first purpose-built hotel. It was visited by the Duke of Kent in 1819 and by the future Edward VII in 1856. The poet Rupert Brooke stayed here in 1909.

In 1800 the area of the eastern promenade was still un-developed rough land where, in the 18th century, ships had been built for the Newfoundland and coastal trades. It was here on the corner site of Fore Street that construction of Sidmouth's first purpose built hotel began about 1807. In the *Exeter Flying Post* of 23 June 1808, the following appears:

R Stone late of the New Inn, Sidmouth, has taken possession of the York Hotel most pleasantly situated on the beach of Sidmouth, and stables known by the name of The Mews a short distance from the hotel. Neat post-chaises, with good horses and careful drivers.

The concept of a hotel where people went to stay for extended periods was a new one in Regency times. Until then those who travelled stayed at an inn (taverns were mostly drinking houses) and those who wished to reside for a time either rented a house or took rooms according to their means. The York Hotel, as it was then called, quickly acquired popularity becoming, and remaining for over 90 years, the town's premier establishment and still, over 200 years later, it remains a popular hotel.

In the month of October 1819, the Duke of Kent paid a brief visit to the town to inspect Woolbrook Cottage which he was proposing to rent (more about this in the chapter on the Royal Glen Hotel). The Reverend Edmund Butcher tells us that:

Mr Wallis (of the Royal Marine Library) was introduced at the York Hotel to submit the much admired panoramic view for His Royal Highness's inspection of which he expressed his decided approbation and was graciously pleased to accept a copy and say it would afford him much pleasure to show it to her Royal Highness the Duchess.

This was Sidmouth's famous Long Panorama Print.

Richard Stone was the first proprietor of the Hotel, which he rented from Sidmouth Manor for the sum of £21 p.a. for the Head Lease. The Hotel, along with the rest of the Manor, was put up for sale in 1813, but for some reason the sale did not take place. In the gale of 24 November 1824, Richard Stone suffered severe losses when his cellars were flooded, causing destruction of all his valuable wines and spirits, not to mention the damage to the fabric of the Hotel. Richard Stone died on 18 August 1831, aged 54, and was buried in the Parish Churchyard. He was described as 'Master of the York Hotel'. His wife was Ann Taylor of Sidmouth whom he had married on 5 January 1801, and there were eight children, all of whom were named with his wife as beneficiaries in his Will. When the Will was proved, his effects were stated as under £1,500.

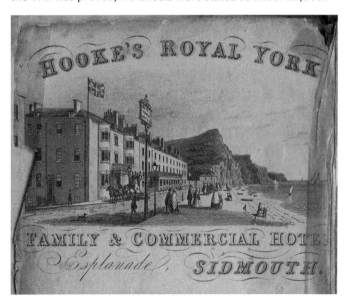

An early advert for the hotel (Sidmouth Museum)

Just before Richard Stone's death, His Royal Highness Prince Paul, brother of the King of Württemberg, and the Father of Grand Duchess Hélène of Russia, who was staying at 8 Fortfield Terrace, arrived to stay at the York Hotel with his suite. It is thought that this visit allowed the hotel to be called 'Royal'

Following Richard Stone's death, the Hooke family took over the hotel and remained for many years. An advert in the press of the time stated:

The Proprietor of the Royal York Hotel in returning his warmest thanks to Royalty, the Nobility, Gentry, Clergy and the Public, for the support he has hitherto received, begs to assure his patrons that it shall be his continued study to merit continuance of their support, by paying every attention to the comfort of those who may be pleased to favour him with their patronage.

The York stables were a little way up the town and were originally those of the London Inn, before they were moved to purpose-built premises in Selly's Yard. Some of the regular coach services, including the evening service from Exeter, set their passengers down outside the hotel where they were met by an assortment of gigs, flys and even sedan chairs, whose use in Sidmouth persisted well into the 19th century.

Lord Charles Wellesley, second son of the 1st Duke of Wellington, stayed at the York Hotel in the summer of 1854. He seems to have been a keen swimmer, for he told a friend that Sidmouth provided the best bathing he had ever enjoyed, so much so that he intended to return another season. It is not recorded whether he ever did so.

The next celebrated visitor was Edward, Prince of Wales, later Edward VII, who stayed at the hotel on 30 September 1856, during the course of a walking tour of the south coast. He crossed from the Isle of Wight in September with his Governor and Tutor and stopped at Poole, Swanage and Bridport, before reaching Sidmouth on the 30th. On 1 October, before going on to Exmouth, he visited Woolbrook Cottage (the Royal Glen) where his mother, Queen Victoria, and grandparents had stayed. The tour was a private educational one and no official publicity was given to it. In an attempt to disguise the Prince of Wales's true identity, he travelled using the name Lord Cavendish.

The following year in June, Miss Angela Burdett-Coutts, later Baroness Burdett-Coutts, heiress of Coutts Bank, and at the time the richest woman in Britain in her own right, stayed at the Hotel with her suite, amongst whom was her companion, Mrs Brown. At the time she was looking for a country retreat, and was investigating the suitability of Sidmouth. Not long after this visit, she acquired a fine house in Osborne Crescent, overlooking Meadfoot, Torquay, where she liked to spend part of the winter and could take a rest from her ever increasing involvement in philanthropic works.

Just across the road from the York stood the large illuminated beacon erected as a marker to guide the fishing fleet back to Sidmouth beach. From a site alongside this beacon it had long been the practice to let off maroons to summon members of the Fire Brigade from all over the town. Unsuspecting guests could be rudely awakened in the night by a resounding report almost on their window sill. 'Big Lamp' as it was always called, was washed away in the gales of 1924 and never rebuilt.

The Proprietress, Miss Wright, was able, in 1907, to advertise 'Weekend inclusive terms, Friday dinner to Monday breakfast 25/-' (£1.25) and in the early 1930s, full board for a week at the height of the season was seven guineas (£7.35).

In the Edwardian era, the adjacent Gloucester House (which became the Faulkner) had illustrious guests, including the actor/manager Herbert Beerbohm Tree. In 1909, the 22 year-old aspiring poet Rupert Brooke was summoned to Gloucester House. His parents were anxious about his new relationships. He had fallen in love with the 16 year-old Noël Olivier. Rupert resented coming but he did write a poem reflecting his new found love. Entitled Sonnet, it is wryly amusing despite the preoccupation with death.

In six years he would be dead himself, a victim of sepsis from an infected mosquito bite whilst on his way to the Gallipoli landings. He died peacefully in a sun-filled cabin aboard a French hospital ship lying in a bay off Skyros, where he was buried in a grave amongst the olive trees, marked by a simple cross.

In WW2, the Hotel was the only one in Sidmouth not to be requisitioned and since the owner was also the Town Clerk to Sidmouth UDC this caused more than a few local 'raised eyebrows'.

In White's Directory of 1850, Henry Joseph Hooke is given as proprietor of the York Hotel and it is strange that the Hotel is again owned by Hooks for, in 1970, it was bought by Freddie and Violet Hook, who had owned the Faulkner Hotel, next door to the York, for 31 years.

Mid 19th century photo of the hotel (Sidmouth Museum)

Freddie was not a Sidmothian, being the son of a Thames lighterman, but his wife Violet was from an old Sidmouth family, the Huckers. Her parents lived in a thatched property in Church Street close to the Parish Church, which was amongst those gutted by fire in 1927. The Hucker family ran Hucker's Luncheon Room adjacent to Fat Face. Freddie was apprenticed in the kitchens of the Victoria Hotel, but moved on to finally become Chef at the Fortfield Hotel. There he cooked for the Duke of Connaught during his stays at the Hotel and, on his marriage, received a wedding present from the Duke – a large ornamental inkwell which the family still have.

In 1939, Freddie bought the small guest house, the Faulkner, next door to the York. With war imminent, visitors were scarce and for the first few months almost no one came. At the outbreak of war, Freddie joined the RAF, leaving Violet to run their guest house as best she could for the duration of the war, with three small children to add to her problems. After the war, together they turned the Faulkner into a thriving hotel, expanding into two more of the houses in York Terrace and eventually taking over the Royal York in 1970. Freddie died in 1990 and Violet some years before, but their youngest son and daughter-in-law continued to run the combined hotels until handing them over to their children who now run a combined business as 'The Royal York and Faulkner Hotel'.

Julia Creeke

The mediaeval Chapel of the Blessed Peter was built before 1322, within the ambit of the Abbey of Mont St Michel in Normandy. It was demolished in 1805, except for a small section of wall.

The Manor of Otterton, of which the sub-manor of Sidmouth formed part, was given by William the Conqueror to the Abbey of the Benedictine Order of Mont St Michel in Normandy. At the time of the Doomsday survey, the Abbot leased to Ottery St Mary, which was in the hands of the Canons of St Mary of Rouen, salt pans and an orchard at Sidmouth. With time, as the settlement grew, there were other temporal affairs to be managed, so the Abbotts retained a Steward who lived at Pinn (just over the brow of Peak Hill on the road to Otterton). So persistent was custom that even down to recent times, the Rolle manorial rents were collected at Pinn Barton Farm.

Part of the original wall of the chapel (SVA)

Each year, the Abbot dispatched across the Channel a group of monks to collect the Abbey's rents and tithes, and deal with any outstanding business or legal matters. However, by 1157, or a little earlier, the Abbot, under pressure from Henry I, had Prior Robert and four monks settled in Otterton in a small Priory, and they now controlled the affairs of the Manor on behalf of their French mother house. King John made several demands of the Priory concerning a Chantry at Otterton and a Chapel at Ladram. The Chapel of St Peter at Sidmouth could

also have been built about this time as a place of worship and refuge for the monks when they came from Otterton to visit their lands in Sidmouth and transact business. Alternatively, it is possible that it was built as a leper chapel.

In the years since the Doomsday Survey, and with the Viking raids now a thing of the past, Sidmouth had started to develop as a small settlement engaged in farming and fishing.

The first record of St Peter's Chapel is in 1322, when the shifting of the River Sid required the boundaries of the Parishes of Sidmouth and Salcombe to be redefined with a line drawn from the Chapel eastwards to the port area (now Port Royal). There was further boundary trouble between the two manors in 1352, when a flood washed away the boundary stones and the Prior of Otterton, Roger de Bueys, and the Dean and Chapter of Exeter, the respective landlords, agreed to appoint a jury of twelve from each manor to agree the new boundaries.

The Chapel of St Peter had been built on the west bank of the estuary of the Sid, which in those days was far larger, as it had not yet begun to silt up and the sea encroach, so the Chapel was well removed from the shoreline. In size it is unlikely to have exceeded 20 x 35ft (6.1 x 10.7m) and in early times would have had a thatched roof and was enclosed by a large wall with a stone arched doorway.

In the French wars of the 14th century, the Prior was several times expelled by the English King, and then re-instated in time of peace, but the final break with France came in 1415, when Henry V presented the Manor of Otterton to his own foundation, Syon Abbey, at Isleworth, Middlesex (a nunnery). Thereafter the monks left Otterton for good and the administration of the Manor of Sidmouth devolved upon a locally based Steward or Provost, acting on behalf of the Abbess.

The possibility that the Chapel of St Peter was a leper chapel arises because of similarity with the equally small St Mary's Chapel at Honiton, founded to provide shelter and a place of worship for these unfortunates. However, whether the Chapel was used by monks or lepers, it probably remained in the possession of Syon Abbey until the Dissolution. Thereafter, it may have continued in religious use, either in connection with the Parish Church, or for lepers. At some stage its religious use ceased and it found a new secular trade as a drinking house near the beach, 'for many years known by the Sign of the Anchor'. In the Survey of the Manor of Sidmouth of 1764, Samuel Sandford is given as tenant and the yearly value £8. The property is described as 'a dwelling house in Town formerly the Chapel now the Anchor consisting of a Kitchen, two Parlours, Cellar, Buttery and four chambers with a garden in the Marsh'.

Later, when the 'Anchor' moved to new premises, the former chapel became part of a dwelling, the occupant of which is reputed to have kept some kind of school. Was it perhaps a lace school, where, in the 18th century, the young learnt their craft from an older woman, whilst at the same time learning by repetition simple lessons? Lastly, the Feoffees of Sidmouth used it as a meeting place for dealing with the affairs of the town's poor – that is, until the floor, which was rotten through neglect, almost fell through. A local builder acquired what was left of the old Chapel and in 1805 demolished it, building in its place a pair of houses, known as 'Marlborough Place'. Much later, Mr Field, whilst carrying out some extensions to his premises, came upon some very large stones which were obviously of some antiquity and were thought to belong to part of the Chapel wall. Also demolished in 1805, was the old mediaeval Market Cross which stood not far away in Market Place.

Twenty years later, the houses of Marlborough Place were assailed by the fury of the gale of November 1824. The sea had encroached considerably since mediaeval times as there was no sea wall to keep it out, only a large shingle embankment which was all but swept away. The houses were extensively damaged, the ground floor rooms filled with shingle: afterwards a horse and cart was often seen backed up to the ground floor windows as men shovelled out great quantities of shingle, to clear the rooms and unearth the parlour carpets. Entirely devastated, their pretty front gardens were an expanse of sand, shingle and mud and it was some time before the houses were re-occupied.

Beyond the houses of Marlborough Place was Portland Place, a terrace of lodging houses set well back from the

A panel from the interior of the building (Sidmouth Museum)

Promenade with gardens in front which also filled Prospect Place. At the turn of the 20th century these were all demolished and the alignment of the buildings which replaced them was totally changed. RW Sampson, the buildings' architect, brought the line of the buildings forward, which resulted in the loss of the gardens of Prospect Place and is why Dukes (formerly the Marlborough Hotel) is set back with its forecourt in front, which was once part of the Prospect Place gardens.

History has sadly left almost nothing but the small Gothic arched doorway, now inside the hotel, and a little section of stone wall on the outside, to show what was once the site of Sidmouth's ancient Chapel of St Peter, although the alignment of the narrow road outside is probably even older.

Julia Creeke

The Red House was completed in 1891, and much enlarged in 1902 to become the Fortfield Hotel. The Duke of Connaught wintered at the hotel on occasions in the 1930s. It was demolished in the 21st century and replaced by the Sanditon apartments, named after Jane Austen's last, unfinished, work.

Sir Joseph Leese, MP and Recorder of Manchester, built a house on a site which was the greater part of what remained of the old Fort Fields and was known as 'Back Fort Field'. The house was built in brick and known as the 'Red House'.

Sir Joseph was a distinguished county cricketer, and all five of his sons were also fine cricketers, playing for Winchester School, one captaining the first XI, and they were often seen playing on the Sidmouth Ground.

About 1902, Michael Healey, who had been Manager of the Knowle Hotel, acquired the Red House and extended it, making it very much larger, and opened it as the Fortfield Hotel. Later Colonel Balfour, Lord of the Manor of Sidmouth, who had already been involved in the construction of the Victoria Hotel, bought the Fortfield and added it to the Manor Estates, running it under management. Throughout the 1930s,

The Duke of Connaught outside the Fortfield Hotel (Sidmouth Museum)

Eddie and May Russell ran the hotel on his behalf, Eddie Russell having previously worked in the Manor Estates Office.

In the autumn of 1931, the Duke of Connaught, last surviving son of Queen Victoria, decided that on account of the Depression he should winter in England, rather than travel to the Continent, and since his Equerry, Major Berkeley Levett, lived at Cottington and was a friend of Colonel Balfour, Sidmouth seemed an ideal choice. Thus the Duke took up residence at the Fortfield Hotel for the first of his stays in Sidmouth, on 28 October 1931.

The Duke was frequently seen out walking accompanied by Major Berkeley Levett, and would buy fish from the local fishermen direct from their boats as they landed, carrying it back to the hotel, strung through the gills, to be cooked for him by the hotel's chef, Freddie Hook. From time to time various of his numerous relatives visited him and the Fortfield saw a succession of royal visitors, including Princess Louise, Duchess of Argyle, Prince and Princess Arthur of Connaught, Prince Gustav Adolf of Sweden, ex Queen Ena of Spain, Princess Ingrid of Denmark (later Queen) and Lady Patricia Ramsey, the Duke's Daughter, who was an accomplished artist. The Duke stayed at the hotel on three occasions between 1931 and 1934.

Like most of Sidmouth's hotels, the Fortfield was requisitioned during WW2 to form part of the Medical Training Depot, with lecture rooms on the ground floor and sleeping quarters above. After it was de-requisitioned and returned to

The Fortfield Hotel (Sidmouth Museum)

Colonel Balfour by the War Office, it was sold by him and the Manor Estates. It remained a hotel until early this century when it was closed, the owners citing that they wished to retire, and it was rapidly becoming uneconomic.

They sought planning permission from the District Council for re-development but were initially refused and negotiations dragged on for several years. Then in 2010, with the hotel empty, there was a fire in the north wing which the fire service managed to extinguish, but it did extensive damage. Just months later there was another huge conflagration which completely burnt out what remained of the old hotel. Eventually, there was agreement to redevelop the site with flats, now renamed 'Sanditon' after Jane Austen's last unfinished novel which is believed to be set partly in Sidmouth.

There is uncertainly as to whether Jane Austen ever stayed in Sidmouth, although she could have visited the town. The only extant reference to Sidmouth in Jane's own words is in a letter of 8 January 1801 where she says 'Sidmouth is now talked of as our summer abode'. In old age, Cassandra, Jane's sister, told her niece Caroline a memory of the 1801 summer. Jane had fallen in love with a young man, probably in Sidmouth. The possible suitor was a clergyman, who sought permission to see Jane again. Jane and her family readily agreed. He left the town and soon afterwards they received a letter reporting his unexpected death.

Julia Creeke

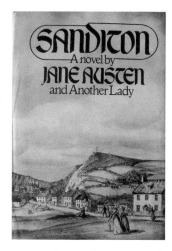

An edition of Jane Austen's novel 'Sanditon' showing Clifton Place and Peak Hill

55 SIDHOLME *originally Richmond House*

Richmond House, from an old print after the painting by George Rowe, 1826 (Sidmouth Museum)

A late Georgian house, with aristocratic, banking and scientific connections, most noted for the magnificent Music Room added in the Victorian era. Childhood home to Frederick Lindemann, the principal scientific adviser to Winston Churchill in WW2.

In 1824, an enterprising wine merchant, William Barrett, built six moderate sized villas on a high ridge of former agricultural land, four to the north and two to the south, which he named Elysian Fields. There was a gated entrance from Temple Street to the new development. Richmond House, as it was then called, was the last villa on the right and Cumberland Cottage its near neighbour.

Mr Barrett sold or rented his properties, which included The Shrubbery and Balsters on Temple Street, and which are still standing. He was reluctant to pay Poor and Church Rates on his unoccupied rented houses. Although the local judiciary occasionally found in his favour, he frequently paid fines and also served time in Exeter County Jail. Despite these setbacks, Richmond House was leased to various wealthy tenants until 1847 when it was bought by the Reverend Augustus Hobart who was a minor member of the aristocracy; his brother was the 5th Earl of Buckinghamshire.

It is not clear why the clergyman chose Sidmouth but he had, for various reasons, become disenchanted with the Anglican Church and, although only in his early 50s, he had retired from the ministry. His official title was 'clerk in holy orders without cure of souls'.

His first marriage to Mary had resulted in six children but, following her death after the birth of the last child, he married his first cousin, Isabella, and had a further seven children. Much of his working life had been in a small Leicestershire parish, Walton-le-Wold. The Sidmouth household consisted of Augustus, then 53, his wife Isabella 49, and their five youngest children. There were only three servants; a cook and two housemaids. Almost immediately the house name was changed from Richmond House to Richmond Lodge. Perhaps it sounded more refined.

In 1849 Augustus's brother died, childless, and Augustus became the 6th Earl of Buckinghamshire. He considered moving to a larger property befitting his new status but he compromised by taking out a sizeable loan and, over the next three years, he purchased six acres (2.4 ha) of adjacent

Earl of Buckinghamshire in later life (Sidmouth Museum)

farmland. In 1854 he started to build what was to become his legacy, the Ball or Music Room. The Great Exhibition of 1851 is likely to have influenced the internal fittings. Its main function is implied by the name but it was also used as a private family chapel. This building, which includes the Billiard Room, was separate from the main

Music Room 1931 (Sidholme Archives)

house but connected by a glazed walkway. The floor area was greater than the 'parent' building.

When the Ball Room was completed in 1855, the lights were fitted with pipework for gas: 236 burners which can still be seen in the wall sconces. In 1860 he purchased the adjacent Cumberland Cottage, renamed it Richmond Cottage, and subsequent tenants were given long leases.

The Earl was a rather reclusive man and, apart from the occasional balls organised by the Countess, he rarely intruded into Sidmouth life. However, in 1860, he reluctantly found himself the spokesman for those who were opposed to the Parish Church restoration and the subsequent installation of the newly-commissioned western 'Queen's Window'. It was felt, probably by the majority of the population, that the proposals reflected an attempt to introduce Anglo-Catholicism into the church. It was not until 1867 that a compromise was made, by which time many local citizens had forgotten the reasons for the initial dispute, and the Earl returned to his former private lifestyle. In 1873 the Countess died, and three years later the Earl moved to the Buckinghamshire family seat at Hampden House near Great Missenden, and Hampden was added to the family name. He died in 1885, a week short of 92 years and the oldest peer in the land. He was buried, according to his wishes, in Sidmouth Parish churchyard.

The house had been sold in 1876 to Benjamin Davidson, a wealthy bank agent for the Rothschild dynasty. He arrived with the famously beautiful Olga and their three young children.

Olga had previously married in 1865 Mr O'Brien but was separated not divorced from him. He died in 1876 and Olga, learning this, married Benjamin a year later. Sadly, the following year, he died aged only 55 years. He is buried in Salcombe Regis churchyard, on the very periphery of their land, which may reflect his Jewish origins. The inscription on the gravestone 'Perfect husband, perfect father' is unlikely to be hyperbole as he made very generous provisions for his wife and children. His Will left £15,000 to Olga as well as the Sidmouth estate during her lifetime. After her death, the estate transferred to his son, Gilbert. Additionally he left £40,000 to Gilbert and £20,000 each to his daughters, Blanche and Dora, and a further £10,000 each for all the children's education.

Olga remained a widow for almost six years and during this time directed significant alterations to the building. The Music Room was incorporated into the main body of the house. The new hall and staircase allowed stairs down into the Music Room. The Countess's attractive bowed window, a feature of the previous exterior wall, was preserved and can still be seen in the hall. Another major alteration was the 'addition' of next door Richmond Cottage, the former Cumberland Cottage, into the eastern aspect of the main house.

In 1884 Olga married Adolf Lindemann, a German water engineer, who had previously enjoyed a business friendship with her late husband. One of their first decisions was to rename the house Sidholme. Soon they had a family of their own, Charles in 1885, Frederick 1886, Linda 1887 and James 1891. James was known as Septimus, or Sepie, as he was Olga's seventh child. Olga insisted that the children be brought up as Anglicans, similar to her other children, rather than the Roman Catholicism of the Lindemanns.

Olga gave considerable financial support to Adolf's developing commercial venture, which eventually was highly successful. However, in the 1880s, 1890s and first decade of the new century, the Lindemanns were not always in residence at Sidholme, presumably to save costs.

Adolf was an accomplished astronomer, and built an observatory on the top of a summer house (the site of which is now now within the grounds of The Laurels). He also built a science laboratory (the present Hotel Annexe) where he encouraged his sons, Charles and Frederick, to join him. Olga took great delight in developing the nine acres (3.6 ha) of grounds and employed a head gardener and a further six under-gardeners.

Olga died in 1927, and the house reverted to the ownership of her eldest son, Gilbert Davidson. Adolf graciously moved out and spent his last years in Marlow. The eventual sale of Sidholme in 1930 coincided with the Great Depression and the £8,000 paid by the Methodist Guild Holidays group, was an excellent bargain.

Frederick Lindemann had not lived at Sidholme since the turn of the century but nevertheless was saddened by the sale. He was now an eminent physicist and already a close friend of Winston Churchill. Known as 'The Prof', and always a controversial figure, he became Churchill's personal scientific advisor in WW2.

Sidholme was the third British location primarily aimed at 'Guilders' – young Methodists who were keen to have economic holidays with like-minded colleagues. In the 1930s there were about 250,000 Guilders nationwide, reflecting its importance and popularity. The house was called a hostel rather than a hotel and guests were expected to help the paid staff. Some structural changes were made, including provision of male and female cloakrooms. The bedrooms typically had six beds. The official opening was on 8 April 1931 in the Music Room. This room was left largely unchanged except that wallpaper now covered (and still covers) the painted Italianate female figures carrying musical instruments.

In 1942, Sidmouth hotels, including Sidholme, were requisitioned by the RAF, primarily by the Medical Training Establishment and Depot (MTE & D). Although the RAF vacated the buildings following D-Day, Sidholme was then converted into a temporary residential nursery under the compulsory Government Evacuation Scheme and it was not until 1947 that it was returned to the Methodist Guild.

The period from the late 1940s to the mid-1970s represented the zenith of the Methodist Guilder concept in its original form, as proposed before the war.

*Olga Lindemann, artist unknown
(private collection)*

In 1987 major restoration and new building work began, which lasted almost three years. In order to help finance this initiative, the Methodist Guild sold land at the top of the gardens, which included the tennis courts, putting green and summer house. Flats in parkland, The Laurels, now occupy that site. In 1990 the new extension was completed consisting of an additional dining room/conference room known as The Richmond Room, with three new bedrooms above.

The heart of Sidholme remains The Music Room. It is approached through the main entrance on the west side, into the hall and entered on the ground floor through double mirror doors. A more interesting route is from the top of the stairs and through the glass doors. The focal points are the beautifully painted organ and the large cut-glass central chandelier. There are six very tall, attractive, arched sash windows which extend to the cornice. On the west and east walls are marble fireplaces, with original heating radiators on each side. (The western fireplace has no chimney.) The tall mirrors over the mantles have Rococo frames, and are both ornate and gold. The most striking feature is the ribbed vault of the ceiling which includes, in the centre, a painted canvas of cherubs and mystical animals on a blue background. The cherubic theme continues in the patterned wallpaper and, more evidently, in the frieze above the cornice. The Coat of Arms of the Buckinghamshires is above both the organ and the staircase. The crest is a bull, and the side supporters a stag (buck) and hound.

A volunteer group, Friends of Sidholme Music Room, has raised money to restore the organ (2015) and the central large chandelier, which was the first of the seven chandeliers to be repaired and restored (2018). Friends of the Lost Garden in Elysian Fields are redeveloping the landscape of the gardens.

Non-resident visitors to Sidholme are encouraged to see this splendid room but should first ask permission at Reception.

Nigel Hyman

SIDMOUTH SAILING CLUB

Recreational competitive sailing in Sidmouth dates from early Victorian times, and the town's first regatta was held in 1847, encompassing both rowing and sailing races. The Sidmouth Corinthian Sailing Club was founded in about 1895. The club became dormant in WW1 and started again in 1936.

Sidmouth has a long-established sailing tradition. For centuries, local fishermen under sail have launched and recovered to the beach that at times has shown utter contempt for this often-fragile human activity. The name 'Port Royal' has an association with the eastern end of the beach, adjacent to the mouth of the River Sid. In bygone days the town was a centre of shipbuilding prowess, which is alluded to in Sidmouth's Coat-of-Arms. The heraldic motif shows a ship representing one of three built in the town and sent to the relief of Calais under Edward III in 1336.

Saxton's 1575 map of Devonshire shows three places along the South Coast of England in bold print, namely Plymouth, Dartmouth and then Sidmouth, good evidence that Sidmouth was a thriving seafaring town. Indeed, after the colonisation of North America, West Country fishermen pursued their catch in the waters off Newfoundland. The Newfoundland Trade, as it became known, grew throughout the 1600 and 1700s. Ships and boats were built in Sidmouth and crewed by local men. Often the route was circuitous, involving heading to Spain and Portugal in the early part of the year for salt and then across to the fishing grounds. The return trip was often back to Spain with the preserved catch and eventually returning to England in the autumn with the remainder of the salted fish, cod liver oil and wine. The Follett family of Sidmouth Manor profited nicely from this mercantile exchange.

Raw materials for the town, including coal, would be delivered by sea. It would have been a common sight to see large two-masted brigantines just off the shore, with long-boats transferring the cargo to the beach. While at anchor, these vessels would have a local pilot aboard, a fisherman with sound local knowledge, to advise on weather conditions, ballast and holding. The pilot may also have guided the ship to another local port, such as Exmouth or Teignmouth. Other small ships suitable for the purpose could be beached on the sand and their cargoes unloaded onto the sand or straight into a horse and cart. As the tide came in, the vessel would refloat and could then be kedged out into deeper water ready for departure when the wind permitted.

The story of recreational sailing in the country can be traced to the late 1600s. King Charles II, and his brother James, Duke of York, later King James II, took a great interest in all things maritime. King Charles had been presented with a yacht – the *Mary* on his return to the English throne and, during his reign, owned seven royal yachts. The brothers and their crews would race against each other from time to time. This spawned an interest in sailing for recreation among other members of the nobility and other gentlemen 'of means'. The sport grew throughout the 1700s and, in the latter part of that century, it started to establish a foothold in the South West, although still dominated by those of wealth. The Starcross Club was formed by Lord William Courtenay and his friend Sir Laurence Palk of Haldon in 1772. In 1792, John Seale of Dartmouth offered his yacht to Mr Henry Studdy, a wealthy shipbuilder and landowner, to take his family from Sidmouth to Dartmouth. Studdy used vessels made in Sidmouth for the Newfoundland fishing trade. Seale's family would later be known for its association with Seale-Hayne College, near Newton Abbot.

In the early 1800s, the West of England was truly awakening to the phenomenon that is recreational sailing. It was in 1815 that, arguably, the most pre-eminent yacht club in the world was formed, eventually to be renamed The Royal Yacht Squadron. From Cowes on the Isle of Wight, its wealthy and influential members, many of whom were from South and East Devon, could indulge themselves. Henry Studdy was a member of the Royal Yacht Squadron and his family eventually became involved in the West of England Sailing and Yachting Conference, which established rules for sailing and ratified small-boat design.

In the mid-1800s regattas were becoming popular, such as the Royal Torbay and the Teignmouth events. It was in this period, specifically 1854, that the accomplished marine and landscape artist, Robert Charles Leslie, brought his young family to live in Sidmouth. (More about Robert Leslie is given in the chapter on 10 Fortfield Terrace.) He knew much about boating from his time on and around the Thames, and as a child had met the artist JMW Turner. Shortly after arriving in

Sidmouth, Leslie was eager to take to the water as he had not been afloat for months. Boldly, he approached 'a weather-beaten-looking man...as he landed on the beach after a night's work among the crabs and lobsters in a small fourteen-foot boat'. The fisherman, one Harry Conant, was to become a longstanding friend. On this occasion, Leslie paid one shilling for the use of *England's Rose*, rigged with a lug-sail forward and a mizzen aft. In his book, *A Waterbiography* he wrote, 'I had a delightful cruise in her along-shore under the lofty cliffs'.

Harry Conant was an accomplished sailor, having sailed in the coal trade, and began life on board a small west-country coaster. He was also a gifted rigger and sail-maker, and 'carpenter enough to keep his own boats in repair'. Of course, these were useful skills for Leslie to have in his friend. In the 12 years he lived in Sidmouth, Leslie first built *Foam*, and then a small tender and eventually a 45ft (13.7m) Bermudan-rigged sloop called *Rip Van Winkle*.

As for regattas, in his writings, Leslie tells us of a wealthy gentleman, who around 1860 put up prize money for a regatta. However, this was not Sidmouth's first regatta because the following appeared in the *Western Times* of 25 September 1847:

Sidmouth. A regatta is announced to take place at this pleasant watering place on Tuesday next; there will be two sailing races and two rowing races, and a punt chase. After which, various rural sports, including donkey and biped racing, climbing a pole, and jumping in sacks, will take place for the amusement of commons.

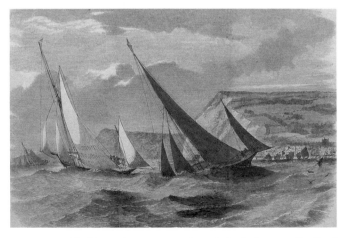

Yachts racing at an early regatta (private collection)

149

In the 1860 regatta, of which Leslie writes, there were separate races for large and small boats, the latter including fishermen who fancied their chances. The regatta got underway in deteriorating conditions, with rain and driving spray, such that boats had trouble seeing the racing marks. It is not clear exactly how the race finished but, of the small boats, the fishermen had the upper hand before returning to the beach in 'half a gale'. The yachts, not suited to landing on a beach, proceeded instead to Exmouth under storm canvas.

Little is known from that regatta until the formation of the Sidmouth Corinthian Sailing Club in 1895. Corinthian, in this sense, usually meant amateur but rules allowed for paid hands, provided the owner was helming. Again, sailing was mostly the preserve of the well-to-do, although it was certainly becoming more accessible, with sailing boats such as the West of England Conference 14ft (4.3m) dinghy, also known as a WEC 14, being more affordable. For the 18 years the Club existed, the Rt. Hon. Sir JH Kennaway, Bart., CB, Mr CE Roberts Esq, JP and George Pidsley Esq, were President, Commodore and Vice Commodore, respectively.

These WEC 14ft dinghies, initially had a standing gaff rig but this rapidly evolved into the Bermudan rig, and were to be the predecessors from which the famous 14ft International dinghy developed. These are a prestigious class still racing today in either the classic timber-hulled class or the more modern hulled boats with modern rigs: they race both nationally and internationally, with a World Championship held every two years. Sidmouth is an unlikely place to have played a

International 14ft dinghy on the beach

significant role at the very beginning of the development of dinghy-racing as we know it today. The International 14 dinghy was used in the 1948 and several subsequent Olympic Games.

It is clear there were some fine and successful sailors in the Club, in particular the Hon. Secretary, Mr GH Vallance (owner of the local Brewery which bore the family's name – Vallances) and Mr Jack Trick, whose names feature heavily as winners of local races, as well as races in the east of Start Point sailing scene. George Vallance had a notable rivalry with Ivy Carus-Wilson of Teign Corinthian Sailing Club. In her writings, she often highlighted the 'sharp practice' by the Sidmouth man. Nevertheless, on 29 June 1911, in *Phantasm*, against the top names from Devon and Cornwall, Vallance pulled off a stunning win in the West Bay Dinghy Cup; Carus-Wilson in *Myosotis* was fourth.

It is not fully understood what brought about the demise of the Sidmouth Corinthian Sailing Club in 1912 but there is some evidence of ill feeling, as reported in the minutes of an AGM in the local newspaper, and the fact that fewer boat owners were taking part. This was likely because of the disharmony and the fact that Mr Vallance, being comparatively wealthy compared with the other members, could afford to build new and ever faster boats of the most up-to-date designs. He continually won most of the races, with the result that many of the other members lost heart and ceased to race in their older out-dated boats. Ivy Carus-Wilson was to marry Morgan Giles, the well-known Teignmouth designer and boat builder. She related how, when the dinghies had to be taken to other towns to race, it being too far to sail them there, they would be loaded into empty coal trucks and taken by rail. When they arrived, they were so dirty from the coal dust that they were loaded onto a horse and cart and taken down to the beach where they were washed out, before any racing could begin. After which they went back the same way as they had come. Otherwise, the racing crews were willing to sail the dinghies long distances, such as Sidmouth to Teignmouth, just to take part in races.

WWI and the subsequent depression may have played a strong part in why little is known of that period, albeit fishing certainly survived these difficulties. However, with wealth spreading and modern processes making boats easier and cheaper to produce, it was obvious that recreational sailing would get going at Sidmouth once more. In 1936, 'owing to the noticeable increase in numbers of sailing craft in Sidmouth, it was suggested that a sailing club be formed'. A public meeting was called and held in the London Hotel

(1 Fore Street – see separate chapter). At the first meeting it was decided to call the club Sidmouth Sailing Club, a name it proudly retains to this day, albeit there was acknowledgement that the 'Sidmouth Corinthian Sailing Club existed some years ago and which enjoyed many years of fine sport'. The elected officers of the club were: Chairman Mr WM Trump, Vice Mr H Skinner, Treasurer Mr W Ardley, and Secretary Mr JAC Field. Mr Ardley, the proprietor of the London Hotel agreed that the hotel could be used as the club's headquarters and a noticeboard was to be hung outside. At the first AGM in 1937, Dr MacLeod assumed the role of President.

The first Sidmouth Regatta of the new era was arranged for Saturday 29 July 1939. At that time, however, the prospect of war with Germany was not an abstract concept. Times were changing. At a Special Meeting in the London Hotel on 12 July 1940 it was highlighted that 'military precautions against invasion by the enemy had begun to be made on the parade... It was inevitable that the season would have to be concluded at once'. Arrangements were made for the safe custody of the Challenge Cup, funds were placed in the Devon & Exeter Savings Bank and a balance sheet and results of racing were inserted in the local press.

The war dragged on and members' destinies varied. However, with eventual victory in Europe and a lessening of the load placed on the town by war, the time was ripe to revive the Club. On 25 October 1945, an AGM was held in the old Sea Cadets Hut that stood on the western side of the present entrance – Sidmouth Sailing Club re-emerged. The newly elected officers were: President Dr MacLeod, Commodore Mr G Channing, Treasurer B Gibbs, and Secretary Mr ST Chard. It was agreed that the Sea Cadet Hut would become the new Club HQ, albeit with very limited facilities. In 1946, discussions took place regarding the possibility of acquiring the Old Coastguard Building, now the Sidmouth Lifeboat Station, but until the building was renovated, meetings of large numbers of members were held in Hope Cottage (now Sidmouth Museum – see separate chapter). The outlook for the Club could now be considered very satisfactory and thoughts were directed to such things as improving the launching ramps, starting a 'junior' section and, in 1952, a new design of 13ft (4m) utility dinghy by Mr Fish. Drawings were presented and included 'patterns in hardboard to enable the members to build to the identical design of the prototype'; this design was to become known as the 'Sidmouth Redshank One Design', with royalty fees of two guineas. One Redshank

Sidmouth Redshank One Design dinghies racing in the 1950s (Sidmouth Museum)

was to be purchased for the Juniors at a total cost of £120. In all, nine Redshanks were built. These were attractive little boats with varnished clinker-built hulls and bright scarlet sails.

In 1954, the Club was approached by the Sea Angling Club in order that they also could also use the Club House for weighing fish and preparing refreshments. After considerable discussion the Hon. Secretary was instructed to write 'regretting their inability to comply with the request, it being felt that too great a risk... having regard to the value of sails being stored'.

Topical even today, the then Sidmouth Urban District Council (SUDC) highlighted that the County Council was 'planning comprehensive development of the Eastern Town but so far no proposals...interests of the Sailing Club are not forgotten'. A new political era had dawned. At an Annual Dinner in 1965, the Charmain of SUDC raised hopes of the Club getting quite a good club-house when future development of Eastern Town took place. He told the Club not to delay in putting forward proposals for its needs. A sub-committee was rapidly formed. Much discussion about sources of grants and other ways of raising money took place. The target was £6,000; the club would have to raise £4,000. It was decided to build a model of the proposed club house.

Major RM Phelips, who had previously had architects draw up plans for a small harbour, stated his intention to donate

Fleet drawn up on the beach in the 1970s (Sidmouth Museum)

£8,000 towards the cost of a new building on the Sailing Club site, but such a building was to provide joint amenities for both the Sea Angling Club, which was his passion, and Sidmouth Sailing Club. A Special Meeting of the Sailing Club was held in Hope Cottage to consider:

> the report of the General Committee describing the proposal for a joint Clubhouse ...and having considered the situation as regards finance, Planning Permission and the offer by the Local Authority to lease land for the project, hereby authorises the General Committee to take steps in consultation with the Sea Angling Club as may be necessary to bring about the building of the proposed premises as planned. The meeting further expresses its gratitude to Major RM Phelips ...for his very generous offer of £8,000 which has made such a project possible.

Regrettably, Major Phelips died early in 1968. However, his Will made provision for a bequest of £8,000 for the building of the new joint club house and this, along with a grant of £7,288 from the Department of Education and Science, went a long way to covering the eventual cost of the present building, which was opened on 27 June 1970 by Miss B Phelips, the niece of the late benefactor. A plaque in memory of Major Phelips is situated just inside the main foyer. The final cost of the building was £22,293. In 1980, an extension was added to the present building to provide a galley (kitchen) and garage for safety-boats.

At the time of the new club opening, various classes of boats had already been adopted including Scorpions, a boat particularly suited to the challenging sea conditions produced by the prevailing south-westerly winds, the '420' and the ubiquitous Mirror, named after the Daily Mirror, which sponsored the design with the aim of getting sailing to the masses. The masses came! Presently, the Club supports other classes, such as the Topper, which is perfectly suited to young people, and the Laser, raced by such Olympic legends as Sir Ben Ainslie, who has sailed at Sidmouth in his formative years.

Just as in 1965, once again in the second decade of the 21st century, the Local Authority is considering the future of the Eastern Town, known more affectionately to the sailors as Port Royal. Will financial arguments regarding pressures of land-use dominate, or will the amenity value attached to our sailing heritage hold sway? Will it be the 'age of sail' or the 'age of tall buildings', or an element of each? Time will tell.

The Club has been proud to host many high-profile sailing events including, as at 2018:

Mirror World Championships: 1988.
Mirror Nationals: 1994.
Scorpion Nationals: 1995, 2004 and 2013.
Laser Masters Nationals: 2007.
Laser Masters World Qualifier: 2008 and 2009.
Laser 2000 National Championships: 2010.

Alastair Watson

57 SIDMOUTH WAR MEMORIAL SERVICE MEN'S CLUB

now known as the 1922 Social Club

Built by public subscription as a social venue for men returning from the Great War, the club was opened on 22 June 1922 by General Sir John Hart Dunne, a colourful character who was the most senior military person locally at the time.

General Sir John Hart Dunne (b.1835 – d.1924) had retired to 6 Fortfield Terrace and was greatly respected locally, hence the request for him to officiate at the opening of the club.

The Club was built by public subscription, primarily for the benefit of local servicemen, past, present and future.

Its declared purpose was 'to keep alive and cultivate the spirit of patriotic comradeship to which the Country largely owes its recent salvation.'

It was thought that over a thousand men from the wider Sidmouth district, or with local connections, served in uniform in WWI. They served in every wing of the armed forces and the merchant marine, in military hospitals, and in all the major theatres of the war. Over 150 died.

Before the war ended, local people were already expressing strong commitment to fund a memorial to honour those who had died. There was also strong feeling that an additional memorial would be needed to mark the end of hostilities and remember the sacrifices made by the town.

A number of options were mooted, including a War Memorial Hospital, a free library, outdoor recreation facilities, a social institute for servicemen, a harbour and a new town hall. However, the returning servicemen were emphatic in their view that a social institute should be established, dedicated for use by them. That option prevailed.

A site for the social institute was identified and ultimately purchased in August 1920 for £1,000. The name adopted for the scheme was the Sidmouth War Memorial Service Men's Club.

The site was a two-storey late Georgian house built in around 1825 called 'The Retreat,' on the corner of Church Street. In the 1850s, it had been a residence for Curates at the Parish Church opposite, and later it was where the author,

Stephen Reynolds was living at the time of his death in February 1919. The house had the advantage of a large yard, stretching back along Church Street. It had a further advantage of being within sight of the War Memorial to the Fallen, which was planned for the churchyard – it was finally unveiled there on 20 February 1921.

Sidmouth architect RW Sampson – who had already designed the Memorial to the Fallen – was commissioned to prepare a design for the club, adapting The Retreat and building a substantial new wing. The new building was to include two main facilities for members – a large reading and recreation room, and a billiards room.

The initial design for the new wing was grand, featuring a tower with cupola at each end, and a Venetian window in the centre. However, the scheme as built lacks these features and is more straightforward and utilitarian in design, no doubt reflecting the prevailing financial limitation. The alterations and the new extension cost £478 in total.

When the 86 year-old General opened the club on 22 June 1922, he was greeted with applause when those present were

General Sir John Hart Dunne (front of steps) opening the Club (Sidmouth Museum)

reminded of his service in previous wars. He gave what was said to have been a 'happy speech, full of humorous reminiscence,' and spoke of the virtues of comradeship and loyalty. He expressed his fervent hope that the club would be 'a haven of rest and social enjoyment' for returning service men.

To mark the occasion, he opened the door to the club with a large hallmarked ceremonial silver key, engraved in dedication to him. This key is now held by the Sidmouth Museum, in its original presentation box.

The club was re-named the 1922 Social Club in 2015.

General Sir John Hart Dunne's experience of war started almost 70 years earlier when, as a young officer, he landed on the Crimean Peninsula with the Royal Scots Fusiliers. He fought in almost every major battle of the Crimean War (1854-56), in conditions equally as atrocious, if not worse, than those experienced in the Great War.

He is however best remembered for his prominent role in introducing the Lion breed of dog (Pekinese) into Britain. In brief summary, he took one from Peking (now Beijing) and presented it to Queen Victoria. The little dog was an instant favourite with the Queen and she named it Looty.

This story began in 1860, when he was stationed in India with the 99th Regiment of Foot and they were sent to join the Franco-British forces in the Second Opium War with China. This war came about as a result of the western powers seeking to expand their trading rights in China. John Hart Dunne kept a journal of his experiences during this period and it was published in 1861 as *From Calcutta to Pekin.*

In order to get to their objective, Peking, the Franco-British forces had first to capture the Taku forts defending the Pei-Ho River. Captain Hart Dunne – as he was then – tells in dramatic terms in his journal how he hoisted the union flag over the northern fort, in competition with the French.

A deeply unpleasant and regrettable sequence of events then unfolded. Before Peking surrendered, the invading armies ransacked the Emperor's Summer Palace, a place of exquisite beauty outside the city walls. The Chinese then brutally murdered a number of prisoners, including a *Times* correspondent. In retaliation, the British High Commissioner to China, Lord Elgin, gave the order for the Summer Palace to be set ablaze.

It was in that maelstrom that Looty was found.

One version of what happened says that soldiers found five lapdogs running around distraught near the body of a lady – perhaps the Emperor's aunt – who had committed suicide. Another version, which has a certain ring of truth about it, says

Looty was found curled up in a wardrobe.

Whatever the case, it is indisputable that five dogs were brought back by British officers. Two would end up with the Duchess of Wellington, two with the Duchess of Richmond and one was presented to Queen Victoria in April 1861 by twenty five year-old Captain John Hart Dunne.

Looty was a Lion Dog, an ancient breed with a long association with the Chinese Imperial Court. Because they were royal pets, ordinary people were expected to treat them royally – it is said that at one time common people had to bow down if one of the dogs went by.

From different accounts, we learn that Looty was around five years old when brought to England, was about eight inches (20 cm) high and had long silken hair. And she was alluring.

Captain Hart Dunne certainly appears to have been bewitched by Looty. He wrote in his journal: 'I have been able to retain... a pretty little dog... a real Chinese sleeve dog. It has silver bells around its neck. People say it is the most perfect little beauty they have ever seen.'

Nonetheless, he complained that she was 'very dainty about her food'. She preferred boiled rice with chicken and gravy mixed in rather than the food given to the other dogs. He insisted that 'Looty was going to get the same food as the others and after a little fasting and coaxing [she] will come to like the food that is good for her'. The evidence suggests he was being overly optimistic about this.

Once in Queen Victoria's ownership, Looty lived comfortably. The Queen had a portrait of her painted by Friedrich Keyl at Windsor in 1861, which was exhibited at the Royal Academy the following year. The Queen gave a replica of this painting to Captain Hart Dunne and perhaps later in life he displayed it at his home in Sidmouth.

The Queen also released a facsimile portrait

'Looty', painted at Windsor by Friedrich Keyl, 1861. Royal Collection Trust/©Her Majesty Queen Elizabeth II 2018

of Looty to newspapers and magazines, fuelling the national fascination with the little dog.

Looty enjoyed celebrity across the Atlantic as well. *Harper's Weekly* gossiped that the other royal dogs took exception to her because of her 'oriental habits,' which suggests that Looty was continuing to insist on her own dietary requirements. It is also possible to imagine Looty being aloof towards the other dogs. American gossip also said that the Princess of Wales was so concerned about Looty's isolation that she pleaded with the Queen to be allowed to take her to Sandringham. It is not known whether any of that was true, although the Queen did bring a male Pekingese across from China to keep Looty company.

Harper's Weekly observed that, 'the breeding of this species of dog became a diversion in fashionable society.'

Looty lived on for eleven years after arriving in England. Her story still attracts interest and she can justifiably be regarded as one of the most famous dogs in history.

John Hart Dunne's association with Looty clearly did him no harm. He was promoted to Lieutenant-Colonel in 1865, Major-General in 1881 and General in 1893. He served as Lieutenant of the Tower of London from 1894 to 1897, and then became Commanding Officer of the Wiltshire Regiment. He retired from the army in 1902, but remained Honorary Colonel of the Wiltshire Regiment for life.

General Sir John Hart Dunne died in April 1924, aged 88, and is buried in Sidmouth Cemetery.

John McCarthy

Major John Hart Dunne in 1865

58 SPRING GARDEN

An 18th century house, home in the 1820s to Rear Admiral James MacNamara, a swash-buckling naval officer of the Napoleonic wars, famous also for being found not guilty of manslaughter following a duel in Hyde Park.

The Dukes, a wealthy Otterton family who had acquired the Manor at the Dissolution of the Monasteries, owned lands stretching over the crest of Peak Hill and down the east side to adjoin those of Sidmouth Manor. Still today, their successor, Lord Clinton, owns woodland along the eastern crest of the hill, the last remnant of that ownership.

In 1753, Mrs Duke agreed a mortgage which allowed Sarah Strode to purchase from John Burrough half an acre (0.2 ha) of pasture, called 'Mary Garden' and a dwelling house, together with a cider mill, pound, implements and outhouses. Sarah Strode remained only six years before Samuel Cawley, on 17 March 1759, became the owner, purchasing for £110 'a parcel of land ½ an acre severed from one close or pasture known as Mary Garden and a dwelling house thereon built, an orchard and watercourses'. Until recent times, a spring rose in one corner of the garden and still there is a well in the basement. Interestingly, this deed mentions the heirs of Sir William Knight as being the owner of the adjoining property on the southern side i.e. Woodlands, and the histories of the two properties were for a time closely linked (see chapter on Woodlands Hotel). Samuel Cawley was a man of some substance, leasing a number of properties from Sidmouth Manor, and on his death 'Mary Garden' remained with his widow, Jane, for life and then to her son Samuel Cawley (junior).

For over 30 years, there is no mention of the house, its

owners or occupants but, in 1810, the Reverend Edmund Butcher informs us that W Fellowes MD, was living in the house as neighbour of Lord Gwydir and Lady Willoughby (Lord Gwydir's wife was titled in her own right). Two years later, on 25 December 1812, Samuel Sander and others sold for £720 'messuage, tenement, dwelling house and walled garden known as 'Spring Garden' in possession as tenant of Dr Fellowes', to the Trustees of Lady Willoughby of Eresby.

Lady Willoughby's sister, Elizabeth, had married the Duke of Hamilton, but the marriage ended in divorce and, on 19 August 1800, she married the 1st Marquis of Exeter, but was widowed four years later, leaving her to bring up the nine year-old son and heir. She lived not only at Burghley, but at the Exeter's London house in Whitehall Gardens and later at her house in Roehampton. She visited her sister Priscilla, Lady Willoughby, in Sidmouth and during those visits stayed at Spring Garden, her visits being remarked upon and mentioned in contemporary writings.

Lord Gwydir died in 1820 and, leaving the contents of his Sidmouth house 'Old Hayes' (Woodlands) to his wife, she put it up for sale. Its buyer was Admiral Sir Henry Digby, and shortly afterwards he also bought Spring Garden, which was next door. This was already an old house which had been modernised and used often as a residence for guests of the Gwydirs. Into it now moved another retired Admiral, Rear Admiral James MacNamara, Senior Rear Admiral of the White, a quite outstanding officer and one of the great daring-doers of the Napoleonic Campaigns.

Admiral MacNamara had been in the *Victory* with Lord Hood, who promoted him to Commander, and in 1795 he went to the *Southampton,* a frigate with the Light Squadron, serving with Nelson trying to drive the French from Genoese territories. The next year, Admiral Sir John Jervis gave him the opportunity to show his consummate skill as a seaman. Jervis on the *Victory* had discovered a French frigate working into Hieres Bay near Toulon and, wishing to prevent her at all costs reaching Toulon, summoned MacNamara on board *Victory* telling him 'Bring the enemy ship out if you can: I'll give you no written order but I direct you to take care of the King's ship'. MacNamara wasted no time and his own letter written to Jervis afterwards tells what happened:

I pushed through the Grande Passe and hauled up under the batteries in hopes I should be taken for a friendly vessel as I got within a pistol shot of the enemy's ship before being discovered, I cautioned the Captain whereupon he snapped his pistol at me and fired a broadside. I laid him instantly on a broadside and Lieutenant Lydiard at the head of the boarders entered and carried all in about 10 minutes, although he met with spirited resistance. After lashing the two ships together I found some difficulty in getting from under the battery and was not able to return through the Passe before 6 o'clock this morning.

It wasn't long before he came to the attention of Nelson, when he attempted to capture the Spanish Brig *El Corso* in a hard gale. The first attempt to get a boarding party across failed, as only one man, the Coxwain, got on board. MacNamara was not going to see him lost and made a second dash – this time he was successful and the Spanish vessel surrendered. The weather was now so awful that for 48 hours the prize was commanded by the Coxwain. The action was conducted in shoal water in a gale

HMS Southampton. Painted by Clements Good
(Hull Maritime Museum: Hull Museums)

and typified MacNamara's brilliant seamanship. There were more heroics when he attempted, whilst commanding the *Cerebus*, to take on an entire Spanish fleet – he set fire to one and scattered the whole.

MacNamara's next exploit, however, gained him more notoriety than his entire Naval career. Captain MacNamara was riding in Hyde Park in 1803, accompanied by his Newfoundland dog when a fight broke out between the latter and one belonging to Colonel Montgomery of the Life Guards. The two officers exchanged heated words after the Colonel dismounted to separate the warring parties. The result was a challenge to a duel that same evening at Chalk Farm. Both men were wounded, the Colonel mortally. The hastily convened Coroner's Court returned a verdict of Manslaughter and Captain MacNamara was taken into custody and the same month put on trial at the Old Bailey. MacNamara conducted his own defence in the most eloquent manner. He ended it saying 'Gentlemen I am a Captain of the British Navy. My character you can hear from others, but to maintain any character in that station I must be respected. I hope to obtain my liberty through your verdict and to employ it with honour in defence of the liberties of my country'. Whereupon he called on the likes of Nelson and Hood plus many others to speak on his behalf – the Jury retired and ten minutes later returned a verdict of 'Not Guilty'.

MacNamara returned to sea and continued his Naval career. He married late in life and, although his main residence was at Bath, he spent some time in his later years in Sidmouth living at Spring Garden next door to his old friend Admiral Digby. He was remembered in the town for the magnificent set of duelling pistols which, from time to time, were taken to the local gunsmith for cleaning. He died in 1826, the year his friend, Admiral Digby, inherited his family seat at Minterne, Dorset, and left Sidmouth.

Spring Garden continued to be part of the Old Hayes (Woodlands) property until it was conveyed away in 1840. About this time, the old house was largely demolished and rebuilt in a more fashionable and grand style. It became the home of Henry Carslake and his wife Esther. Henry Carslake was a brother of John Carslake of Cotmaton (see chapter on Cotmaton Hall).

In 1828, Spring Garden was rented by another sister of Lady Willoughby, the Dowager Duchess of Northumberland. These sisters from quite ordinary parents had all succeeded in marrying into the highest levels of society. The Duchess had just lost her husband and she spent six months in Sidmouth.

In more recent years, Spring Garden was the home of Dr and Mrs Tom Fison, both of whom worked tirelessly for the local community. Dr Fison was in general practice in the town for 35 years. He was Chairman of the Hospital Comforts Fund and over the years put together a fine collection of antique medical instruments which are displayed at Exeter University Medical School. Tom Fison first came to Sidmouth in the 1920s to stay with his great aunt who lived at 'Redcliff', now the Harbour Hotel, and returned to the town after the war. He had many interests outside medicine, including ornithology, and his patients might have been more than a little surprised to see him chasing round Mutter's Moor on a summer's evening 'Churr-rring' loudly hoping to attract nightjars, much to the delight of his grandchildren.

Julia Creeke

The TOWER of SIDMOUTH PARISH CHURCH

The tower dates from the 15th century, having been left intact when the body of the church was rebuilt in Victorian times. It contains a mediaeval tolling bell. Above the west door is the stained glass window given by Queen Victoria in memory of her father, who died in Sidmouth in 1820.

The tower is the main surviving part of Sidmouth's mediaeval church, built in the mid-15th century, which was largely swept away in 1860, when the church was rebuilt to accommodate the growing population. It is not the first church tower in the town, as excavations in 2009 showed that an earlier 12th century church, on the same site, had a tower towards its east end. In mediaeval times, the tower would have served many purposes. In addition to calling the faithful to worship, the tolling of the bell would have been the only timekeeper for most of the population, and would have served as a warning in times of danger – such as in 1340 when the French raided and burnt Teignmouth along the coast. The tower would also have provided a beacon for fishing boats returning home, and a lookout for raiders or shoals of fish.

Tower dating from the mid 15th century (Sidmouth PCC)

Today, it marks the historic centre of the town.

The tower is 75 feet (23m) high and 25 feet (7.6m) square at the outside of the base. Inside, the base is 14 feet (4.3m) square and the platform at the top is 18 feet (5.5m) square. The spiral staircase has 105 steps. Above the west door is the Queen's window, given by Queen Victoria in memory of her father, the Duke of Kent, who died in 1820 during a visit to Sidmouth when she was just eight months old. The Queen was invited to make a gift to the new church when it was rebuilt in 1860. However, disagreements between the vicar and the Earl of Buckinghamshire, who was principal funder of the rebuilding, led to Sidmouth's local historian, polymath and member of the restoration committee, Peter Orlando Hutchinson, travelling to Osborne House to petition the Queen to withdraw the offer.

It was to be another six years before a new vicar, the Reverend Clements, was able to celebrate the installation of the window we see today, made by Ward & Hughes of London. The main glass panels show Christ in Glory at the top, Jesus with the Children in the centre, and depictions of eight Christian virtues on the sides. At the bottom is a frieze of five scenes from the life of St Nicholas. The colours are vibrant, especially when illuminated by the evening sun. The Queen's window is of Bath stone and was originally part of the 1860 rebuilding. Following serious erosion by rain and salt, the stonework was completely replaced and the windows re-leaded in 2016.

The bell chamber is at the top of the tower, with tracery designed in 1908 by RW Sampson. It is said that the church had three bells in the 15th century, one of which survives as the Sanctus bell, now tolled for funerals and at the communion. This bell weighs 7cwt (356kg) and bears the inscription 'Est Michi Collatum, I.h.s. Inslnd Nomen Amatum'. By the early 18th century there were five bells and in 1875 this was extended to a full octave peal in the key of F#, the tenor weighing 12cwt (610kg). With the exception of the old

HM Queen Victoria, painted by Franz Xavier Winterhalter, 1859 (V&A)

Sanctus bell, the peal was recast in the lower pitch of E in 1972, the tenor now weighing 18cwt (914kg). In 1990, two new treble bells were added from the bequest of Lady Olive Fleming, widow of Sir John Ambrose Fleming, inventor of the thermionic valve (see chapter on Greenfield), to give an augmented peal of 10, reckoned amongst the finest in the South West.

The platform at the top commands a spectacular view of the town and is surmounted by a flagpole and a weather-vane in the shape of the *Mary Rose*, installed in 1992 to commemorate Mrs Margaret Rose, a Sidmouth resident. The pennant beneath is dated 1809. It is recorded that the curate, ringers and guests had dinner on the platform on the day of Queen Victoria's coronation in 1837. In 1873, Peter Orlando Hutchinson designed pinnacles for the tower, like those seen on many other Devon churches. However, by 1967, not just the pinnacles, but much of the top of the tower had become unsafe. During the subsequent rebuilding, the pinnacles were not replaced.

Brian Golding

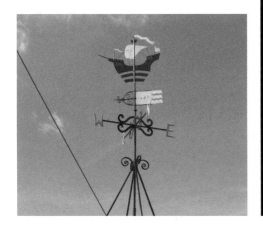

Mary Rose weather-vane atop the Tower (Sidmouth PCC)

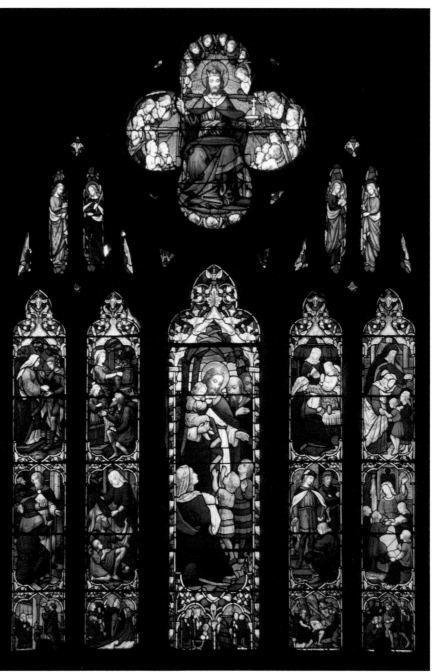

West Window donated by Queen Victoria (SVA)

Dating from the 1400s, this was originally a single hall with a central hearth and cruck roof. In Tudor times a first floor was inserted, with a fine decorated screen dividing the space at ground floor level.

This is undoubtedly one of Sidmouth's oldest buildings, whose purpose and date of construction lies hidden in mediaeval history. That it has been very closely connected with the Manor of Sidmouth is certain, for it was still in the possession of the Lord of the Manor when it was put up for sale for the very first time in 1919.

Sidmouth had formed part of the Manor of Otterton, which included Harpford, Venn Ottery and Yettington plus various other hamlets, and was thus very large. The Doomsday Book tells us that when Edward the Confessor died, the Manor of Otterton was in the possession of Countess Gytha, widow of the once powerful Earl Godwin of Wessex and mother of King Harold, who was killed at the battle of Hastings. Its Saxon steward at this time was Yngoful, who lived at Pinn and was responsible, on behalf of the Countess, for seeing that the land was being properly cultivated by those working it.

Following the defeat of Gytha's army at Exeter and her flight to Flanders, William the Conqueror seized the Manor of Otterton, giving it to the Benedictine Order of Mont St Michel in Normandy. It was the most valuable of all the Abbey's English possessions and, to manage its secular administration on the Abbey's behalf, the Abbot retained, as in former times, a Steward living at Pinn, but by 1157 a prior and four monks were permanently settled in a small Priory at Otterton.

With the creation of parishes – Sidmouth in 1259 – the monks lost much of their clerical work. During the French wars of the Plantagenets, the fortunes of the Priory ebbed and flowed: Priory lands were twice seized by the Crown and then, in more peaceful times, were restored. Finally in 1415, Henry V gave the Manor of Otterton, including Sidmouth, to the Abbey of Syon at Isleworth in Middlesex (this was a nunnery), a royal foundation of his own. But Syon did not maintain the Priory at Otterton and thereafter no religious body occupied the buildings. As the River Otter gradually silted up, Sidmouth began to overhaul Otterton in size and importance and there were growing maritime interests in trade and fishing.

It may well be that the construction of Tudor Cottage, a small hall house of typical mediaeval cruck construction, dates from this time and that it served as both a residence for the Steward and administrative centre for the Manor.

Early in the reign of Henry VIII, as relations between church and king worsened, the Abbess of Syon granted a lease of the Manor of Sidmouth for 99 years to Richard Gosnell, possibly hoping it might save Syon's position. But in 1537 the smaller monastic houses were disbanded, and two years later came the final Dissolution. The Crown seized all monastic lands but, although the Abbey of Syon was disbanded and the nuns pensioned off, the lease granted by the Abbess to Richard Gosnell was left in place, with the Crown now landlord.

In mediaeval times most small settlements had a Church House where the Church Wardens brewed the Church Ales.

No one living in a Parish was permitted to brew ale, only small beer (often drunk in lieu of water whose purity was frequently suspect). The selling of Church ales at parish gatherings to celebrate religious festivals was, in mediaeval times, one of the major sources of finance for the maintenance of the Parish Church. The Church House provided a venue for these gatherings and perhaps Tudor Cottage started life as a Church House, but later, as Sidmouth grew in size, its former use was abandoned.

During the reign of Henry's father, Henry VII, the hall house with its central hearth and cruck roof was altered to provide more comfortable living conditions. A plank and muntin screen dating from 1503 was used to divide the hall into two ground floor rooms and a first floor was inserted to make a solar above the parlour as was the fashion of the times. This plank and muntin screen was painted with the royal arms of England impaled with a Bishop's mitre and two pallium against a background of the cosmos and crescent moons orbiting round the frame. The strapwork design included floral emblems of the New World. The reasons for the painted screen and the significance of the decoration are not fully understood, although the house was probably the seat of the Manor Leat Court, and justice by this time could not be administered except under the Royal Arms. Those Arms could have been added to give the Court authority to administer justice on behalf of the sovereign.

It has not been possible to discover who occupied the house at this time. There is little doubt that the history of this ancient building is inextricably linked to both the Manor and Church, although its exact use remains obscure.

When the floor was inserted in the 17th century, the open hearth would have been replaced by the present external chimney stack. This is of especial interest in view of the easily visible fire insurance plaque, which consists of animal faces, on the outside of the chimney.

Gradually, as times changed and fashions altered, the house became out-dated, reduced to two humble dwellings, and the screen plastered over and forgotten. The house would, until the mid 19th century have enjoyed an open prospect down to

Screen showing the Royal Arms and emblems of the New World (SVA)

the sea, being situated on rising ground in a street known, until 100 years ago, as Silver Street. The name was of very ancient origin being either derived from the Latin word for wooded or more likely from the Saxon 'scylfe' meaning a slope.

In the early 1970s, during renovations, it was decided to remove the partition between the two downstairs rooms and, on stripping away some old lath and plaster, the screen was rediscovered. The original paintwork was executed by a highly skilled artist or artists. It is possible that it was started in the reign of Edward VI but completed towards the end of the century in the reign of Elizabeth I. It underwent professional restoration and conservation under the supervision of the Devon County Archaeological Service and is now revealed in its full glory – a rare survival from the Tudor period.

The house is privately owned and there is no public access.

Julia Creeke

VICTORIA HOTEL

Built in 1902 by Colonel Balfour, Sidmouth's Lord of the Manor, the hotel was immediately popular for its modern facilities such as rooms en suite and garages for cars.

John Edmund Hugh Balfour inherited the Manor of Sidmouth on his 25th birthday in 1869. He had been left a minor when his parents died and the Manor, which had been purchased by his father, was placed in the hands of Trustees. The Manor at this time was in poor financial health and the Trustees sought to improve this state of affairs. Over the years some areas of land were sold off, but they made a substantial investment when they purchased the Knowle and turned it into a very successful hotel.

When Balfour inherited the Manor he sought to continue this policy. He felt that Sidmouth was without a top class hotel and sought to remedy this, but the areas of land suitable for such a building, and which were owned by the Manor, were very limited, particularly if it was to be close to the sea.

One area which was considered suitable comprised part of the gardens of Woolbrook Glen (now the Royal Glen Hotel). The site as it stood was deemed not to be sufficiently large for what was envisaged. The south-eastern corner was occupied by Westpark Cottage, which had been built early in the 19th century and can be seen in the Long Print of Sidmouth Sea Front, just peeping out of the trees. For many years it had

Hotel at its opening in March 1904

been home to members of the Heffer family (other members of this family lived opposite in Heffer's Row), the last to occupy it being 'old' Tom Heffer. In the intervening years it had been enlarged and after his death it became a guest house. The house was surrounded by substantial trees and the whole of the southern part of the proposed site was very well wooded. There was no space to extend the site westwards because both Westcliff Hall and Redlands had already been built on the land fronting Manor Road.

Eventually, in order to build the hotel, a considerable area of the grounds of the Royal Glen was acquired, along with Westpark Cottage, which was demolished, and most of the trees on the site felled, to improve the view from the new building.

By this time, RW Sampson had become the architect to the Manor Estates, and he was asked to design the new building, construction of which commenced in 1902. He planned a building which was very different in appearance and far bigger than anything he had previously designed. When the size of the new edifice was discovered, many Sidmouth residents were appalled and complained that its size represented a 'blot on the landscape' and disfigured the western view along the Promenade. It was the largest single building in the town and its architecture was very different from anything seen in Sidmouth up to that time, so that it certainly exuded an air of grandeur. The building cost some £30,000 to build, and a further wing to the west was added in 1907.

The hotel opened in March 1904, with many guests arriving by a special train which had been laid on from London's Waterloo Station, and completed the journey in the record time of 3 hours 40 minutes. There was an inaugural dinner at which Major Hastings, Steward to the Manor Estates, presided, the guests of honour being Sir John and Lady Kennaway. There were an enormous number of doctors invited, which seems strange, but perhaps the hotel proprietors were seeking to encourage them to send their patients for rest and recuperation at the hotel, emphasising the benefits of Sidmouth's sea air and mild climate. Somewhat unfortunately, the guest speaker chose as his subject Sidmouth's new drainage scheme. The guests were treated to a six course dinner which included *Selle d'agneau de Sidmouth à la Cosmopolite* and, predictably, *Pudding Victoria*.

The hotel had 45 rooms, including some suites of bedroom, sitting room, dressing room and bathroom, and, remarkably for the time, some of the best bedrooms had en suite bathrooms. It was possible also to rent a private sitting room, and there was accommodation for guests' servants and, even at this early date, provision had been made to accommodate motor cars.

The hotel had been furnished by the Barnstaple firm of Shapland & Petter and a contemporary account stated:

For the extremely bright and comfortable fitting up of the establishment, Messrs Shapland & Petter have executed their commission in a manner which challenges comparison with the very best that can be seen in any hotel. The Manager, Mr Macguire, has been instructed to run the hotel on liberal terms, with reasonable charges, a generous table and good service is to be expected. The Victoria certainly has everything the most fastidious can desire. A feature of the hotel is several complete suites of apartments on the first floor – sitting room, bedroom and bathroom – the decoration of these is especially good and the furnishing is of the choicest possible character. The Drawing Room is exquisitely furnished, the Billiard Room with its tables is very striking, the Lounge is comfortable and commodious and the Dining Room arranged with a number of small tables will provide for one hundred guests.

Sidmouth Mills, at the Ford, had remained a working mill into the 20th century. The water-wheel had been replaced by an oil engine and the surplus electricity it generated was supplied to the newly built Victoria and Fortfield Hotels as well as to the Parish Church. An advert in the 1918 *Sidmouth Ward Lock Red Guide* describes the electric lights in both of these hotels. This was at the time the height of modernity because much lighting was still by gas.

The tariff shown in the hotel's first brochure makes interesting reading. (Please note that one guinea = £1.05p, and that 1/- is one shilling and there were 20 shillings to the pound. 1/- is equal to £0.05 or 5p; 1/6 is one shilling and 6 pence. There were 12 pence in a shilling, so 1/6 is about 7p, and 0/3 is about 1p). Boarding terms were 3½ to 5 guineas per week, suites being by separate negotiation. For shorter stays the terms were:

The staircase hall

Private suites of apartments	16/- per day
Bedroom – single	3/- per day
Bedroom – double	6/- per day
Child in bedroom	1/6 per day
Private Sitting Room	8/- per day
Full board for guest's servants	7/- per day

Fires	Sitting Room fire	2/- per day
	Bedroom fire	1/6 per day

Night lights 0/3 each (No charge for electric lights)	
Hot bath in bathroom	1/6
Cold bath	1/-
Hip or sponge bath in bedroom	0/6

Table d'Hôte daily at separate tables –	
Breakfast	3/-
Luncheon	3/-
Dinner	5/-

À la Carte meals in the Coffee Room varied: breakfast was from 2/- to 3/6 according to dishes selected. Luncheon was from 1/- for sandwiches to 3/- for the hot dishes. Dinner varied from 3/- for a joint and vegetables, to 5/- for four courses, five courses were 6/-. Afternoon Teas were 1/6 and tea or coffee by the cup 0/6 (0/9 if you wanted it in your room).

By the time the second brochure was printed, sometime after the Great War, prices had increased. Full board terms were from 6½ to 8 guineas per week and a double room was 12/- and a suite 35/-. A five course dinner was 7/6 although afternoon tea was still 1/6. Guests could still have a fire in their bedroom, but it would now cost them 4/6 per day, but the charges for baths had disappeared and board and lodging for visitor's servants was 12/- per day. The hotel garage now made ample provision for guests' cars:

> The Hotel Garage, containing large private lockups, is modern in every respect and has two covered wash yards and an inspection pit. Mechanics and washers are always available.

Both brochures lay great stress on the health benefits of a stay by the sea, and the mildness of Sidmouth's climate. The first outside amenity listed in both is the Sidmouth Brine Baths, how close they are to the hotel, and the excellence and benefit of the treatments offered, which are compared with the best continental spas. A pre-Great War guide book to the town has a whole chapter on the Victoria Hotel, praising its comfort and amenities, and says:

> Its proximity to the Baths, an institution which contributes much to Sidmouth's distinction as a health resort, will be much esteemed by the hotel's visitors who come here for special treatments.

A 1911 newspaper advertisement mentioned only three features: electric lights, the lift, and French chefs. During the Great War, an advertisement from the same paper now added that both management and waiters were English. The emphasis on 'Englishness' was a sensitive local issue as the hotel's main competitor, The Knowle, had recently had their unfortunate German manager arrested as an undisclosed alien. (See Knowle Chapter)

George Bernard Shaw (1856–1950) was fond of visiting Sidmouth and was captivated by the atmosphere. He stayed at the Victoria Hotel in April 1937 during a period when his health was suffering, thought to be caused by his vegetarianism; he returned on another later occasion. He is said to have used the fire escape to avoid being accosted by guests and autograph hunters in the hotel lobby. John Irvine, a friend of Shaw's for over forty years and who lived in Seaton, introduced him to a number of Devon writers including Eden Phillpotts, who in his 1951 autobiography, *From the Angle of 88*, remembers: 'I can see him at Sidmouth scattering scraps for the seagulls while the great silver birds swooped round him'.

Early in WW2, the War Department requisitioned the majority of Sidmouth's hotels for the war effort and allocated these to the Air Ministry who in turn used them to house the Medical Training Depot. RAF Sidmouth was unlike other enclosed RAF stations since it occupied a large part of the town. The imposing Victoria Hotel, which pre-war had been accustomed to providing luxury holidays and short stays for those of affluent means, now became the Depot's Headquarters. It remained so until early 1944 when the Depot was transferred elsewhere. There was an inspection of personnel on the Cricket Field each week followed by a parade through the town led by the Depot's Band. The Band also led the weekly Church Parade. After the Depot transferred from Sidmouth, for the remainder of the war, the hotels were used for convalescence or rest and recuperation, with many Canadians amongst those who were sent to enjoy Sidmouth's sea air and relative peace and quiet.

John Betjeman (1906–1984) is now remembered primarily as a poet and author, but amongst his other important achievements were talks on the radio, and television appearances, as well as editing the famous Shell Guides to the English Counties. He wrote the *Devon* (1936) guide himself and described Sidmouth as 'caught in a timeless charm'. He persuaded his family that Exeter was about halfway between their home in London and their destination in north Cornwall and, in so doing, he often visited Sidmouth. The Victoria Hotel was his residence for longer stays, and he also took refreshments at the Hotel Riviera, which allowed him to watch passing holiday-makers. Across from the Victoria are the Connaught Gardens which he described in a radio broadcast about the town in 1949 as:

> …a modern piece of Italian-style gardening on a cliff top, with views, through arches, of red cliffs five hundred feet high – in Connaught Gardens if you and I were tropic plants, and sheltered from the sea breeze, we would flower and flower as high as the cliffs themselves, if only the wind would let us.

Later in the same broadcast, likely based on the Victoria Hotel, he continues:

> From our table, what beautiful buttoned-nosed blondes I saw, smiling secretly at young men in club blazers at

neighbouring tables. Tennis-girl queens of Sidmouth! What romances must have started over coffee in basket chairs in the lounge or on the hotel court during a strenuous single.

Sidmouth became a popular place to use as a location for filming in the late 1980s and into the 1990s, until the Council decreed that this caused too much disruption and its use fell away. Stephen Fry (b. 1957), a raconteur, comedian, actor, journalist and author, in one of his weekly columns in the *Daily Telegraph,* described his experience of filming in Sidmouth for the second television series of *Jeeves and Wooster* (1991), which included scenes in the Victoria Hotel grounds, on the Esplanade and the beach:

Do you know Sidmouth? The silver ribbon of time that is the River Sid twists amiably down through Sid Vale, Sidbury and Sidford until it opens into the south coast at Sidmouth. As you can see there are more Sids to be found in South Devon than at a 1950s dog track.

The first performance at Sidmouth by the RAF Red Arrows display team was on 26th August 1974. With their planes based at Exeter Airport, after the display, the air crews returned to Sidmouth to the Victoria Hotel for a reception and to spend the night. Over subsequent years, the team formed a strong friendship with the town and returned to stay at the Victoria. Eventually this burgeoning friendship between the town and the display team was noticed by those in authority and it was ended. The team, having performed at Sidmouth for almost 20 years, was withdrawn. The town was told it had had its fair share of displays and the Red Arrows must give other towns their turn. It was 2014 before the Red Arrows flew again at Sidmouth. By now safety regulations had changed and the Red Arrows had to perform their full display over the sea – so Sidmouth has once again become a favourite location with the team.

The Hotel has frequently been central to the life of the town: for example, a luncheon attended by HRH the Duchess of Kent during her visit in September 1986 to celebrate the conclusion of the Sidmouth Landscape Appeal. This resulted in the purchase of 220 acres (89 ha) of cliff land on Salcombe and Peak Hills for the National Trust, following the raising of £220,000. At the end of the lunch she was presented with a small version of Sidmouth's Long Print.

Another quite memorable event was a visit by the Rolls Royce and Bentley Car Owners Club to the town during one of their annual rallies. The car owners and their passengers chose to stay for the weekend at the Victoria and the hotel car park was filled by a large group of their magnificent vintage cars. So valuable were these cars that 24-hour security guards had to be provided to watch over them when they were parked overnight. On the Sunday morning, before leaving Sidmouth, they paraded along the Promenade and made a splendid sight. The Club has returned to the hotel on subsequent occasions.

Sidmouth seems to have a particular attraction to the literati and another author, Dick Francis (1920–2010), wrote, late in life, *Silks* (in association with his son Felix). One or other of them appeared to know Sidmouth, as the hero's father is dispatched to the town, for his safety, to stay at the Victoria Hotel, although it 'wasn't cheap'!

The hotel currently belongs to the Brend Group of Hotels based in Barnstaple. It has been in their ownership since the 1970s when the late Mr Brend, senior, attended a dinner in London and found himself sitting next to the Chairman of the company who were then owners of the Victoria. In the course of conversation it transpired that the company were considering selling the hotel, whereupon Mr Brend immediately offered to buy it. Rumour has it that he wrote the cheque for its purchase there and then.

Over the years the hotel has undergone various alterations to keep its facilities up to date. The sun lounge was turned into the present lounge, swimming pools have been added, yet much of the hotel remains as it was in 1904 when it was built.

Julia Creeke

The former home of Colonel Charles James William Grant VC, (b.1861 – d.1932) a British Indian Army officer awarded the Victoria Cross in 1891 for conspicuous bravery at the Battle of Thobal, Manipur.

Colonel Grant was born at Bourtie, Aberdeenshire. His family had a tradition of service in British India – both of his parents were born in India into Scottish military families serving there. His father achieved the rank of Lieutenant-General in India.

Charles Grant was educated in Scotland, before becoming a Gentleman Cadet at the Royal Military Academy, Sandhurst. He was commissioned into the Suffolk Regiment in 1882 and then transferred to the Madras Staff Corps of the British Indian Army in 1884.

In 1891 he was stationed at Tamu, on the border between Burma and Manipur, then a semi-independent state. News reached Tamu that the British Residency in the Manipuri capital, Imphal, had been attacked and five unarmed British officers had been taken prisoner. This had come about following a botched attempt by Britain to interfere in power struggles within the Manipuri royal family. Lieutenant Grant – as he was ranked then – volunteered to go into Manipur in an attempt to free the captives. Unknown to him, the prisoners had already been killed by the time he set out.

Seven miles inside Manipur, Lieutenant Grant's column of 80 Gurkha and Punjabi troops came under attack. Following a fire-fight and

Colonel CJW Grant wearing the Victoria Cross

bayonet charge, they captured a defensible position at Thobal. A large part of the Manipuri army then arrived to confront them. He wrote in his notes what he felt when he saw the approaching force: 'I halted in sheer amazement: the enemy's line was over a mile long.'

The defenders started to dig-in and the attackers opened fire on them with two cannons. Lieutenant Grant had the defenders concentrate their rifle fire on the gun crews and successfully drove them back up the hill. However, in the meantime, the compound became entirely surrounded, and Manipuri troops continued to arrive in greater numbers.

The attackers kept up heavy rifle fire throughout the first night in order to deprive the defenders of sleep. Then came waves of infantry assault over the next nine days, which the small group of defenders successfully fought off. At the height of the battle there were over 2,000 attackers. Lieutenant Grant twice spurned offers of safe passage if he would stop fighting and retreat.

To bluff his opponents about the size of his force, he made it known during cease-fires that his name was 'Colonel Howlett', implying that, as a senior officer, he had a whole regiment at his back. He sewed stars onto his shoulder straps to evidence his rank. The ruse worked for a time, and the Maharaja of Manipur dashed off a letter to the British Viceroy of India complaining about the behaviour of one 'Colonel Howlett', requesting that he be recalled immediately.

On the ninth day, with the breakdown of negotiations, the attackers moved-up at 6 am and landed 15 artillery shells in and around the compound. Luckily nobody was killed, although two of the detachment's elephants were wounded. Then came a large-scale infantry assault, which the defenders fought off. At 8 am Lieutenant Grant went outside the compound armed with a 16-bore shotgun and, supported by ten Gurkhas, drove away several hundred of the enemy. He did the same again at 11 am, with just seven Gurkhas, driving away another large group.

The enemy withdrew the next day when they realised a larger British force was moving towards Imphal. This was fortunate because by then the defenders were almost out of ammunition.

The Citation for the award of the Victoria Cross to Lieutenant Charles James William Grant was published in the London Gazette as follows:

For conspicuous bravery and devotion to his country displayed by him in having, upon hearing on 27 March, 1891, of the disaster at Manipur, at once volunteered to attempt the relief of the British Captives, with 80 [Gurkha and Punjabi] soldiers, and having advanced with the greatest intrepidity, captured Thobal, near [Imphal], and held it against a large force of the enemy. Lieutenant Grant inspired his men with equal heroism, by an ever-present example of personal daring and resource.

All of the Gurkha and Punjabi troops serving under Grant were also decorated for their bravery.

After the battle, he joined the larger British force moving towards Imphal. In further fighting, his horse was shot from beneath him and later he was hit by a bullet that went through the base of his neck and out the other side, taking fabric from his shirt and tunic with it. Writing about this soon afterwards he said: 'feeling the wound with my fingers and being able to speak and feeling no violent flow of blood I discovered I wasn't dead quite yet, so I reloaded my revolver and got up.' He didn't receive medical treatment until the position he was attacking was captured.

Later in his career, now promoted to Colonel, he went on to command the 89th and then the 92nd Punjabis. He retired to England in 1913 to live at Knightsbridge in London, then re-enlisting with the Royal Scots Regiment in 1914 on the outbreak of WWI.

After the war, he and his wife Mary moved down to Devon and finally they came to Sidmouth to build Western Field within a very large plot next to Greenfield, the home of Sir John Ambrose Fleming. The house had a servants' wing and was crammed with mementos of a life in British India.

Garden front of Western Field in the 1960s
(courtesy of Poppy Houldsworth)

Colonel Grant died at Western Field in 1932 and is buried in Sidmouth Cemetery – the only VC holder buried in East Devon. Mary Grant continued to live in the house until her death in 1959 and she is buried with her husband.

Their grave in the cemetery was restored in 2014 by the Sidmouth Branch of the Royal British Legion and was dubbed 'The Tiger's Tomb' by the *Sunday Telegraph*. That reflected a comment by one of Charles Grant's men that 'he fought like a tiger' when he went outside the compound at Thobal with just a few Gurkhas to drive away large numbers of the enemy.

In the 1980s, Western Field was divided into three separate homes, and a new block containing four flats was built within the grounds, on the Manor Road frontage. The grounds of Western Field remain private, and not open to public viewing.

John McCarthy

63 WOODLANDS HOTEL *formerly OLD HAYES*

A late mediaeval farm house, originally thatched, transformed in the Regency period. It was home in the 1820s to Rear Admiral Henry Digby, a veteran of Trafalgar, with a naval career spanning 58 years. In 1855 the thatched roof was replaced and remarkable Italian terracotta decoration added to the exterior.

Unrecognisable by its own name or that of any owner or tenant in extant mediaeval documents, there is no doubt of the antiquity of Woodlands, for in 1971, during excavations, a previously unknown stone-vaulted well-house, passages and cellars were discovered below the garden terrace and these must have belonged to the original mediaeval house.

In 1598, it is recorded that Sir William Peryam resided at 'Hayes' for a short time: this gentleman had a considerable interest in the Manor of Sidmouth. This is the first mention of the property by name so far located, but as 'Hayes' is synonymous with a hay meadow and is a very old Devonian word it would indicate a pastoral use going back to mediaeval times. It is probable that most of the existing buildings date from Tudor and Elizabethan times, and comprise a house and barns now welded into one dwelling, with massively thick cob walls (straw, clay and often cow dung mixed together).

The house known as Old Hayes enjoyed a peaceful and sheltered location, looking out over fields and orchards and, in the late 18th century, there were few other buildings in the area. In 1788, Sir William Pole owned the old Manor, for, in that year, he sold 25 acres (10.1 ha) of his land on Peak Hill to Emmanuel Baruh Lousada to enable him to begin construction of Peak House. (More about Emmanuel Baruh Lousada can be found in the chapter on Peak House.)

Around 1800, the Reverend J Coplestone was living there, turning one of the barns into his private chapel. From one of the landings inside the house, the bell for the chapel is still visible. He had been Vicar of Offwell, near Honiton, where he and his wife had six children born to them. In the Parish Church, a tablet records Caroline Coplestone born in 1788 and died in 1880 and who was one of his two unmarried daughters. They spent most of their lives living in a house in Fortfield Terrace.

What made Lord Gwydir decide to settle in Sidmouth in preference to other fashionable seaside towns is unexplained, but the old house appealed to him and he purchased it about 1806. He immediately set about altering it into a most picturesque thatched cottage orné, spending a great deal of money in the process. A new west front was built overlooking the garden, allowing a suite of reception rooms to be formed, all of which were decorated in fashionable Regency style. So keen was Lord Gwydir to see that the work was done as he wished that he rented a house in Fortfield Terrace so as to be on the spot to oversee operations. He rented from Sidmouth Manor the small but adjacent Crammer's Orchard for the large sum of 8 guineas a year (£8.40) and shared the lease of a coach house and stables on the opposite side of Cotmaton Road (now Gwydir Cottage) with Mr Andrews of Fortfield Terrace.

'Old Hayes', 1817. From Butcher's Sidmouth Guide, 1820 (Sidmouth Museum)

Lord Gwydir's 'Woodland Cottage', (the name the house bore in his lifetime) was in the van of fashion as Regency England had just discovered the pleasures of the seaside.

Peter Burrell (Lord Gwydir) was not an aristocrat, being the son of Peter Burrell, a Commissioner of Excise, and his wife, Elizabeth, whose father, John Lewis, lived in Hackney. He was born in 1754 at their house in Upper Grosvenor Street. In 1761, he was sent to Eton and ten years later entered St John's College, Cambridge. He served two periods as an MP, first from 1776-80 for Haslemere, and from 1782-96 for Boston. He had entered Parliament as a Tory, but, following the 1783 Coalition, voted with Whigs against Pitt and was a keen supporter of the prosecution of the American war against the independence of the colony.

He was described by contemporaries as a man of great elegance, with a fine deportment, athletic, an able speaker and possessed of considerable personality. He was also an able cricketer, although the playing career (1785 to 1790) of the now Sir Peter Burrell extended to just nine known first-class matches. He played for Kent in a couple of matches, although he was a Londoner by birth, and his family seat was then in Sussex. He was a very useful batsman, as indicated by his highest innings of 97 playing for the White Conduit Club v Gentlemen of Kent at White Conduit Fields on Thursday 30 June and Friday 1 July 1785.

It was with this personable man that Priscilla Barbara Elizabeth, daughter of the 3rd Duke of Ancaster and his second wife Mary Parton, fell greatly in love. She fretted so much that her mother feared for her daughter's health and finally permitted the union. They were married at Ancaster House in Berkeley Square on 23 February 1779, though it was said by those that knew them well that he was 'never naturally partial to his wife'.

By the death of Priscilla Burrell's brother, the 4th Duke of Ancaster, the Barony of Willoughby of Eresby descended to her and to her sister jointly. This was also the hereditary office of Lord Great Chamberlain. Peter Burrell, now knighted, had been nominated as their deputy and, although the office was largely ceremonial, he nevertheless superintended the arrangements for the trial of Warren Hastings.

On 16 June 1796, he was created Baron Gwydir, taking the title from his wife's ancestral estates in Caernarfon, but his wife's title took precedence over his and she was thus always known as Lady Willoughby. Lord Gwydir was settled on his estate at Langley Park, Beckenham, Kent, and Woodland Cottage was his seaside retreat.

As a result of family connections, he moved in the highest social circles and was a friend of the Prince Regent, frequently dining with him in Brighton, and Woodland Cottage was visited by many of his society friends. The garden was a particularly picturesque feature and much commented upon because of a loggia along the north side supported by pollard oak trunks, and roofed with rustic branches with the bark left on. There were plantings of roses and honeysuckle which twined up; the whole terminating in a little room of similar design, all surrounded by orchards. When Lord Gwydir was not in residence, visitors were admitted to house and garden to view.

Vice Admiral Sir Henry Digby

In 1819, in a letter to a friend preserved in the Royal Archives, the Duke of Kent mentions that there was 'The possibility of receiving the offer of the loan of Lord Gwydir's Cottage at Sidmouth'. In the event, he decided to give preference to renting Woolbrook Cottage (Royal Glen), being closer to the sea. It seems likely that the house had not been in regular use by Lord Gwydir or his family for some time, for he was badly affected by gout and a year later, on 29 June 1820, he died in Brighton aged nearly 66; the funeral taking place at Edenham, Lincolnshire.

On the death of Lord Gwydir, Brooks and Co, of 28 Old Bond Street, London, were retained to dispose of Woodland Cottage and part of those original particulars of sale are still extant.

When Henry Digby bought Woodland Cottage from the estate of Lord Gwydir, he was already a Rear Admiral with a distinguished naval career stretching back to 1783.

He was a commander by his middle-20s and established a reputation as a highly successful and aggressive prize-taker. In 1799, his capture of the treasure ship, the *Santa Brigida*, further increased his personal wealth and he was said, at the time, to be the richest man in the English fleet, having won £60,000 in prize money, the equivalent of about £4 million now.

His sixth command, in 1805, was HMS *Africa*. She was an old, small ship with 64 guns and thought by some to be too small and slow to be part of any major naval engagement. Nevertheless, on the eve of Trafalgar she was one of the 27 ships-of-the-line. Due to poor weather and not being able to keep up with the rest of the fleet, she missed the signal in the night and found herself, shortly before the battle, far north and isolated. Nelson sent the signal '*Make all sail*' meaning her to pull back, but Digby interpreted it as an instruction to join the main fleet; a 'misunderstanding' that a young Nelson would have recognized. *Africa* weaved between enemy ships firing broadsides and eventually joined five other British ships surrounding the giant Spanish flagship, the 136-gun *Santissima Trinidad*. With amazing audacity, Digby decided to add her to his prize tally and sent his first lieutenant, John Smith, with a small party to board and accept surrender. A Spanish officer on the quarter-deck politely refused saying that the ship had stopped firing but would soon resume battle. Smith apologised for his mistake and took his escorted party back to the ladder and returned to the *Africa*; a wonderful example of chivalry in war observed by both sides. The flagship was in fact grievously damaged and surrendered soon after. In further encounters *Africa* was badly damaged but remained afloat; 62 men were killed or injured.

In 2006, in an Antiques Roadshow programme, a damaged book was shown with the inscription:

This book was shivered [fragmented] in this manner by a whole shot, knocking to pieces the bookcase, off Cape Trafalgar on 21 October 1805, on board the Africa (64 guns). Signed Henry Digby.

Digby received £973 prize money and a subsequent government grant of over £2000.

Further promotions were to come: to Vice Admiral in 1830, and he was still in the service in 1841 at which time he was Commander-in-Chief at Sheerness. On his retirement in 1842, he was made a Grand Commander of the Order of the Bath, but died the same year at Minterne in Dorset, the family seat of the Digbys. He had left Sidmouth in the early 1830s when he inherited Minterne – his diaries are still preserved in the Library there. When he died aged 72 he had served continuously in the Navy for 58 years, one of the longest naval careers on record.

Jane Digby was the only daughter of Admiral Digby and his wife Margaret Coke of Holkham Hall, Norfolk. Margaret was celebrated for her good looks and their young daughter Jane was to take after her mother. She was headstrong and very attractive with dark violet-blue eyes and a fine pale complexion. Her parents allowed her to come out into society at the young age of 17. Lord Ellenborough, a man with serious political interests, was captivated and, although about 12 years older than Jane, they married. Jane, however, soon got bored with married life and eventually her dalliances caused Lord Ellenborough to sue for divorce. In early 19th century England, this required the consent of Parliament and a very public and scandalous law suit ensued.

As a result of the divorce, Jane left England for the continent and soon an Austrian Count was her partner. By him she had two children but sadly the daughter had a mental condition. After some years with the Count, boredom set in again and she left him to bring up the children, and set off on her travels. Advised not to return permanently to England, she went to Athens, became a close friend of the Queen of Greece, and built a fine house in Athens. Her mistake was to fall in love with a Macedonian bandit who was a favourite of the Queen of Greece, who placed Jane under house arrest.

Jane had always wanted to see the ancient city of Palmyra and so set off for the Middle East. Arriving in Damascus, she was advised that consent to travel to Palmyra was needed from the Bedouin sheik in whose ancestral territory it lay. She sought him out and he agreed to take her there. That was the beginning of the most unlikely love affair – she was a Christian, and 17 years older than the Sheik. After several further adventures, she settled down to live in Damascus, building a house there. When the Sheik was in Damascus they lived together, and when she went into the desert with him she wore traditional Bedouin robes.

Jane eventually returned to visit England and was reunited with her parents. Admiral Digby had been repeatedly fearful that Jane's behaviour throughout her life would prevent her having a place in society but, to his credit, he never wavered in his devotion to her. When he died in 1842 Jane was so upset that she made herself 'ill with weeping'. Her social position had been affirmed when Edward VII, as Prince of Wales, on a visit to the Middle East, met Jane at her home in Damascus. This house still stands, though now in poor condition. When she died, she was laid to rest in the hills outside Damascus. It seems unlikely that she ever visited Sidmouth.

In the mid 1830s, Shirley Newdick, a wealthy and cultured man, was living at the Cottage, and it was he who laid out the gardens and planted many of the trees which still exist. He re-aligned the lower section of Mill Lane (now Cotmaton Road) which produced the present east/west staggered cross-road. This allowed a southward extension of the garden to include the stream. This flowed through the garden in a formal channel, and he built a boundary wall which he planted with climbers. The great Monterey pine also dates from this period. The garden, which was modest in size, had always been largely orchard, and Shirley Newdick relaid it to lawn with more formal plantings.

Shirley Newdick is given as a shareholder in the company which was formed in 1836 for the purpose of constructing a harbour at the western end of Sidmouth beach. In the event, after raising a considerable sum of money, the project fell through and shareholders lost their entire investment. Much of the money was lost by the engineer in charge deciding to build a tunnel through part of Salcombe Hill for a railway to Hook Ebb, beyond Salcombe Regis, for the purpose of bringing stone from a quarry there for the harbour. Two foundation stones were laid with much ceremony and a stub of one wall built at the end of the Promenade: that was as far as the project got before the money ran out. The railway engine ordered arrived by sea and was off-loaded at Exmouth and brought to Sidmouth over Peak Hill with much jubilation, but when it was put on the rails, it wouldn't fit in the tunnel. It was

One of the gables ornamented with Italian terracotta – the colour is claimed to be as originally intended (SVA)

said that the rails were relaid on the Promenade and, for a summer, the engine gave visitors rides up and down. A railway engine in Sidmouth at this early date would have made it probably the first steam engine in Devon.

The last of the 19th century owners, whose alterations were to form the building as we know it to-day, was Henry Johnson, who was to acquire the Cottage in 1855. Henry Johnson had travelled widely and been living in Italy for many years. However, the wars and political upheavals associated with Italian reunification caused many British residents to quit Italy. Henry Johnson was a wealthy man and sought to continue his life in Mediterranean climes in an English setting, but, finding the enormous thatched roof in poor condition, decided on a permanent solution to thatching. He therefore ordered from Italy elaborate composition stone decoration for the newly-formed gables and roof ridges and had it all shipped to England. The old thatch was replaced with elaborate hexagonal slates, which were expensive because of the wastage and losses in cutting them. The name was changed to Woodlands. It was now the building we know today.

Subsequent owners maintained the charm of Woodlands and made no obtrusive alterations. About 1918, paying guests were first accepted and in the late 1920s it became a hotel when Mr Ferry with his sisters leased it, one sister continuing to run it after her brother's death until the lease ran out. Woodlands remains one of Sidmouth's architectural gems.

Julia Creeke

The present offices of Sidmouth Town Council in Woolcombe House occupy the surviving part of one of the oldest buildings in Sidmouth. Its modest exterior belies a spectacular interior.

The earliest documentation relating to the house is from 1698, although it likely dates from the 15th century. Unfortunately little is known of the building's early history until the 19th century. AE Chandler was a local historian and the first curator of the Museum, which was then located in Woolcombe House. In the 1950s he made a case that this house, or in any event this location, was the Manor house. Ascerton, was one of the five 'sub-manors' of the mediaeval Sidmouth Manor. The others were Radway, Cotmaton, Woolbrook and Bulverton. The Otterton Cartulary indicates that in 1262 land was granted to Jordan of Ascerton. Peter Orlando Hutchinson, in the second volume of his History of Sidmouth writes: 'It appears to have been situated at about

Town Council headquarters (SVA)

half a mile north of the town on the Exeter Road and between Brewery Lane, so called, and Cox's Lane. The ancient name was Ascerton, or in its common abbreviated form, Ascton, as it usually appears in the Cartulary of Otterton.' Hutchinson and his colleague, Heineken, attempted without success to find a suitable building, but Chandler argued for the Woolcombe House site, an attractive but unproven suggestion.

Peter Child, the former County Historic Buildings Adviser, examined the property in 1997 and 2018. What survives of the original house are two bays dating from the 15th century. The high quality of the roof structure indicates that it was a house of some status, irrespective of any manorial history, occupied by a prosperous farmer or a member of the minor gentry. It is difficult to be precise about its original form as both archaeological and map evidence indicate that half the original building is lost, but there are sufficient clues left in the remaining structure to enable a probable reconstruction.

The house (almost certainly originally thatched) would initially have been completely open from the ground to the roof, probably along its entire length, with an open hearth or hearths on the floor. Without the present floor (of what is now the council chamber) which was inserted in the 17th century, the lavishly decorated visible under-surface of the roof would have been even more imposing than it is today.

It uses typical Devonian 'jointed cruck' trusses consisting of vertical posts in the side walls onto whose curved tops are tenoned the principal rafters of the roof. The truss at the west end of the building (and currently hidden behind the flags) has additional braces under its collar so as to give the whole truss the form of a pointed Gothic arch. This is known as an 'arch-braced' truss and is a sign of a house of higher status. The present council chamber room has a central roof truss with easily visible mortices for studs, and holes for stakes indicating that there was once a partition dividing this space into two, with the section to the east probably a private chamber and the section to the west, part of the principal room or 'hall' of the house.

The demolished section beyond the hall to the west, if the house followed the common convention in Devon, consisted of further bays containing a passage across the house and, beyond that, a service room for working and storage.

When the floor was inserted in the 17th century, the open hearth was replaced by an external chimney stack at the front, and fireplaces, both very fine and still present, on the ground and first floors.

The 1840 Tithe Map for Sidmouth shows the house to be twice as long as it is today. The 'new' western section was built before 1888, the date of the first edition OS 25" map when the plan of the building is shown in its present form.

In 1834, the house passed to the Holmes family who were builders, and would become carpenters and wheelwrights to the Balfour Manor estate later in the century. The taller part of the outbuilding was used for making wheels and coffins and included a sawpit. (The attractive thatched outbuildings may have been a barn, if this was a farmhouse originally, and had cobbled floors.) Houses on nearby Water Lane were built and occupied by members of this well-known Sidmouth family and 'Aunt Cathy's [Holmes] Walk' is along the river path adjacent to the allotments from Lawn Vista Bridge to the bottom of Water Lane.

In 1911, Woolcombe House was put up for sale to pay off business debts and was advertised as having a 'commodious builder's yard with workshop and gardens'. The auction bidding at the Royal York Hotel started at £300 and reached £680. The successful purchasers were Annie Leigh Browne, who divided her time between Sidmouth and London, and her sister, Lady Lockyer. Annie Leigh Browne had given financial assistance to help the town's first hospital 25 years earlier, and she was buying stretches of land adjacent to the river to protect and enhance the landscape. (See chapter on May Cottage for more on Sidmouth's first hospital.) Her reason for the Woolcombe House purchase was, similarly, philanthropic. Within a year she had developed and improved the grounds, with both lawn tennis and croquet facilities. Asking 'nominal' charges, she was specifically attracting trades-people, office workers and shop assistants. Meetings for up to 60 people took place on the first floor in the house and, again, for only a small charge.

Several new activities started during the Great War. In 1915 a Naturalists' Club was formed, affiliated to the Sid Vale Association. There was a wide range of weekly talks costing

Under-surface of roof with Devonian 'jointed cruck' trusses (SVA)

only 1d (0.4p), ranging from migration of birds, tree recognition, evidence of evolution and the modern-sounding 'wild life gardens'. On the first floor, Mr Ernest Bonner arranged local fossils, shells, feathers, crystals and old prints for public display on two days a week. (This collection continued through the 1920s but then went into storage in the outbuilding.) A junior branch of the Sid Vale Association was formed and young members were allowed small plots of land to plant vegetable seeds and take away their own produce. Additional ground belonging to the house was used, during the war years, to cultivate potatoes which were offered to the Red Cross Military Hospital, Peak House.

In 1916 Miss Browne offered free use of the facilities to enable Belgian refugee children in the town to learn English. Two sisters, Mademoiselle Donnet and Miss Marshall were appointed teachers. In the same year, a Maternity and Infant Welfare Centre was available on the ground floor.

In 1923, classes were available for local young adults to learn practical skills including carpentry, wood-carving, leather work and engineering drawing, which might enable them to more easily find employment. Miss Browne was looking to help the less well-off in the community and 'education' in the broadest sense was a guiding principle in her life.

In the inter-war years, practical sessions were offered to the Junior Branch of the SVA. These included painting and

Mary Lockyer (left) and Annie Leigh Browne
(Sidmouth Museum)

drawing, as well as scientific talks organised by Miss Browne's sister, Lady Lockyer, who was herself an experienced astronomer.

In 1936, Annie Leigh Browne died, aged 84 years. In her Will she left management of her estate, which included Woolcombe House, to her very close friend, Mary Stewart Kilgour.

During WW2, the building was used as the town's Information Centre in the event of any emergency and as a more general Citizens Advice Bureau, finally closing in 1946.

AE Chandler, the Chairman of the Sid Vale Association, had long considered Woolcombe House a suitable location for the town museum and the plans reached fruition in 1950. Miss Kilgour requested that the previous collection of Annie Leigh Browne and Lady Lockyer be taken out of store to become the first displays. The Sidmouth Urban District Council was responsible for heating, lighting and decoration, and Mr Chandler became honorary curator. The opening ceremony was in July 1950 and was attended, amongst others, by the 87 year-old Lord of the Manor, Colonel Balfour, and the 98 year-old Miss Kilgour. The Museum was open all year, although the opening hours varied according to the time of the year. It was invariably open on Sunday afternoons. The displays were on the first floor with cases against the side walls and flat cases running down the centre.

The Museum moved to Hope Cottage (see separate chapter) at the top of Church Street in 1970. Since that time Sidmouth Town Council has been based at Woolcombe House. The meeting chamber and magnificent timber ceiling should be seen by more of the local population as well as visitors. The friendly staff are agreeable to morning visits if the room is not in use, and permission can be requested at the front desk.

Nigel Hyman

Back cover illustrations, clockwise from top left:

Beatrix Potter at 'Hilltop', her Lake District home
Grand Duchess Elena Pavlovna, by Karl Brullov, 1830
(State Russian Museum, St Petersburg)
Royal Glen Hotel
Colonel CJW Grant wearing the Victoria Cross
Marino Lodge

Cover by Giles Sadler, Thorn Tree Design

FURTHER READING

Barnard C. and Barnard R. *The Knowle Sidmouth: a stately pleasure dome, a house and history*. Sid Vale Association, 2013.

Barnard C. and Barnard R. *A Case of Murder: Sidmouth and the Kent family.* Sid Vale Association, 2013.

Bray R. *I give you Sidmouth*. Market Press, 1935.

Brownlee S. *Sampson's Sidmouth*. Sid Vale Association, 2009.

Butler J. *Peter Orlando Hutchinson's Travels in Victorian Devon 1846 -1870*. Devon Books, 2000.

Butler J. *Peter Orlando Hutchinson's Diary of a Devon Antiquary 1871-1894*. Devon Books, 2010.

Cornish JG. *Reminiscences of a country life*. Country Life, 1939.

Cornish V. *The scenery of Sidmouth*. Cambridge University Press, 1940.

Cornish V. *A family of Devon, their homes, travels and occupations*. King bros. and Potts, 1942.

Creeke J. *The story of Sidmouth's Long Print*. Sid Vale Association, 2013.

Creeke J. *A picture in time: Sidmouth's Long Print*. Sid Vale Association, 2014.

Creeke J. *Salcombe Regis: an anthology, 700 years of village life*. Friends of Salcombe Regis Church, 2015.

Dilworth T. *David Jones, engraver, soldier, painter, poet*. Jonathan Cape, 2017.

Hardy C. *Elizabeth Barrett-Browning: Sidmouth letters and poems 1832-5*. Sid Vale Association, 2012

Hyman N. *Sidmouth: people and places*. Sid Vale Association, 2014.

Hyman N. *Sidmouth's literary connections*. Sid Vale Association, 2016.

Hyman N. *Richmond House to Sidholme*. Sid Vale Association, 2017.

Hyman N. *Stephen Reynolds: author, fisherman and home front hero*. Sid Vale Association, 2019.

Lane R. *Old Sidmouth*. Devon Books, 2001.

Leslie RC. *A Waterbiography, 1894*. Republished by Ashford Press Publishing with Introductory Note, 1985.

Linehan C. *Peter Orlando Hutchinson of Sidmouth, Devon, 1810-1897*. Maslands, Tiverton, 1989.

McFadzean C. *Sidmouth's Lace*. Sid Vale Association, 2016.

Miles R. Sidmouth scientists. Sid Vale Association, 2015.

Reynolds S. *A Poor Man's House*. 7th edition. Halsgrove, 2001.

Sid Vale Association. *Sidmouth: a history. 3rd edition*. Sid Vale Association, 2015.

Summerscale K. *The suspicions of Mr Whicher*. Bloomsbury, 2009.

Sutton A. *A Story of Sidmouth*. Townsend, Exeter, 1959.

Travis J. *The Rise of the Devon Seaside Resorts 1750-1900*. University of Exeter Press, 1993.

The Sid Vale Association promotes conservation and heritage, the Museum,
and facilities for recreational and cultural activities in the Sid Valley
To find out more about the Association go to:

www.sidvaleassociation.org.uk

ISBN 978-0-9934814-8-2